D1526815

This study investigates the historical and political conditions which have contributed to the current state of the Protestant community in China, and the kinds of spirituality and religious life that it has evolved. The authors draw on extensive fieldwork, and offer fascinating insights into the beliefs and practices of a little-documented section of Chinese society. They show that healing, protection, and vengeance by gods have been deep-rooted elements of Chinese religiosity for several hundred years, notions appropriated by Christians who now emphasize the powers of Jesus. Chinese Protestantism is seen to result from an interesting blend of the old and the new, and comparative material is adduced which sets Protestantism side by side with Catholicism and Buddhism, the two religions in China of comparable scope. A wide range of sources are utilized by the authors, and these lead to one of the most complete and detailed surveys of Christianity in China ever produced.

PROTESTANTISM IN
CONTEMPORARY CHINA

CAMBRIDGE STUDIES IN IDEOLOGY AND RELIGION

Religion increasingly is seen as a renewed force, and is recognised as an important factor in the modern world in all aspects of life – cultural, economic, and political. It is no longer a matter of surprise to find religious factors at work in areas and situations of political tension. However, our information about these situations has tended to come from two main sources. The news-gathering agencies are well-placed to convey information, but are hampered by the fact that their representatives are not equipped to provide analysis of the religious forces involved. Alternatively, the movements generate their own accounts, which understandably seem less than objective to outside observers. There is no lack of information or factual material, but a real need for sound academic analysis. 'Cambridge Studies in Ideology and Religion' will meet this need. It will give an objective, balanced, and programmatic coverage to issues which – while of wide potential interest – have been largely neglected by analytical investigation, apart from the appearance of sporadic individual studies. Intended to enable debate to proceed at a higher level, the series should lead to a new phase in our understanding of the relationship between ideology and religion.

PROTESTANTISM
IN CONTEMPORARY
CHINA

ALAN HUNTER and KIM-KWONG CHAN

*Department of East Asian Studies,
University of Leeds*

CAMBRIDGE
UNIVERSITY PRESS

Published by the Press Syndicate of the University of Cambridge
The Pitt Building, Trumpington Street, Cambridge CB2 1RP
40 West 20th Street, New York, NY 10011-4211, USA
10 Stamford Road, Oakleigh, Melbourne 3166, Australia

First published 1993

Printed in Great Britain at the University Press, Cambridge

A catalogue record for this book is available from the British Library

Library of Congress cataloguing in publication data

Hunter, Alan
Protestantism in contemporary China / Alan Hunter and Kim-Kwong
Chan.
p.   cm. – (Cambridge studies in ideology and religion)
Includes bibliographical references and index.
ISBN 0 521 44161 7
1. Christianity – China – History. 2. Protestants – China.
3. China – Religion. I. Chan, Kim-Kwong, 1958–. II. Title.
III. Series.
BR1288.H86 1993
280'.4'0951–dc20   92-39148 CIP

ISBN 0 521 44161 7 hardback

VN

This book is dedicated with love to
Joy and Adelina

Contents

List of figure and tables	*page* xi
General editors' preface	xiii
Acknowledgements and notes on the text	xv
List of abbreviations	xix
Map	xx

Introduction

Christianity fever?	1
Characteristics of Chinese Christianity	4
A note on methodology	8
Information sources and academic work	13
The structure of this work	18

1 The social and political context

1949–1979: the Party triumphant	21
Reform in China after 1979	28
Social control and human rights	36
The legal framework and religious policy	47
Institutions	53

2 A survey of the Protestant community

Reporting statistics	66
The official church	72
House churches and autonomous communities	81
Representative leaders	88
Politics of the church	93

3 The historical legacy

Protestants, politics and the Chinese Communist Party	105
The denominational churches	113
The independent churches	119
The social gospel	123

Revivals, evangelism and charismatic trends   126
Continuities 1920–1990   135

4   Protestantism and Chinese religious culture
Prayer and the indigenous tradition   141
Healing   145
Charismatic phenomena   152
Morality   155
Sin, suffering, salvation   158
Conversion   163
Church growth since 1979   168

5   Varieties of Christian life
Introduction   176
An official church?   179
Christians in Xiamen   185
House churches in Xiamen   191
The Apostolic Church   199
The witness of Brother Huang Detang   210

6   Buddhism and Catholicism
Buddhism in the 1980s   219
The revival of monastic life   222
Lay Buddhism   226
Buddhism and the Protestant church – some comparisons   229
The Roman Catholic church in China   236
The Church in the post-Mao period   238
Catholic religious life   244
Developments after 1989   248
Catholics and Protestants   251

7   Into the 1990s
The church in 1992   257
Congruency, indigenization, transformation   265
Final thoughts   271

Bibliography   281
Index   289

Figure and tables

Figure 1   Administrative structure of the Chinese   *page* 63
            Protestant church

Table 1   Official estimates of Christian numbers in   68
            selected provinces, late 1980s

Table 2   Explanations for conversion to or   169
            continued adherence to religions in
            modern China

xi

General editors' preface

Only twenty years ago it was widely assumed that religion had lost its previous place in western culture and that this pattern would spread throughout the world. Since then religion has become a renewed force, recognized as an important factor in the modern world in all aspects of life, cultural, economic and political. This is true not only of the Third World, but in Europe East and West, and in North America. It is no longer a surprise to find a religious factor at work in areas of political tension.

Religion and ideology form a mixture which can be of interest to the observer, but in practice dangerous and explosive. Our information about such matters comes for the most part from three types of sources. The first is the media which understandably tend to concentrate on newsworthy events, without taking the time to deal with the underlying issues of which they are but symptoms. The second source comprises studies by social scientists who often adopt a functionalist and reductionist view of the faith and beliefs which motivate those directly involved in such situations. Finally, there are the statements and writings of those committed to the religious or ideological movements themselves. We seldom lack information, but there is a need – often an urgent need – for sound objective analyses which can make use of the best contemporary approaches to both politics and religion. 'Cambridge Studies in Ideology and Religion' is designed to meet this need.

The subject matter is global and this will be reflected in the choice both of topics and of authors. The initial volumes will be concerned primarily with movements involving the Christian religion, but as the series becomes established movements involving other word religions will be subjected to the same objective critical analysis. In all cases it is our intention that an accurate and sensitive account of religion should be informed by an objective and sophisticated application of perspectives from the social sciences.

The relation between religion in general, and Protestant Christianity in particular, and Marxist Communism in China is significantly different from the interaction in Europe or in Latin America. Protestant Christianity in China was a fruit of the missionary movement of the last one hundred and fifty years. On this ground, as an alien implant, as well as the standard Marxist antagonism to religion as a false and disabling reality, the Protestant churches have been subjected to steady official opposition and periods of intense persecution, particularly during the Cultural Revolution. This book is the first substantial and carefully researched study of how the Protestant churches have responded to this situation and how far their belief and way of life has been affected by the situation. The authors have been painstaking in their research, and have produced an authoritative study which fills a real gap in the literature showing the various ways in which Protestant Christianity has responded to an aggressive and hostile ideology, securely based since the 1940s in the institutions of the State.

DUNCAN FORRESTER AND ALISTAIR KEE
New College, University of Edinburgh

Acknowledgements

The research for this book was supported by many people and institutions. Our greatest debt is to the individuals in China who have shared their experiences with us over the past years. Many are Christians who have borne witness to their faith in an extraordinary fashion over the last decades. It is a moving experience to come close to these people.

We would also like to express our appreciation of the assistance given to us by non-believers who have professional or personal connections with the Christian community. In particular we are grateful to scholars in the Chinese Academy of Social Sciences; Fudan University, Shanghai; Hangzhou University; the Shanghai Academy of Social Sciences; and Xiamen University.

Hong Kong Baptist College generously provided accommodation and other assistance, and special thanks are due to Lauren Pfister and Carver Yu of the Department of Religion and Philosophy.

We also received great help from various Christian research centres, notably the Chinese Church Research Centre, the Christian Study Centre on Chinese Religion and Culture, and the China Department of the Council of Churches for Britain and Ireland. It has been a privilege to meet such figures as Jonathan Chao, Deng Zhaoming, Laszlo Ladany, Tony Lambert, Edmond Tang and Bob Whyte, who were unfailingly helpful and generous in sharing their information. These individuals and their co-workers have made essential contributions to the study of Christianity in contemporary China. Were it not for them, the field of study would be far less developed than it is today.

We are grateful to the Department of East Asian Studies of the University of Leeds, and especially its Head, Don Rimmington, who was responsible for co-authoring several earlier papers, initiating the original research, fund-raising, arranging links with Chinese institutions and shaping the project as a whole. This enterprise was, of course, expensive. The major part of the costs was covered by a grant from the Leverhulme Trust, and we received additional donations from the Hong Kong Baptist College Research Committee, the Sino-British Fellowship Trust and the Universities China Committee in London. The Christian Nationals Evangelism Commission Fellowship Church in Hong Kong also supported our work. We would like to acknowledge the generosity of these institutions, without which the research could not have proceeded.

NOTES ON THE TEXT

1. We have attempted to make this book as accessible as possible to readers who do not have a specialist knowledge of China. Two reference works that can be recommended are *The Cambridge Handbook of Contemporary China* by Colin MacKerras and Amanda Yorke, which has a particular focus on the past decade; and *The Cambridge Encyclopedia of China* edited by Brian Hook, which contains a wealth of information on Chinese culture and history.

2. We have used the standard system of *hanyu pinyin* to romanize Chinese terms. Exceptions are a few place and personal names better known in other spellings. We have avoided the use of Chinese words in the text as far as possible.

3. The unit of currency in the People's Republic of China is the yuan. In the 1980s the exchange rate was around six yuan to the US dollar. A factory worker might earn around 100 to 150 yuan per month.

4. There are twenty-six provinces under the jurisdiction of the government in Beijing, of which the five with substantial non-Han populations are known as 'autonomous regions'. The three cities of Beijing, Shanghai and Tianjin with their suburban areas are known as 'municipalities'. Their administration

reports directly to the central government, and in many respects they are equivalent to provinces in status.

Most provinces are divided into about eight prefectures or districts, which in turn are divided into counties. An average county in a typical central province has an area of about 1200–2000 square kilometres, and a population of between 600,000 and 700,000.

5. Chinese names are generally given in standard form, i.e. family name followed by personal name(s). In some cases where an alternative arrangement is well known, for example K. H. Ting, this has been retained in the text. However even in these cases the family name is used first in the bibliography.

Abbreviations

CASS	Chinese Academy of Social Sciences
CBA	China Buddhist Association
CCBI	Council of Churches for Britain and Ireland
CCC	China Christian Council
CCP	Chinese Communist Party
CCPA	Chinese Catholic Patriotic Association
CCRC	Chinese Church Research Centre
CNCR	China News and Church Report
CPPCC	Chinese People's Political Consultative Conference
GMD	Guomindang
NCC	National Christian Conference
NPC	National People's Congress
PRC	People's Republic of China
RAB	Religious Affairs Bureau
TSPM	Three Self Patriotic Movement
UFWD	United Front Work Department
WCC	World Council of Churches

The term 'the Party' is also used as an abbreviation for the Chinese Communist Party.

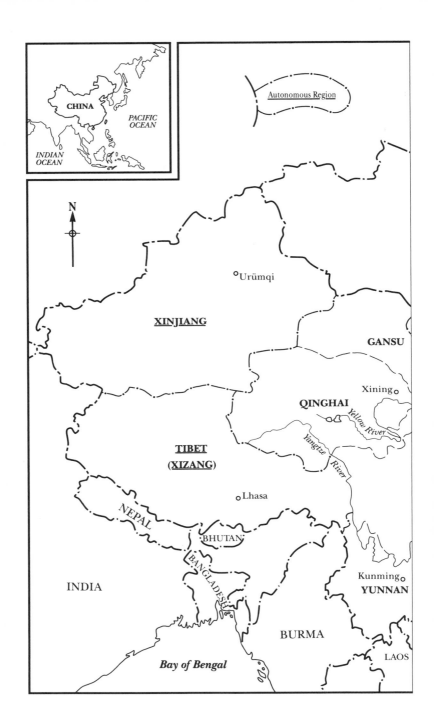

Autonomous Region

CHINA

PACIFIC
OCEAN

INDIAN
OCEAN

N

Urümqi

XINJIANG

GANSU

Xining

QINGHAI

Yellow River

Yangtze River

TIBET
(XIZANG)

Lhasa

NEPAL

BHUTAN

BANGLADESH

INDIA

Kunming

YUNNAN

BURMA

Bay of Bengal

LAOS

FORMER SOVIET UNION

0 _____ 200 Miles
0 _____ 300 Kilometres

MONGOLIA

HEILONGJIANG

Harbin

Changchun
JILIN

INNER MONGOLIA

Huhhot

LIAONING

Shenyang

NINGXIA

Yinchuan

HEBEI

BEIJING

TIANJIN

NORTH KOREA

Shijiazhuang

Taiyuan

SHANXI

Yan'an

Yellow River

Jinan

SHANDONG

SOUTH
KOREA

Lanzhou

Qingdao

Yellow
Sea

Yellow River

SHAANXI

Zhengzhou Kaifeng

HENAN

Nanjing

JIANGSU

ANHUI

Hefei

SICHUAN

Chengdu

HUBEI

Wuhan

Yangtze River

SHANGHAI

Chongqing

Hangzhou

Ningbo

Xiangshan

Yangtze River

ZHEJIANG

East China
Sea

Changsha

Nanchang

Wenzhou

HUNAN

JIANGXI

GUIZHOU

Fuzhou

Guiyang

FUJIAN

Xiamen

GUANGXI

GUANGDONG

Taibei

TAIWAN

Nanning

Guangzhou

Hong Kong (Xianggang)

Macao
(Aomen)

VIETNAM

South China Sea

Hainandao

PHILIPPINES

Introduction

CHRISTIANITY FEVER?

In 1949 there were about one million Chinese Protestants, who worshipped in some twenty thousand churches and chapels, and in countless home meetings. By 1958, after nine years of communist rule, almost all churches had been closed. Strict controls were also in force against Christian meetings held in homes. In August 1966 the Chinese Communist Party (CCP) issued a directive which marked the start of the Cultural Revolution. A campaign was launched against old ideas, culture, customs and habits. Historic buildings, libraries, and works of art were wrecked and thousands of individuals persecuted. Religious institutions were closed, often with violence against personnel and vandalism of contents. For the next decade it seemed that religions, including Christianity, disappeared from China. Their total destruction was an ideal promoted by Jiang Qing, Mao's wife and a leading figure in the Cultural Revolution, who confidently announced that religion was dead. This suppression of institutional religion has few parallels in history, perhaps only the governments of Albania and North Korea having been equally thorough.[1] In some areas the persecution was particularly systematic: for example the county of Pingyang in Zhejiang province was targeted as a 'model atheist district' in which all religion was to be eliminated.

---

[1] As noted by Tony Lambert, *The Resurrection of the Chinese Church*, London: Hodder and Stoughton, 1991, p. 11. Two churches were permitted to remain open in Beijing to serve the diplomatic community. See Donald E. MacInnis, *Religious Policy and Practice in Communist China: A Documentary History*, London: Hodder and Stoughton, 1972, pp. 287–8, for the start of the Cultural Revolution.

Christians continued to meet in secret during this period. Evangelical groups in Hong Kong reported that small prayer meetings were being held in private homes, that by 1974 several hundred people were attending large services in Fuzhou, and that in Wenzhou there were Bible study classes and training sessions. We have also seen mimeographed Bibles and religious literature from the mid-1970s. Towards the end of the Cultural Revolution there was widespread unofficial activity in the Christian community, and also the first signs of a revival of the official church: K. H. Ting, Bishop of Nanjing, was allowed to meet foreign visitors after 1973.[2]

In 1976 Mao Zedong died, the Gang of Four was overthrown and Chinese society started to recover from the chaos of the Cultural Revolution. In 1978, Deng Xiaoping took effective control of government. The Party explicitly repudiated the policies of the past decade, promised greater freedoms and initiated a wide-ranging reform programme. No-one could foresee what the future of religion might be. One could assume that there were far fewer than one million Protestant believers by 1979, after the persecutions, closure of the official church, ideological remoulding of society and lack of contact with the outside world. No new pastors had been ordained since the 1950s, most church buildings were being used for other purposes, there were hardly any Christian publications, no news of religion in the media, no religious education in schools. Would people still have any wish to engage in religious activities? According to Leninist theory, religion will rapidly die out in socialist society, while even less extreme theories of secularization predict its decline in the face of industrialization, urbanization and improved education. And if Christianity were merely a tool of imperialism, as the Chinese people had been told for many years, it would have been in a precarious position by 1978, since foreign influence had been absent for three decades and was still carefully restricted.

In fact, the 1980s saw a rapid growth of Protestant Christianity, which spread markedly faster than other religions. The first

---

[2] See Lambert, *Resurrection*, pp. 9–26 for further information. The *hanyu pinyin* romanization of K. H. Ting, used by some writers, is Ding Guangxun.

church to re-open was in the eastern port of Ningbo in early April 1979, and it was soon followed by more in Shanghai and other large cities. The official church recovered much of its property and revived as an institution. According to its estimates, by 1990 there were some six thousand open churches and fifteen thousand registered meeting points providing for five million believers. It ran seminaries, a publication programme, education for lay leaders, an aid agency, youth groups and many of the other facilities that one might expect of a church. Moreover its legal status was recognized by the government and Christian leaders were able to make representations at the highest political levels.

Meanwhile there had also been a growth of religious activities conducted in homes and other meeting points. Many Christians do not attend the open churches and have organized their own structures. These groups are diverse: some are opposed to the official church for ideological or personal reasons, some are linked to networks in different parts of China, some have contacts with foreigners, others are simple, humble meetings of uneducated people who may understand very little of Christianity. This phenomenon is generally known outside China as the 'house church movement'.[3] We suggest later that this term is becoming inadequate, since many of the house churches have expanded into communities of considerable size and complexity.

The house churches are politically controversial. In the early 1950s, the Chinese government established a sophisticated network of administrative agencies to control religious activities. The system fell into disuse during the Cultural Revolution but was reinstated in 1979. House churches are a challenge to this bureaucratic supervision, since they meet in private and do not recognize the leadership of the official church or government bodies. Also, some have found enthusiastic assistance abroad, which contravenes the government's insistence on no foreign

---

[3] The term 'house church' (*jiating jiaohui*) may have originated from the movement founded by Watchman Nee (Ni Tuosheng) in the 1930s, which promoted meetings in private homes led by lay persons. In China, the term 'meeting point' (*juhuidian*) is also commonly used.

interference in China's religious affairs. Among the house
churches' most vocal supporters have been evangelical groups in
Hong Kong, who have encouraged them by importing publications, transmitting radio broadcasts, training evangelists and
donating money. Moreover they have published material that is
embarrassing to the official church leadership.

It has been claimed that the house church movement has
grown in an extraordinary fashion, that there are fifty or even
one hundred million underground Christians in China. Such
claims are wildly exaggerated, but there has been a dramatic
increase in religious activities, especially of Protestantism and of
folk religion, since 1979. By 1989 this was acknowledged by
Chinese research institutions, and began to acquire the name
'Christianity fever', which has since been used in official Chinese
publications.

Religion gained a higher political profile after 1989. The top
leadership of the CCP, dismayed by the challenge to its power in
spring of that year, attempted to intensify its ideological control
over society. It was aware that religious organizations, especially Christian ones, had been influential in opposition to the
communist governments of eastern Europe. Stricter regulations
were promulgated, and rumours spread that a crackdown on
religious activities was imminent. In 1990, Chinese government
officials reportedly feared that 70 per cent of the nation's
religious activities were out of control, while Premier Li Peng
called for attacks on the underground churches. Other senior
leaders warned of a transfer of allegiance, especially in the
countryside, from the CCP to religious organizations.[4]

CHARACTERISTICS OF CHINESE CHRISTIANITY

The reports of 'Christianity fever' raise many questions. In the
short term, how reliable are the reports? What are the true
numbers? Will the church become a force in Chinese politics?
On a deeper level, the phenomenon raises important questions
about Chinese society and religion, and about the nature of

---

[4] *China News and Church Report* (CNCR) 1805, 28 June 1991; *International Herald Tribune*, 1
July 1991, p. 6.

Christianity, or at least its Protestant tradition. Is the growth comparable to that in South Korea or Latin America? Are Chinese people transferring allegiance from their traditional religions to a western import? Can we identify explanations for these changes in the context of economic reform, industrialization and increased contact with the outside world?

Two themes to be developed in this book are the historical and political conditions that have contributed to the current state of the Protestant community in China. The Protestant missionary enterprise coincided with a period when traditional Chinese culture was in crisis, Chinese governments were ineffective, the country often in a state of war, and when foreign power was at its height. The missionaries met strong opposition to their work: they and their Chinese converts were generally despised and rejected by the population. Many Chinese officials also opposed Christianity as a foreign religion, and later the Guomindang (GMD) and the CCP attacked it, sometimes violently, as a tool of imperialism.[5] The foreign connection has diminished dramatically, but Christians are to some extent still protected by foreign support: the CCP would face severe international pressure if it were to adopt outright repressive measures. Besides, the government since 1979 has been relatively tolerant of religion, and the church itself is now probably strong enough to withstand any administrative pressures that might be applied. At the worst, more Christians would be obliged to practise in secret, and that could easily backfire on the government. Thus politically and historically, Christians form a minority social group that has suffered repeatedly from persecution but has finally achieved a measure of security.

We will briefly anticipate some sociological explanations for the recent spread of Christianity. The 1980s was a period of radical transition in the countryside, seeing the rebirth of family farming and a market economy, and at the same time a liberalization of political controls. The economic changes brought greater prosperity to many, but also more uncertainty.

[5] Guomindang (or Kuomintang) is the name of the nationalist party, founded by Sun Yat-sen and led for many years by Chiang Kai-shek, that ruled China from 1926 to 1949.

Traditional rural isolation was increasingly broken as people travelled and traded far more, and there was greater contact with the outside world. There was perhaps a sense of loss of identity. Meanwhile health provision continued to be very poor, and women in particular may not have benefited from the reforms: some observers suggest their status deteriorated over the decade. At the same time there was far less rigid social control after the abolition of the People's Communes in 1979/80 and less pressure to display political conformity. In short, most families had more cash, more freedom to participate in religious activities, and also perhaps more anxieties which they needed to assuage.

In cities, disaffection with the CCP was widespread by the late 1980s among intellectuals, a number of whom developed an interest in Christian thought and traditions. There were reports of some conversions among Chinese students abroad and even on the campuses of universities in Beijing. This interest, however, seemed to remain rather superficial and limited. Christianity in China has yet to evolve an intellectual dimension equivalent to its spiritual life. Neither has it made much impact on industrial workers, although one source of converts has been retired people seeking relief from loneliness or ill-health. With some exceptions the growth rate is probably slower than in the countryside. The core of many congregations is still elderly people who were practising Christians before 1949.

Christian life in China often revolves around two poles: church, or meeting point, and home. There are over twenty thousand registered church buildings at which communal worship takes place, often close in liturgy to European or North American models. Most such churches are served by pastors affiliated to the official church organization, the China Christian Council (CCC). Many churches have activities such as Bible-study classes and prayer groups.

Many believers find weekly attendance at church insufficient for their spiritual needs, and so home activities of various kinds are important. Retired people, usually female, are often among the most fervent disciples. At their home meetings, prayer and personal testimony play an important role, especially accounts of healing. Many believers interpret their lives as a series of minor epiphanies or miracles. Belief in ghosts and devils is still widespread, and prayer in the name of Jesus thought to be an effective remedy against possession and evil spirits. These informal home meetings are an effective opportunity to conduct personal evangelism among neighbours, for example by convincing them of the powers of Jesus. Supernatural healing, protection and vengeance have been a deep-rooted element of traditional Chinese religiosity for several thousand years. Moreover, the political climate positively favours informal oral communication: many subjects are officially taboo and the information network is tightly controlled. Serious obstacles are put in the way of anyone who wishes to conduct research on religion, so it is usually difficult to verify or disprove particular stories. It is easy for tales of the supernatural to flourish.

In Chinese folk religion, prayer is essentially petitionary, seeking health and wealth in particular. This is reflected in the Chinese Christian tradition. We were frequently told that a main reason for conversion is hearing of or experiencing healing by Jesus, which appears to be a common phenomenon in China today. Other testimonies relate to the achievement of wealth, safety at times of accidents and God's revenge on enemies, all popular themes in traditional Chinese religion. But these concerns were often a first step towards a deeper understanding of the religion, and believers would later turn to Jesus as personal friend and protector, source of eternal life, Son of God and saviour of mankind: the Christological emphasis is on the role of Jesus as Saviour and Healer. Among many groups the sense of sinfulness and the need for repentance is strong, and they may insist on the need for a rebirth experience, sometimes to be witnessed by glossolalia or other psychic phenomena. Behavioural changes, for example being less quarrelsome, are seen as a reliable indicator of sincerity and piety.

The lack of trained leadership for the huge numbers of believers in rural areas is apparent. Heterodoxy can easily arise as peasants integrate the new religion without a strong church tradition. In some places folk beliefs are suppressed by the local government while Christianity is tolerated, which makes it an attractive alternative. Protestant/folk religion syncretism has produced self-appointed Messiahs, eschatological predictions, mass spiritual healing and so on.[6] Some Christian groups, on the contrary, are extremely strict and tolerate no accommodation with what they perceive as heterodoxy.

As regards ethics, Christianity is known in some areas as the religion which can ensure harmony in the family, especially in the relation between mother- and daughter-in-law, which is notorious in Chinese culture as a breeding-ground for family arguments. Christians also claim a disproportionately high number of 'model workers' and low number of criminals in their midst. Even Li Liuwan, one of the six Vice-Presidents of the PRC, praised the positive moral influence of Christianity during a visit to Wenzhou in 1991. However the collation of crime statistics as well as religious ones is problematic in China, and we are not certain to what extent these claims are justifiable. Rubinstein concludes his recent study of the church in Taiwan with the words:

> What the history of Taiwanese Protestantism teaches is that Chinese society has once again demonstrated a unique ability to force alien traditions to transform themselves into patterns with which the Chinese people are most comfortable. Such a process of Sinification was at work in the centuries when Buddhism first entered China and slowly, but surely, became a Chinese religion. It is clear that this process, this steady societal pressure for change and accommodation, is at work again.[7]

Is this true in the People's Republic also? The encounter between two vast traditions, Christianity and Chinese culture, has fascinated and puzzled members of both for hundreds of years.

A NOTE ON METHODOLOGY

A study such as this inevitably raises questions of methodology. The size and diversity of China constitute the first difficulty to be

---

[6] See for example Lu Guangwen, 'We Must Guard Against Heterodox Sects', *China Study Journal*, vol. 6 no. 2, August 1991, pp. 72–3. Chinese popular religion is discussed below in chapter 4.

[7] Murray A. Rubinstein, *The Protestant Community on Modern Taiwan: Mission, Seminary and Church*, Armonk, New York and London: M. E. Sharpe, 1991, p. 155.

confronted. The Han Chinese inhabit a vast land mass, almost ten million square kilometres of contrasting terrain: mountains, deserts, alluvial plains and coasts, some parts poor and arid, others rich and fertile. Economic activity ranges from space technology to subsistence farming and hunting. Apart from the Han, other ethnic and linguistic groups in China include speakers of Turkish, Mongolian and Tungus languages who migrated from Central Asia; speakers of Sino-Tibetan languages in the far west; and numerous small groups in south-west China who speak Austro-Asiatic languages.

In the west, national boundaries have accustomed us to think of specific local cultural identities. We are likely to see the differences rather than the similarities between a Swede and a Spaniard for example. The absence of these boundaries in China may tend to conceal the ethnological diversity of the Chinese population, although each Chinese province has the population and area of a medium-sized European country. The use of a common script may also conceal real linguistic differences, and the formal national culture masks a tremendous variety of local cultures. There has so far been little ethnographic charting of the population, and it is often difficult to appreciate the significant differences that may exist between one province and another, even one district and another. Economic and social diversity is equally pronounced. Some districts have seen rapid industrialization in the past twenty years; there may be areas only fifty miles away where the modern world has barely impinged.

To speak of 'Christianity in China' is only useful at a high level of abstraction, as when talking of 'Christianity in Europe'. There is no 'typical' city or province. Religion in Shanghai means something very different from religion in Lanzhou; Zhejiang is not the same as Qinghai. A striking example is the relative lack of success of evangelization in Guangdong despite more than a century of intensive efforts and easy access. One should be careful when generalizing from case studies. The research agenda at present should include detailed local investigations that could eventually provide data for broader conclusions. Religion in modern China has been a relatively under-researched topic, and so writers have to operate on a high level of generality, which is a serious weakness. It also reflects a weakness of social science research on China in general. In the modern era there is no readily available set of provincial or district level surveys to which one can refer for accurate data with regard to religion. For example, if one wished to collate information on a particular province's religious heritage and current situation, and their correlations with local politics, industrial development, central government policy or health programmes, there is no ready-made solution: one would be obliged to piece together the information for each area in a painstaking and lengthy process.

The reason is not hard to find. On the western side, scholarship on modern China has been influenced by the agenda of governments, particularly that of the USA, which viewed China as an ideological and possibly military threat. Research was to a considerable extent focused on economic and political rather than cultural questions. Moreover China was isolated internationally and access to it extremely difficult. In the 1980s progress was made in social science and arts research on China, but funding is difficult to obtain and much remains to be done. East–West relations have eased markedly since the 1970s, however, and the outlook for future study seems good.

Chinese sources need to be evaluated with care. Official publications reflect two important traditions of the CCP, which came to power after a thirty-year armed struggle. First, its political culture was strongly influenced by the demands of guerrilla warfare. The emphasis was on the strict control of intelligence in a military environment, rather than on a public information network for civilian administration. After 1949 the Chinese leadership constantly feared that it might be involved in a major war with the USA, which it confronted in Korea and Vietnam, the USSR or Taiwan. To secure political authority it placed rigid limits on the flow of information. Consequently many fields of study – local history, economics, social developments, political trends – were accessible only to those with a right to know, which was determined by status in the Party.

Second, publications in China are supposed to conform to

guidelines laid down by the CCP Department of Propaganda. According to Mao Zedong himself, the function of the press is 'to organize, to stimulate, to agitate, to criticize and to propel'. Its most important task is: 'to select issues and to present convincing arguments to attack the various shades of opportunism, conservatism and destructive capitalism, to assure the establishment of socialism, to conquer pessimism and to mobilize aggressivism'.[8] In short, 'the press is an instrument of class struggle' and 'the journalistic battle front is where the sharpest and fiercest political ideological battles are fought'.[9] In practice this meant that news would be published when it promoted government objectives, rather than to air controversial issues (or to make profits for shareholders).

This level of information control was not maintained after 1979. Hundreds of new journals were authorized, many of which pushed back the frontiers of censorship, and unofficial publications made an appearance.[10] Chinese people listened regularly to foreign radio and TV broadcasts, thousands worked or studied abroad, and China itself opened to western tourists, academics and business people. In the freer atmosphere, even the most staid publications began to report scandals as well as successes. Nevertheless there is undoubtedly much important information, on religion as on other questions, held in archives not open to western, or most Chinese, scholars. Likewise, the overall process of social mapping has improved but still remains under-developed. Sociology and anthropology were among the disciplines suppressed after 1949 and especially during the Cultural Revolution. China has few university departments in these disciplines, and their work often faces restrictions. Some government offices such as the Cultural

[8] Letter by Mao to journalists, dated 12 January 1958, in *Xinhua banyuekan* (*New China Fortnightly*), Beijing, 25 February 1959, p. 160.
[9] Lu Dingyi, 'Speech on the Twentieth Anniversary of the New China News Agency', *Renmin shouce* (*People's Handbook*), Beijing: Dagongbao, 1958, p. 144; Deng Guo 'Socialist Revolution on the Journalistic Front', *Xuexi* (*Study*), no. 8, 18 April 1958, p. 2.
[10] See Jia Lusheng, 'The Second Channel', translated extracts with an introduction by Guo Xiaolin in *Index on Censorship*, vol. 18 no. 2, February 1989, pp. 20–2. Also Michael Schoenhals, 'Unofficial and Official Histories of the Cultural Revolution', *Journal of Asian Studies*, vol. 48 no. 3, August 1989, pp. 563–72.

Bureaux conduct research, but the results are not made public.

Other problems are posed by administrative constraints on religion. Since 1949 a variety of policies on religion have been adopted, which at times have been extremely severe. Since 1979 the policy has been far more liberal, but government agencies do still exercise control over religious activities. The limits on what they permit the foreign researcher vary from place to place and from year to year. The southeastern coastal provinces are relatively open; interior provinces and Beijing itself more tightly controlled. The mid-1980s were liberal; the period after the suppression of the 1989 democracy movement was not. A consensus for the ground rules seems to be that interviews with leaders of the official religious organizations are nearly always permitted, as is occasional attendance at official religious activities such as church services. Private conversations with believers and with Chinese scholars are also unlikely to attract official displeasure. The situation is less clear in other respects. For example, would a foreign researcher be allowed to conduct joint research with Chinese scholars? To have interviews with police or government officials? To maintain regular attendance at religious services, or conduct repeated interviews with pastors or believers? These might be considered more sensitive issues, and would need considerable negotiation to gain permission.

Some methods of inquiry are almost impossible. For example access to archives on religious questions, systematic observation or survey work and contacts with house churches were certainly not permitted in the early 1990s. Foreign researchers have to bear in mind that interviewees in religious organizations are obliged to report foreign interest to officials, and that some pastors have been subjected to detailed questioning after receiving foreign guests. They should also be aware that many statements to visitors are purely formalistic: information collected during guided tours, for example, can be regarded in this light.

To summarize our experiences, we believe that one can gain a good understanding of the national situation, and a detailed grasp at the micro-level in certain specific places. To do this one has to compare material from different sources such as material from Hong Kong research efforts, usually Christian based;

survey of the mainland press; conversations with scholars and believers in China; personal observation on a selective basis; study of other areas of Chinese life. We do not hold sufficient data for a comprehensive analysis of the phenomenon of Christianity in China, but the insight one gains from these sources is more than superficial or impressionistic.

INFORMATION SOURCES AND ACADEMIC WORK

Any analysis of the Protestant community in China is faced with these problems of data collection. We have attempted to deal with them by using a wide range of sources which have been checked and compared. First, both writers have visited numerous churches and meetings in China, and held discussions with a wide range of individuals including believers, pastors, academics, administrators and government officials. Unfortunately we are not able to refer to specific persons who are sources of information, especially concerning political questions, in any way which would jeopardize their security. We cannot pretend to any detailed knowledge of the top leadership of the official church, and have not had the benefit of personal discussions with them. Their views can be consulted in various publications described below.

Second, we have made a thorough examination of available written sources, which we review briefly here. They can be considered in five categories: work by Chinese academics; reports in official Chinese publications; research work by organizations outside China; confessional works by Chinese Christians; and books on the Chinese church written outside China.

The most important centres for research on religion in China are the Institute for World Religions in the Chinese Academy of Social Sciences (CASS); the Centre for Religion in the Shanghai Academy of Social Sciences; the Nanjing Institute for Religious Studies; the Religious Studies Institute of Sichuan University and the Centre for Research on Christianity of Hangzhou University. Of these, the Nanjing Institute has focused on Protestant churches. Much research in these centres has been

subject to ideological constraint, approaching religion as a
social phenomenon that requires investigation with a view to
policy recommendations. Typical papers begin with praise for
the CCP's religious policy, criticism of the Cultural Revolution,
and quotations from Marx and Engels who are said to provide
the basis for a scientific understanding of religion. Some papers
then present reports of fieldwork, although many appear only to
repeat material acquired from government agencies of the area
under consideration. Most papers end with a reaffirmation of
Party policy and the need for its correct implementation. We
were informed that all academic research on religion is considered sensitive and subject to careful scrutiny before publication.[11]
Religious studies as a discipline is still weak, but of great
importance for the future. It will probably be a fruitful area for
co-operation between Chinese and western scholars.

Tianfeng, a monthly journal of around sixty pages, is the organ
of the Chinese official church. It expresses a pro-government
political position, for example supporting the changes in policy
after June 1989. Articles include reports of meetings, speeches by
church and government officials, observations on church life,
extracts of sermons and devotional material. The overall
impression is of a formal and carefully vetted publication. The
Amity News Service was established in Hong Kong in 1992 to
provide an English language conduit for church leaders, and
another important source of information has been interviews
with spokespersons who have been authorized to talk to
foreigners. The Chinese press also carries occasional stories
about religion. As described above, such publications conform
to politically determined guidelines.

Various organizations monitor the Chinese press, translate
items into English, and publish their own research findings. Here

[11] David Yu provides a good survey of this kind of work in 'Religious Studies in China at
Crossroads', *Journal of Chinese Religions*, no. 18, Fall 1990, pp. 167–72. A significant
publication is *Zhongguo shehuizhuyi shiqide zongjiao wenti*, edited by Luo Zhufeng,
Shanghai: Shanghai shehuikexueyuan chubanshe, 1987. This is available in English
as *Religion under Socialism in China*, translated by Donald E. MacInnis and Zheng
Xi'an, New York and London: M. E. Sharpe, 1991. Two journals *Zongjiao (Religion)*
and *Dangdai zongjiao yanjiu (Contemporary Religious Studies Review)* are published in
Nanjing and Shanghai respectively.

we mention three of the most important as far as the Protestant church is concerned: the Chinese Church Research Centre (CCRC), the Council of Churches for Britain and Ireland (CCBI) China Department, and the Christian Study Centre on Chinese Religion and Culture. The Hong Kong-based CCRC monitors the religious situation in China. Among its publications are a weekly news-sheet in English entitled *China News and Church Report* (CNCR), a bi-monthly journal *Zhongguo yu jiaohui* (*China and the Church*) and several books. The centre takes note of official information but regards it with scepticism, using letters received in Hong Kong, personal observations, interviews and leaked internal documents to formulate its own views. Its work has been sharply criticized by senior church leaders in China, for publishing anti-Chinese, unpatriotic material. Our own research has tended to confirm that done by the CCRC, although in our opinion it over-estimates church growth. This probably arises from its enthusiasm for house church groups and weaknesses in methodology. House church leaders may exaggerate the strengths of their own groups and report high numbers of believers in particular counties. CCRC researchers have sometimes been tempted to extrapolate provincial or even national figures from such reports. However, they have undoubtedly provided a major resource for materials on the contemporary Chinese church, collating and publishing many documents that would otherwise not have been made public.

It may also be relevant to note that the Centre is one section of China Ministries International, an overtly evangelistic organization that perceives its role as facilitator of the conversion of China to Christianity. Its director Dr Jonathan Chao is also president of a Christian college in Taiwan, and the organization has founded a graduate school, a seminary and a lay training institute in Hong Kong and a seminary in Taiwan. Chao and his co-workers are committed to evangelistic work inside China.

A number of church groups in Britain initiated an ecumenical China Study Project Committee in the 1970s, which later became the China Department of the CCBI. The Department is responsible for liaison between British and Chinese churches and has also been active in research. Its first director, Bob

Whyte, wrote an informative and balanced account of the history of the Chinese church, and also initiated a bulletin now known as the *China Study Journal*.[12] Each issue has two sections, the first having interpretative articles and the second, which so far has been more substantial, providing a translation service from the Chinese religious and secular press. It covers not only Christian churches but religious and national affairs, Islam, Buddhism and Daoism, providing an excellent source of reference for Chinese religions in the 1980s. The political orientation of the Department and its publications has tended to be neutral, contrasting with the anti-communist tone of some evangelical groups: the CCBI maintains good relations with the official church in China.

The same is true of the Christian Study Centre on Chinese Religion and Culture, based in Hong Kong. As well as housing a library and reading-room, the Centre publishes two important journals, *Ching Feng* and *Bridge*. The former publishes longer articles on a variety of topics related to religion in East Asia, for example Christian literature, Confucian philosophy and religion in Hong Kong and China. *Bridge*, edited by the scholar and journalist Deng Zhaoming, is devoted to the church in China. It provides reports on grass-roots Christian activities all over China, based on first-hand observation that makes it virtually unique as a source of information. Deng reports on open churches but he is also critical of many official positions.[13]

Confessional writing by Chinese Christians is naturally important as source material. Writings of the official church can be conveniently surveyed in English in the yearly *China Theological Review* which translates articles mostly from the *Nanjing Theological Review*, produced by the CCC in Nanjing. The CCC has also published collections of sermons and educational materials. Evangelical groups in Hong Kong, for example Christian Communications Ltd, publish occasional

---

[12] Robert Whyte, *Unfinished Encounter: China and Christianity*, London: Collins, 1988. The journal was previously known as the *China Study Project Journal*.

[13] Other journals and research groups include *China Talk* published by the Hong Kong Liaison Office of the United Methodist Church; and *Tripod*, a bulletin of the Holy Spirit Study Centre, an important Roman Catholic research group in Hong Kong.

devotional works in English. *Prayers and Thoughts of Chinese Christians* provides an overview of Chinese Christian spirituality.[14] Hong Kong publishers such as Tien Dao produce numerous books on Christian spirituality and collections of personal testimonies in Chinese.

A small number of works on the Chinese church are essential reading and have been referred to frequently in this study.[15] We do not have space here for a critical review, but should mention at least two works that afford differing perspectives. Anthony Lambert's *Resurrection of the Chinese Church* is a detailed account of church life between 1979 and 1990, covering the same period as our own work. Mr Lambert is China consultant for the Overseas Missionary Fellowship, and has visited China numerous times from his base in Hong Kong. His book reflects this personal experience, and is also valuable as a reference work since it makes full use of documentation supplied by the CCRC and other agencies, and has a realistically critical assessment of official material. The book is stronger on description than analysis, which is characteristic of many publications from evangelical sources; theological or metaphysical explanations are often offered where a social scientific approach might seem more appropriate.

Philip Wickeri's *Seeking the Common Ground*, which focuses on the history and theology of the Protestant interaction with the CCP, presents a far more positive view of the official church. Wickeri displays great erudition, has an excellent grasp of available documents, has conducted personal interviews with important participants and makes an impressive contribution to the history of the Chinese Protestant movement. However we agree with the reviewer in the *China Quarterly* who finds 'there is

[14] Chan Kim-Kwong and Alan Hunter (eds.), *Prayers and Thoughts of Chinese Christians*, London: Mowbray, 1991.
[15] The most important include: Richard C. Bush, *Religion in Communist China*, Nashville: Abingdon, 1970; Chan Kim-Kwong, *Towards a Contextual Ecclesiology: The Catholic Church in the People's Republic of China, 1979–1983*, Hong Kong: Phototech Systems, 1987; Lambert, *Resurrection*; MacInnis, *Religious Policy* and also *Religion in China Today: Policy and Practice*, Maryknoll: Orbis Books, 1989; George N. Patterson, *Christianity in Communist China*, Waco, TX: Word Books, 1969; Philip L. Wickeri, *Seeking the Common Ground: Protestant Christianity, The Three Self and China's United Front*, Maryknoll: Orbis Books, 1988.

something about the basic assumptions underlying his narrative which troubles. There is a sense of *déjà vu* about reading much of this book, as if it were written during the 1950s.'[16] The *déjà vu* lies in Wickeri's apparent belief in the sincerity and benevolence of the CCP, in particular its united front policy, a belief now shared by few other observers. Wickeri will probably continue to be an important interpreter to the west of the official Chinese church's views: in 1991 he became the first foreigner to be ordained in China for over forty years. Lambert's and Wickeri's works are thus rewarding in terms of understanding the Protestant experience in China; they also illustrate the divergent interpretations of it made by foreign scholars.

More widely, we have consulted the ever-growing body of scholarship concerning life in the People's Republic of China, references to which are made as appropriate. With all the above material, and including the present work, the reader is well advised to be aware of the limitations of any particular author, methodology and source material. China is a vast continent, its information systems are under-developed and all observers have their blind spots. Nevertheless the country and its religious life are becoming more transparent and the careful student, we believe, can piece together a clear understanding of the situation as a whole and some of its undercurrents.

THE STRUCTURE OF THIS WORK

Murray Rubinstein, introducing his book on Christianity in Taiwan, states '[my] basic approach is eclectic. It combines traditional historical methods of presentation with analytic and descriptive modes derived from such fields as theology (and its subfield of missiology), anthropology, and comparative religion.'[17] Most writers on Christianity in the PRC have likewise adopted an eclectic approach, although few of them have been so explicit about it. We feel this is inevitable at present: to understand Christianity in modern Chinese culture needs a variety of perspectives.

[16] James T. Myers, book review, *China Quarterly*, no. 127, September 1991, pp. 636–8.
[17] Rubinstein, *Protestant Community*, p. 12.

Our intention in this study is first to clarify the socio-political changes of the 1980s that made such an impact on the Christian community. The Chinese state has a pervasive influence on social life, and relations with the CCP inevitably influence the doctrines, practices and ecclesiology of the church. Moreover it is difficult for the outsider to grasp what it is like to live in China today, since human rights and other issues are sometimes reported in a sensational way by western media. The first chapter explains the context of current religious policy and the administration of religious affairs.

Chapter 2 presents a survey of the institutions, church life and other components of the Protestant community in the 1980s. It is descriptive rather than analytical. The material is unusual, some of it reported here for the first time. We also note that different sources at times provide conflicting information, and attempt to discern the background to this problem.

Chapters 3 and 4 focus on two major strands of interpretation. First we suggest that the current church is the outcome of a historical process, with roots in the missionary enterprise and the response of Chinese to that period of evangelism. Many of the characteristics of the church today can only be understood against this background. Further, in chapter 4 we suggest that Chinese Christianity should be analysed with reference to a range of cultural and psychological factors, in particular traditional Chinese religiosity.

Chapter 5 provides reports on grass-roots Christian life, illustrating the diversity of Protestantism inside and outside official structures. There are few published accounts of Christian communities, partly because much attention has been focused on state–church relations and politics. Also, it has not been possible for foreigners to observe and interview systematically, nor have Chinese academics been able to publish many case studies. Here we have attempted at least some preliminary reporting.[18]

[18] Two books that may be consulted for further accounts are Jonathan Chao and Richard van Houten, *Wise as Serpents, Harmless as Doves: Christians in China Tell Their Story*, Pasadena: William Carey Library, 1988; and Raymond Fung, *Households of God on China's Soil*, Geneva: World Council of Churches, 1982.

Protestantism is, of course, by no means the only religion in China, and it is helpful to view its problems and successes in comparative perspective. In chapter 6 we describe Buddhism and the Roman Catholic Church as the institutional religions of comparable scope. The comparison highlights evangelism as a key feature of Protestantism's success, and highlights the differing political positions of the three communities. For reasons of space we are not able to consider Islam and Buddhism in areas such as Tibet and Xinjiang, nor can we examine the significant impact of Protestantism among the non-Han people of southwest China. These are topics that demand specialist research, and are not directly relevant to our focus on Protestantism in mainstream Han culture.

Finally, in January 1992 the Fifth National Christian Conference was held in Beijing. This forms a convenient point to close our narrative, in the uncertain political atmosphere that prevailed after the traumas of 1989. We also offer some final thoughts on broader issues that emerge from this study.

CHAPTER I

The social and political context

1949–1979: THE PARTY TRIUMPHANT[1]

In October 1949 the CCP announced the foundation of the People's Republic of China. The next three years saw the high point of popular support for the new government, but the situation soon became more tense with the outbreak of the Korean war when the Chinese people were called on to 'aid Korea and resist the US' by means of voluntary military service, financial contributions and massive demonstrations. At the same time the CCP stepped up its efforts to revolutionize China: not content to rule, the communists intended to transform Chinese society. This entailed expropriation of the capitalist class and the creation of an egalitarian society through ideological campaigns, thought reform, public accusation meetings, mass arrests and intensive social control. All industries were nationalized by the mid-1950s and thereafter ran on command lines adopted from the Soviet Union, China's main ally. The state was effectively a one party system, with the theory of proletarian dictatorship as its ideological justification. There was undoubtedly repression, but also progress: China finally freed herself of foreign control, and standards of public health, education and welfare improved.

There were parallel developments in the countryside. By 1952 most land had been redistributed, in the following years it was

---

[1] Readers who wish to study the history of China after 1949 have a vast choice of material. Among many other sources we can recommend the *Cambridge History of China*, general editors John K. Fairbank and Denis Twitchett, vols. xiv and xv, Cambridge University Press, 1987 and 1992. The following paragraphs provide a very brief account of some of the major events.

collectivized and by 1958 People's Communes were set up over most of China. They remained in operation until the early 1980s, the evidence suggesting that they were inefficient as production units, although they did have a number of advantages over family farming: they were less patriarchal, could mobilize labour for public works and limited polarization between income groups. In the late 1950s the whole of China, and especially the rural areas, was devastated by catastrophic policy decisions. In 1958 Mao Zedong initiated a mass movement known as the Great Leap Forward, in the course of which the Chinese nation was instructed to overtake the USA and Britain. Absurd projects, such as the building of millions of tiny blast furnaces, led to a massive waste of natural resources. Misguided central directives on agriculture, coupled with the poor harvests of 1959–61, led to famines in which millions died. In the early 1960s the Party leadership adopted more pragmatic economic policies and Mao himself was edged out of power, but he responded by a gradual mobilization of support for extreme left-wing policies, culminating in the Cultural Revolution. The latter was launched in 1966 as a mass movement of students who were instigated to attack the Party hierarchy, endorse Mao's claim to supreme leadership, and destroy all remnants of the old society. People with suspect backgrounds, particularly intellectuals, were persecuted, sometimes tortured and killed; soon the situation threatened to degenerate into complete anarchy, and the military was called in to form a *de facto* government. In the mid-1970s, power was held by a clique which earned the hatred of most of the Party leadership, and the country as a whole, and which became known as the Gang of Four, their names a symbol for persecution, divisiveness and chaos under the guise of a purist ideology. After 1976 power returned to a more orthodox alignment of senior officials inside the Party apparatus, and eventually Deng Xiaoping emerged as leader of this faction, which he led until his semi-retirement in 1989.

The period from 1949 to 1979 was traumatic for the churches.[2] In 1950 and 1951 the CCP evolved a strategy for

---

[2] Bush, *Religion in Communist China*, is an excellent study of the situation before 1970. Whyte, *Unfinished Encounter*, chapters 6 and 7, discusses the period from 1949 to 1979.

dealing with religious organizations. The main purpose was to ensure that they would support the new government; in the case of Christians it also meant cutting their links with foreigners. The Party believed that religion, a product of feudalism according to Marxist theory, would soon die out in the new social order, but believers had to be controlled in the meantime. Religious leaders who would co-operate with the government in this programme were found relatively easily in Buddhist, Islamic, Protestant and Daoist circles; only the Catholics, who were deeply anti-communist, resisted for several years. These individuals were appointed to run various 'Patriotic Associations', which have operated until now as the official leadership structures for their respective religions, working in close co-operation with the government.

A group of men and women was selected from the Protestant movement to serve as leaders for the new church. Several of them were Christians who sincerely believed in the political programme of the CCP. The Party was at the height of its prestige in the late 1940s and many Christians, especially in student circles, were genuinely supportive of it: they felt that their religious beliefs were no reason not to support the CCP, and that its programmes for social reform were in accordance with Christian ethics. Others were secret Party members who had been sent to work within the church. In July 1950 the group published a manifesto, approved by Premier Zhou Enlai, which constituted the blueprint for the new church movement. All Protestants in China were urged to sign it and some 400,000, about half the total Protestant membership in China, had done so by 1952. Its aims were explicitly stated as: 'Under the leadership of the government to oppose imperialism, feudalism and bureaucratic capitalism . . . to purge imperialistic influence from within Christianity itself; and be vigilant against imperialism, especially American imperialism, in its plot to use religion in fostering the growth of reactionary forces.'[3]

Lambert, *Resurrection*, pp. 9–27, provides some information on Christianity in the Cultural Revolution.
[3] For this and other texts of the period see *Documents of the Three Self Movement* edited by Francis P. Jones, New York: National Council of Churches, 1963.

The most immediate tasks were to end reliance on foreign personnel and financial aid, and to create a unified church structure under governmental control and supportive of governmental policies. The methods adopted were denunciation meetings, political study and thought reform. Those who refused to co-operate were subjected to harassment and imprisonment, and missionaries were singled out for attack to hasten the process of independence. Relatively few were imprisoned, but all had their freedom of movement curtailed and those on furlough were unable to renew their visas.

The tactics were generally successful. By 1952 all but a handful of missionaries had departed, foreign funding had stopped and several senior Chinese churchmen took refuge abroad. Soon the new organization, which in 1954 adopted the name 'Three Self Patriotic Movement' (TSPM), became the most powerful institution in Protestant circles. The TSPM Standing Committee took all important decisions concerning the church under the direction of the newly established Religious Affairs Bureau. The National Christian Council and its affiliated institutions were dissolved, as were the denominational structures. Colleges and hospitals that had previously been Christian run were handed over to the state. From this time on the church would have only a minimal involvement in social welfare.

There were intense efforts to rework Christianity in accordance with Party guidelines, and to indoctrinate pastors with the resulting ideology. Support of the Soviet Union became a Christian duty. *Tianfeng*, the official TSPM journal, congratulated Stalin on his birthday and published an article by K. H. Ting praising the suppression of the Hungarian uprising in 1956. Christian teaching was brought into line with the prevailing trend in Chinese politics, namely to emphasize struggle and hatred of enemies. There was a strong insistence on this-worldly rather than other-worldly concerns, and a tendency to proclaim a justification by works rather than by faith alone. Christian social ethics were reworked to avoid the charge of 'reformism', one of the main communist heresies of the time. Such modifications in doctrine were exactly paralleled in

Buddhist circles: Buddhists were obliged, for example, to abandon their traditional pacificism and contribute towards the purchase of a bomber for use in Korea.

An early consequence of the communist takeover was that it was no longer socially advantageous to be a Christian. Before 1949 it had been a common complaint that many Chinese, the so-called rice-bowl Christians, were attending church to curry favour with westerners. After 1949 the situation was just the opposite: it was soon evident that belonging to a religious organization would bring only trouble. Only those who were deeply committed took the risk of continued participation.

One important development in the 1950s was the TSPM's announcement of a 'post-denominational era'. Denominations were criticized as relics of imperialism and Christians were told to organize themselves into one united church movement: only TSPM churches were permitted to operate.[4] Most urban churches were closed, the buildings usually handed over to other work-units as a patriotic gesture. In Shanghai the 200 churches still open in 1957 were down to twenty-three by 1958; in Beijing, sixty-five churches were reduced to four. The pulpit became a forum for political propaganda. Pastors were instructed to preach on topics such as anti-imperialism and the leading role of the CCP in the reconstruction of society, which led to disillusion among the congregations. Many Christians were targeted for attack, either as supporters of the GMD, as having contacts with foreigners, or as rightists. In addition, Christians went to remote provinces, either as a punishment, or to evangelize, or as a measure of political protection for their families. Finally, many believers had strong personal objections to particular TSPM leaders who had been responsible for denunciations. Most pastors had left for factories or labour camps, and congregational attendance was very low. The situation became even worse in the mid-1960s and during the Cultural Revolution it seemed that the CCP had achieved its objectives in the sphere of Christianity at least, while similar conclusions were being drawn about the state of Buddhism.

[4] For this sequence of events see Francis P. Jones, *The Church in Communist China: A Protestant Appraisal*, New York: Friendship Press, 1962, pp. 156–7.

It is easy to understand why churches were attacked during the period: they were both symbolic and actual links with imperialists, as were international trading companies or banks, which were also expropriated. The CCP did not tolerate ideological diversity in any field, particularly when war with the USA appeared likely. The ease with which the churches were taken over suggests that under their impressive exterior they did not command a great deal of popular support, and that is probably close to the truth. Even in cities with a relatively strong Christian community, Protestants rarely amounted to more than 1 per cent of the population, and even then were split into denominations. The only church institution that held out for several years was the Catholic Church in Shanghai, which was not fully tamed until the mid-1950s, mostly because of its deep-rooted mass support in districts of the city. To control it needed repressive action against the majority of the population there, which the Party was reluctant to undertake.

The religious policy of the CCP certainly played a role in the closure of rural churches, but the transformation of work practices and institutions in the countryside was equally important. The rural population came under great pressure during the most radical phases of CCP rural policies. Millions starved, and those who survived were exhausted and regimented. Cash incomes were minimal after the creation of the communes, so support for churches would have been extremely difficult, and in any case it is doubtful that a pastor could have bought food even if he had money: provisions were distributed only in exchange for work-points. With possible minor exceptions, all churches were closing down by the early 1960s and closed from 1966 to 1979. Such pastors as remained were bi-vocational or unable to function as pastors at all.

The story of the institutional church until 1979 is one of collapse. What of the home meetings where the majority of Christians worshipped? Here there is greater difficulty in assessing the situation owing to lack of evidence. It seems probable that for about twenty years the Christian movement went truly underground, not only in the sense that believers had to hide their activities from the police, but in the more profound sense that religion ceased to have a significant meaning in society. The CCP came to power with massive support from peasants and working people who had suffered terrible oppression and war for the past thirty years. Dramatic upheavals took place in the course of land reform as the whole structure of rural society changed several times in two decades. In the cities there were equally dramatic changes and the whole of China was swept by a communist fervour. It must have seemed as though a new world was coming, whether in pain or joy. There is every indication that all religions declined rapidly in the period, a process accelerated by persecution. There were intensive campaigns against practitioners of popular religion and the Buddhist monasteries were hard hit by land reforms. The period from 1950 to 1976 was the high point of the project to exert total control over society.

During the Cultural Revolution the attempt began to break down, showing the contradictory nature of that movement. On the one hand CCP ideology was at its most extreme, but on the other, policy implementation was haphazard and chaotic, often verging on anarchy. Millions of individuals moved around the country, often unwillingly, in the process of factional fighting, administrative sanction, rustication, terms in labour camps and work in border regions. The economic situation was precarious, most people surviving on a restricted diet and with a minimum of consumer goods. Social and cultural life was strictly regimented. Yet at this time, a few reports began to emerge of illegal religious activities, both in cities and the countryside. At first they were probably spontaneous meetings of old groups of friends and family, which gradually spread their influence through personal evangelism. Possibly the utter disillusion with the Party and widespread insecurity made people receptive to the Christian message. Then, as Deng initiated his reforms in 1979, city and provincial governments recalled the old TSPM officials to oversee the reopening of churches. This marked the starting point of a remarkable Christian revival.

REFORM IN CHINA AFTER 1979

In 1991, during an informal conversation in Beijing, a senior government official gave his impression of western analyses of religion in modern China. He felt that they tended to make two main errors: to isolate religious policy from the overall political situation, and to ignore the complex relationship between policy intention, implementation and reaction:

The fundamental orientation of our government since 1979 has remained constant. First we want to raise the standard of living throughout the country by economic reforms and development. This will ensure that the majority of the population supports us. Secondly we must hold everyone within a certain framework, namely socialism. China is a huge country with enormous problems. If we let every group say and do just as it pleased there would soon be chaos. But these days we mostly use persuasion. It is counter-productive to use the methods of dictatorship unless absolutely necessary.

Religious people think they are special. There again so do intellectuals and so do journalists. In fact all policies concerning these people are essentially the same. They are part of the overall ideological control mechanism. The basic principle is simple: if they are obedient, then we treat them well. If they are not, then we discipline them. It is quite interesting that when they want to break the law they all appeal to different principles. Christians say they must obey God, journalists claim they are serving the public, intellectuals say they are developing culture. But from our point of view these excuses are all irrelevant. We treat these people as an administrative problem.

The other point is that it is a highly complex matter to develop a policy, implement it and get people to obey it. In every area there are three main actors. First is the Party leadership which formulates the policy. They have certain ideas which they wish to put into practice. Second are the lower-level cadres. They have their own reasons. They may want to adopt the policy or they may not want to, for countless reasons. Third is the target population, those for whom the policy is devised. Again they may approve of it or they may not. All sorts of results can appear. So when you consider religious policy I suggest you consider these aspects, not just the formal documents.

On reflection this seemed sound advice. Religious life in the 1980s should be considered in the light of the overall reform programme.[5]

---

[5] There are numerous specialist studies of the reforms of the 1980s. Two good collections

By 1978 the top leadership of the CCP recognized the urgent need for far-reaching changes in economic and political life. Its first priority was the structural reform of agriculture, where productivity was extremely low. Low educational and technical standards were exacerbated by poor management, often caused by the enforcement of central directives inappropriate to local conditions. However the worst problem was regarded as utter cynicism and unwillingness to work on the part of the peasants, allegedly caused by the 'egalitarian distribution system . . . which does not accurately reflect a person's work'.[6]

Before 1978 almost all decisions in rural areas had been taken by Party officials whose target was the fulfilment of state-determined quotas for each locality. The main thrust of the reforms was to allow peasants to sell most of their produce on a deregulated market. Each family now manages its own affairs according to a household responsibility system and, if successful, can improve its income and standard of living. The state has also strongly encouraged peasants to diversify production, for example by establishing food processing and transport in small towns and villages. This should enhance output and provide alternative productive employment for millions of rural workers.[7] Most observers believe that the reforms have been successful in raising living standards and stimulating production, although serious criticisms of the whole process have been voiced, concerning environmental and infrastructural damage, social polarization, and a return to more traditional, patriarchal social relations.[8]

This process inevitably led to the creation of new social forces and a totally different spirit of competition, mobility, diversification and independence among the rural population. The Party had given its full approval to private enterprise with the

of papers are: *Transforming China's Economy in the 1980s*, edited by Stephan A. Feuchtwang, A. Hussain and T. Pairault, Boulder: Westview, 1988; *Chinese Society on the Eve of Tiananmen*, edited by Deborah Davis and E. Vogel, Cambridge: Harvard University Press, 1990.

[6] *Renmin ribao*, (*People's Daily*), editorial, 14 March 1980.

[7] 'Technology Transfer to Rural Areas', *Beijing Review*, no. 25, 22 June 1987, pp. 15–16.

[8] A fierce and eloquent critic is William Hinton, *The Great Reversal: The Privatization of China 1978–1989*, New York: Monthly Review Press, 1990.

slogan 'to get rich is glorious', and the peasants in most areas appear to have responded enthusiastically. The Chinese countryside became the arena for a small-scale but lively capitalism, as people began to travel and trade, searching out markets, products and technology.

The inevitable corollary of this was a massive reduction of state power in the countryside. From the 1950s to 1978, CCP cadres had formed a repressive network across the country, based in offices in market towns from which they effectively dominated the surrounding areas, with the primary task of extracting grains and other foodstuffs from the peasants to supply city markets at depressed prices. It was a rigid, self-serving political bureaucracy inclined 'to issue blind directives, to order unreasonable projects and recommend impractical schemes . . . unable to co-exist with any kind of pluralism, any grass-roots initiative, any lower-level dissent'.[9] The new policies meant a radical down-grading of this power network, and the frontiers of state power were pushed far back. In the 1980s, China's peasants had a substantial amount of autonomy to pursue their own activities, such as religion. Only if the latter became too provocative was there likelihood of intervention.

Urban economic activity was also reformed, although not so comprehensively. At periods in the 1980s, radical programmes for decentralization and competition were discussed, but by 1991 only a few sectors – such as restaurants, tailoring, road transport – had seen the growth of independent enterprises. The vast majority of industrial concerns remained under state control, where planners generally determined production targets, supplied materials, fixed wages and prices. The losses incurred by large state enterprises, their inefficiency, stockpiling, and resistance to change constitute perhaps the most serious problem at the centre of the Chinese economy.[10] In agriculture the major shift has been from state to private farming; in the urban economy it has been from central to local or provincial ownership.

---

[9] William Hinton, *Shenfan: The Continuing Revolution in a Chinese Village*, New York: Secker and Warburg, 1983, p. 757.

[10] *New China News Agency*, 10 October 1991 and *China News Analysis*, no. 1445, 15 October 1991, p. 4.

Provincial governments now have far more power in relation to the centre, especially in the southern and eastern provinces. There are frequent reports of tough negotiations between local and central officials, and also of a growth in inter-regional economic links, as trade deals by-pass central mechanisms.[11]

In 1978 and 1979, the leadership seemed about to initiate a similarly radical programe of political reform. The Party admitted it had made serious mistakes since 1957. Mao Zedong was criticized for over-hastiness and personal, arbitrary rule. The official press endorsed reformist ideas, stressing the need for democratic control over political power. The 1978 constitution granted substantial civil rights, notably in Article 45 which guaranteed freedom of speech and the right to hold public debates. The culmination was a vigorous non-Party movement, especially in Beijing in 1978/79, that demanded democracy, human rights, a thorough reform of the one-party state and repudiation of Mao's career. However in 1979 the CCP leaders decided that such dissent was no longer tolerable and arrested several hundred young activists. Cynical observers concluded that Deng Xiaoping and his faction, having ousted their enemies in the Party hierarchy, had no further use for such unorthodox support. The outstanding dissident editor, Wei Jingsheng, was imprisoned in 1979, and subjected to appalling treatment. The provisions of Article 45 were removed from the constitution: Party theoreticians explained that liberalization had meant freedom to criticize the Gang of Four, not a licence to attack the Party.

The 'four principles', namely the socialist system, the dictatorship of the proletariat, the leadership of the Party and Marx–Lenin–Mao Zedong Thought, were invoked as immutable truths. In 1981, after careful personal consideration by Deng Xiaoping, an official statement rehabilitated Mao's tarnished image: once again 'the Chinese people have always regarded Comrade Mao Zedong as their respected and beloved great leader and teacher'.[12] Conservatives, especially in the

[11] Gu Zhibin, *China Beyond Deng: Reform in the PRC*, Jefferson, NC: McFarland, 1991, p. 45.
[12] See *Beijing Review*, 6 July 1981, pp. 10–39.

military, blamed reformers for undermining the prestige of socialism, the Party and China, and successfully insisted on a return to more orthodox rule.

This campaign set the pattern for the coming decade, a balance of power in the Party élite between reformers and hardliners. Deng Xiaoping himself, undisputed leader throughout the decade, held an ambivalent position. In 1980 he endorsed the principle of the 'institutionalization of democracy and its codification into laws', but he was also a strong advocate for suppression of the democracy movement. Socialist democracy is 'definitely not a democracy which discards the socialist legal system, the Party's leadership, and discipline and order'.[13] He settled for a compromise between hard-line communism and further reforms. The 1980s saw a series of swings of the political pendulum as the two factions temporarily gained and lost influence. By far the most abrupt reversal came in the spring of 1989. Zhao Ziyang, the leading reformist, was dismissed from his posts during the democracy movement. Hard-liners regained control of the Standing Committee of the Politburo and quickly asserted their authority throughout the administration, in education, the media and other spheres. The positive role of Mao in the Chinese revolution was again emphasized as a symbol that hard-liners were in control.

One should be aware of the complexity of taking and implementing decisions in the world's most populous nation. In the highly centralized and authoritarian system of government, the top leaders regularly decide policy on a vast range of issues and tend to exercise great personal authority; since imperial times, power in China has tended to reside in individuals rather than institutions.[14] The extent of consultation depends on the particular issue. Foreign policy, defence and internal security, for example, are handled only by the inner circle and its closest advisers. Even at the most liberal periods they have not been

---

[13] For these quotations and a detailed discussion of the issues see Tang Tsou, *The Cultural Revolution and Post-Mao Reforms*, University of Chicago Press, 1986, pp. 300–12.

[14] Suzanne Ogden, *China's Unresolved Issues: Politics, Development and Culture*, Englewood Cliffs, NJ: Prentice Hall, 1989, p. 87.

open to discussion in the press or other public fora. Similarly in the realm of ideology, the 'four principles' are sacrosanct. Issues reserved for the top leaders are decided with minimum consultation and may be rigorously implemented.

On the other hand many important questions are decided only after consultation extending far beyond the central offices of power. There may be no political opposition in China, but interest groups have many ways to express their views: the controversial Three Gorges Dam project for the Yangtze River, for example, has been discussed by successive Chinese governments since 1911! In the less sensitive areas, negotiations may be prolonged almost indefinitely, or result in compromise solutions whose formulation is vague enough to please all parties. Similar factors influence implementation. When there is no split in the élite consensus, or where top leaders enforce decisions through their personal power networks, matters can be settled quickly. In the 1980s this was often the case when Deng himself took over an issue, for example population policy in 1979/80 or the suppression of the student movement in 1989. Generally speaking, religion did not attract much attention at this very high level, with the exception of a few meetings held in 1990. This is probably an indication that the policy was broadly accepted by all interested parties and did not rate a high priority on the agenda.[15]

An important constraint on policy implementation is the nature of the bureaucracy responsible for the daily administration of China's affairs. In 1982 there were an estimated twenty million state and Party cadres; including administrative staff in schools, hospitals and other units, the entire bureaucracy may have numbered 100 million.[16] A host of hidden processes operated against an efficient command line: policies adopted in Beijing were often compromised by the self-interest of local cadres, informal groups, personal relationships, bargains and

---

[15] One exception was a national religious work conference held in Beijing from December 5–10, 1990, which was addressed by Li Peng and Qiao Shi.
[16] John P. Burns, 'China's Fight against "Bureaucracy": Reform of the State Council, 1981–82' in *China in Readjustment*, edited by Chi-Keung Leung and Steve S. K. Chin, Hong Kong: University Press, 1983, pp. 283–305.

compromises. Loyalties were inevitably uncertain since the Party itself was home to many factions inspired by personalities, political orientation and local interests. The superficial portrayal of the Party as a monolithic entity with efficient totalitarian control over society is a myth.

The treatment of intellectuals illustrates many of these uncertainties. The 'four cardinal principles' were not openly questioned, but the details of the cultural policy itself were continually shifting. The idea that art should serve the Party could be interpreted in many different ways. The journalist Liu Binyan exposed corruption inside the Party. Film-maker Zhang Yimou explored hitherto forbidden themes of sexuality. The popular TV series *River Elegy* treated the whole of Chinese culture as decadent. The Shanghai journal *World Economic Herald Weekly* gave a gloomy assessment of the economic situation. Fang Lizhi advocated human rights and a legal system. Zhao Fusan argued for a more liberal understanding of religion. None of these could be called illegal, but they were on the boundaries of what was permitted. In such a fluctuating situation, government action was bound to appear arbitrary. Some people were chastised, others were not. Intellectuals were often pressurized; on the other hand, being articulate and sometimes with friends in high places, they were ideally placed to sabotage the implementation of strict policies.

The policy on religion should be understood as part of this scenario. It was a secondary issue and rarely attracted élite attention. On the other hand the target population was quite large and there was a substantial bureaucracy devoted to monitoring it. There were numerous cross-currents of interest which resulted in an ambiguous situation, but one which in all essentials conformed to national norms. An article in the *emigré* journal *China Spring* reported the views of an official responsible for the supervision of religion in a region of Hebei:

Based on the experience of the official, there was no uniformity in orders from the central government. Documents often contained contradictions. Thus it was more secure to remain inactive than to execute orders from one of the factions. Why did the policy always change? According to the cadre, the prime reason behind the ever-changing policy was due to the many personnel changes in the central government. In view of such circumstances, 'we who are responsible for the management of religious work must learn to be flexible, or else our heads will be chopped without our knowing why'.[17]

The 1980s thus produced a serious contradiction between conservatism and change. The Party faced a theoretical challenge: it needed to legitimize both the economic reforms and its own dictatorship. The introduction of market mechanisms and rural capitalism had no justification in the Marxist canon, yet the Party dared not question Marxist–Leninism since that would call its own rule into doubt. Similarly, it desperately needed technical and managerial skills from abroad, yet could not allow an open society to receive them. In practice, economic reforms were so pressing that they had to be adopted, and it was left to academics to find a theoretical Marxist justification for them, a project that is still unfinished. In general, pragmatism took precedence over theoretical considerations.

The modernizing economy created new social forces, and people were exposed as never before to ideas, information and foreign influences. In the cities a more relaxed life-style appeared, and young people in particular demanded personal freedoms. In the countryside the network of control was eroded as peasants returned to family farming. Intellectuals began to circulate dissident views and there was a proliferation of unofficial publications. The Party meanwhile experienced increasing public contempt for inefficiency and corruption. After June 1989 the leaders reasserted their determination to maintain orthodoxy: for example there was a concerted propaganda campaign to celebrate the forty-second anniversary of the founding of the PRC in October 1991, which emphasized the goal of socialism under the leadership of the CCP. The need for modernization was not questioned, but it was conceived in terms of economic growth, not social change. The population was repeatedly warned against foreign influences and loss of

[17] *China Spring*, August 1991, edited and translated in CNCR 1836, 16 August 1991. On the question of policy implementation the most important studies are *Policy Conflicts in Post-Mao China*, edited by John P. Burns and S. Rosen, Armonk: M. E. Sharpe, 1986; and *Policy Implementation in Post-Mao China*, edited by David M. Lampton, Berkeley: University of California Press, 1987.

faith in socialism, which were presented as the major threats to progress. The government believed that its economic policy was basically correct, and that it could retain political power by supervision of the cultural and ideological sphere, by rejecting such demands as right of assembly and freedom of publication. The issue of social control, which we examine next, is still central to its strategy.

SOCIAL CONTROL AND HUMAN RIGHTS

The question of human rights is an area of controversy between the Chinese government and western leaders who express concern over detention without trial, summary executions, torture of prisoners and imprisonment for political or religious reasons. These are alleged to be in contravention of the Universal Declaration of Human Rights and other provisions to which China should conform by virtue of its membership of the United Nations. More widely, critics point to lack of individual freedom, the unsound legal system, lack of voting rights, absence of real political debate and strict control over publications. Anger was especially high over the shooting of unarmed civilians in June 1989, and the campaigns of mass arrests and executions in its aftermath.

Do these concerns reflect a kind of intellectual imperialism? Do we have any right to complain if the situation in China does not conform in some respects to western ideals of human rights, legality and democracy? Chinese dissidents in exile and organizations such as Amnesty International tend to argue that every country should be bound by certain international principles, but the Chinese government rejects this view, maintaining that such issues are internal and not grounds for comment, let alone interference, by outside parties.[18] Some western critics may fail to appreciate the extent to which China was humiliated and exploited by foreigners before 1949, and consequently the determination with which it rejects outside interference now. It

---

[18] A comprehensive statement of China's official views on human rights is by the Press Bureau of the State Council of the PRC, *Human Rights Conditions in China*, Beijing, 1991.

is also relevant to explore the differing concepts of citizenship and legality in western and Chinese culture, the traditional place of religion in the state structure and other issues. We do not excuse the violation of human rights in China, but it is important first to understand them in historical and cultural context. An evolution from the present abuses will probably not arise from conformity to western models, but will be a development of China's own traditions.

The relation of the individual to the state is fundamentally different in Chinese society – both imperial and republican – to that which has emerged in most western countries. In China the individual has never, even in theory, held a set of abstract, inalienable rights that he or she could assert against state power. Rather, the state has had the right to impose its will on society. If done correctly, for the benefit of all, the ruler would retain the Mandate of Heaven; if government was irresponsible and destructive, it would eventually be overthrown. The supreme power of the state was mollified by ideological and ethical constraints, such as the benevolence advocated by Confucianism, rather than by constitutional and political traditions. Tang Tsou, a political scientist, sees western societies as based on a different concept: 'The concept of citizenship begins with members of the society viewed as isolated individuals, possessing equally a set of abstract rights, who form themselves into social groups by exercising those rights . . . The rights of the society's members, rather than their duties, are underscored.'[19]

Tang notes that the western model, which it should be remembered is late historically and limited geographically, was already rejected by pre-communist Chinese thinkers, even those who wished to reform Chinese political life: for example Liang Qichao believed that 'Rousseau's liberal thought, however splendid otherwise, was not suited to the purpose of China's state-building'.[20] There is no opportunity here to explore in depth the relation between individual and state in imperial and republican times, but one must recognize that the priorities of the Chinese state under the CCP are totally different from those

---

[19] Tang Tsou, *Post-Mao Reforms*, p. 272.   [20] *Ibid.*, p. 274.

of western democracies. The overriding demand is for economic development, national independence and progress towards an egalitarian society, in the face of which any individual rights can readily be sacrified. One can compare the state with an army: decisions rest with the high command, who will endeavour to maintain their forces in good order to attain their goals. The troops' welfare is not an end in itself, but a means to an end.

Another point is that the development of the modern western state, for example in England, took several centuries, with extension of civil and political rights between the seventeenth and nineteenth centuries, and a more extensive social welfare network in the twentieth. In China this development has effectively been compressed into a few decades, and to some extent in reverse order: the priority of the CCP was to urgently organize some measure of socio-economic welfare for a population which was almost at subsistence level, and to approach the issues surrounding personal freedoms at some future point.

Human rights in China should also be understood in the context of an overriding ideological agenda, of which the main components between 1949 and 1979 were to reinforce Party control over society, to oppose imperialism, to destroy the power of the old ruling classes and to push China towards socialism. An implicit goal was the increase of production, but this was theorized as an essential precondition to the achievement of the main objectives, not as an end in itself. Not only human rights, but the concept of an absolute law that was applied equally to all citizens was irrelevant. In its formative period the Party had no option but to operate outside the law, both against the nationalist government and the Japanese, and it never established a tradition of respect for legal niceties.[21]

The legal system, freedom of expression and related questions were simply not on the agenda before 1979, and the CCP was not in the least apologetic about its programme. On the contrary, it was at perhaps its most confident, arguing that it was proceeding rapidly towards socialism and successfully opposing imperialism: claims that attracted support from many

[21] *Ibid.*, p. 277.

western intellectuals who were vociferous critics of human rights abuses in other countries at the time. Political control and economic commandism were reinforced by comprehensive control of the media, following an earlier dictum of Mao that 'art and literature should serve politics'. Worse, there was a massive death-toll directly attributable to government policy, a huge wastage of human resources in labour camps, the deliberate cultivation of hatred, persecution and social fragmentation.[22] These policies were justified as an essential part of 'class-struggle', which was perhaps the most destructive theory embraced by the CCP after its rise to power. One may have considerable sympathy, or even admiration, for the CCP's intention to eliminate foreign influence, exploitation and the corruption of the previous regime. But it is difficult to justify the attacks made on millions of people for the most trivial of reasons.[23] A profound misunderstanding of the nature of China's problems vitiated the CCP's programme of action. For some thirty years the Chinese people were mobilized in a misguided direction, to attack alleged 'class-enemies' who were really marginal to the situation. More useful undertakings, such as rural reconstruction, industrial and technological development, education and health care were sacrificed, leading to profound hostility, tension and cynicism. The misdiagnosis of China's problems was carried to obsessive extremes after 1966 when rationality in public life entirely collapsed.

When we consider the 1980s, then, it is important to note the tremendous change for the better compared to previous decades, even taking into account the repression after 4 June 1989. The number of quasi-judicial executions, use of labour camps, control over information and individual behaviour never reached anything like their previous dimensions. For most practical purposes the achievement of socialism was tacitly pushed to a distant future, while the nation concentrated on the

---

[22] The most conservative estimates are of 700,000 executions in the first five years of CCP rule, and an undisclosed number of deaths, perhaps many million, in the Great Leap Forward of 1958.

[23] For example for knowledge of a foreign language or taste in music, which were sufficient grounds for persecution as rightism in some years.

development of industry, consumer goods, variety of agricultural produce and a rise in living standards. Of the other major concerns, only the maintenance of CCP power was retained in full. The primary cause of human rights abuse under the previous system – the branding of millions of individuals as 'class enemies' or 'enemies of the people' – was repudiated. It is true that attacks continued on 'bad elements', who were defined as criminals, enemy agents or corrupt profiteers, and that many people were doubtless unfairly prosecuted, but the overall situation was vastly improved. A survey of the level of social control in the 1980s is essential background to understanding the situation for religious believers. To this end we examine three critical areas: freedom of information and publication; freedom of association; and the control or surveillance of individuals.

The role of the main newspapers and broadcasting stations is still essentially to transmit to the nation the concerns of the CCP leadership, filtered through the Propaganda Department. The press refrains from investigative journalism as far as the Party centre is concerned, although it occasionally makes revelations about corruption at lower levels: 'Secrecy within the Chinese leadership permits its scandalous behaviour and policy errors to escape public censure. Here again, Chinese culture has helped shape institutional practices in today's China. Secrecy concerning affairs of state is as old as China: decisions by China's emperors were always made "behind the curtain". Under socialism, the leadership's tradition of secrecy has continued to the point that only a handful of leaders know precisely how and why decisions are made.'[24]

The great change in the 1980s was not so much an improvement in the official press, but rather the rapid growth of alternative sources of information. The most important were journals and books registered by smaller publishing companies of various kinds, often in the provinces; unauthorized publications; and the availability of news from foreign sources. So many publishing houses sprang up in the 1980s that it became

[24] Ogden, *China's Unresolved Issues*, p. 100.

impossible to monitor them all. As in most repressive societies there were dozens of innovative schemes to avoid, pervert or bamboozle Party censors. From time to time there was a purge of these free publications, but they always resurfaced under a different guise. Some of the most controversial writings appeared in publications that had obtained official authorization; some of the famous incidents in intellectual life were concerned with the closure of those that had 'gone too far'.

Other publications were simply illegal. In the late 1980s a rapidly growing number of underground presses sold their books through private booksellers, a system of distribution which became known as the 'second channel'.[25] Unlike the Soviet Union, the role of illegal publications has never been important in China, and there has been nothing equivalent to the *samizdat* literature. However from about 1986 the profit motive began to play its usual stimulating role in the book trade when it was discovered that unofficial publications could be lucrative. Apart from the predictable pornography, the best sales were from unofficial accounts of the Cultural Revolution, and revelations concerning the private lives of top leaders. A few Christian publications are produced illegally, especially by house church groups in southeast China.

Finally, foreign broadcasts are widely heard. Many intellectuals gained their daily news from the Voice of America and the BBC, which must have audiences of hundreds of thousands all over China, and in some cities TV stations like CNN are received. Although viewers are limited in terms of numbers, the news quickly filters to the rest of the population. This is reinforced by other factors: the thousands of Chinese who have studied or worked abroad, translations of foreign books, films and TV programmes, reception of broadcasts from Hong Kong and Taiwan, the influx of foreign students, teachers, tourists and business personnel. Chinese citizens now have access to a range of news sources on international issues, and to some extent even learn about China's domestic affairs from foreign media.

In sum, the availability of information is vastly improved.

[25] See introduction, note 10.

One major difference with the west is that much information is perhaps available, but needs considerable effort to find. The distribution system is chaotic, and many news stories are broadcast only once by foreign radio: it may be difficult to discover further information or to pursue a particular story. Moreover, large areas of national life are still completely off-limits, and one cannot discover the inside story for major political events unless one has personal contacts in high places. Information is still power, and guarded as such.

Improvements in the next area, freedom of association, have been far slower, if not non-existent. The tolerance for social groups outside the direct supervision of the Party is still extremely limited. Religious groups are among the few permitted organizations in the state, which makes them especially sensitive. It is true that there are several trade unions, 'democratic parties' and 'mass organizations', but they are specifically under Party leadership: their task is not to form an opposition, but to assist the CCP in its running of the country.[26] We shall consider later the importance of the patriotic religious movements as examples of these co-opted mass organizations.

Guidelines for publications and associations, whether or not reasonable, are at least relatively consistent. The situation as far as the individual goes presents a more complex, shifting picture. Would a person get into trouble if he/she complained about the government? Went to church? Met foreigners? Joined a demonstration? Left the Party? One of the most frustrating aspects of life in China was uncertainty about what was tolerated and what was not. Offences seemed to change constantly depending on policy shifts, campaigns, attitudes of local officials and other factors. To all the above questions, the answer is that people might encounter trouble, equally they might meet official indifference or even approval. For example contact with foreigners in the mid-1980s was officially encouraged, since Chinese citizens could practise a foreign language, usually English, learn about other societies, perhaps make contacts for study or trade. On the other hand the situation was far more

---

[26] Ogden, *China's Unresolved Issues*, p. 154.

tense after June 1989 and people were told that discussion with foreigners, especially about politics, was undesirable.[27]

On the whole, the following guidelines seem to have been in operation. Freedom of speech in private conversation was widespread. We have participated in numerous conversations in restaurants or other public places where little effort was made to hide personal views. People generally refrained from personal attacks on the CCP leaders in too strong language, but almost any other views, including sharp criticism of current policies, were expressed without much concern; however, controls were far more stringent in formal settings such as meetings, where expressions of loyalty to the Party are expected. There was considerable freedom to pursue personal interests such as music, sports, hobbies or philosophy. Unlike previous decades one did not become a target for attack because one happened to like western music or classical Buddhist texts. On the contrary the 1980s saw a blossoming of private interests of all kinds.

Travel and internal tourism became popular and are no longer closely scrutinized. Travel abroad is more expensive and difficult to organize, but nevertheless possible, and many Chinese in the big cities, if they have not been abroad themselves, know some family member or friend who has been. Perhaps the sense of movement in the economy and social life stimulated an urge to travel, a sense that China is a country on the move.

Far fewer people were victimized for ideological reasons. In early 1979 the Party removed 'class labels' from over four million people who had previously been classified as landlords, rich peasants, rightists and other 'enemies of the people'. Tens of thousands who had been sent to labour camps were returned to society. In pragmatic terms, as long as one did not openly oppose Party rule one was probably safe from persecution. However, the memory of the mass persecutions is still fresh to anybody over the age of forty, and China lives in the shadow of a *gulag* system that has not yet been honestly faced. The legacy of fear may take decades to disappear.

[27] It was reported in 1991 that the leaders of many work-units instructed employees not to meet foreigners without special permission.

Individual life is still more constrained than in most western societies. This is due in part to the close-knit nature of traditional Chinese culture, which has emphasized family loyalty, kinship ties and the responsibility of the individual to society rather than personal freedoms. The authoritarian style of government reinforces these traditions, and imposes limits to personal freedoms as understood in the west. The inculcation of loyalty does exact a toll on personal time and space, since most people are expected to attend political study sessions once a week or so, when Party representatives explain current policy and expect an enthusiastic endorsement. It is still difficult to change one's occupation or place of residence. Most urban Chinese are assigned without choice to a work-unit when they leave school, and usually work there until retirement. Similarly, one still needs permission from several authorities to make a permanent change in one's place of residence, which is not easily achieved, especially for villagers. Regulations on residence may well become even more stringent in years to come to prevent an influx of displaced, unemployed peasants into the cities. Such regulations contribute to the overall frustration of living under the constant supervision of a bureaucracy that is sometimes perversely obstructive.

Perhaps the main constraint on individuals in the 1980s was their knowledge that the system of personal dossiers was still fully operational. Work-units are charged with collecting all kinds of information – including unsubstantiated reports from personal enemies – about employees and collating it in a personal file. This file, which follows individuals throughout their career, contains information on such matters as personal life, political views, work record, contacts with foreigners, reading habits and participation in meetings. In the 1980s this material was rarely used, but everyone understood that the process of information collection was proceeding unabated. Those with unconventional views could thus be easily targeted by the security forces should there be campaigns in the future.

On the whole, then, the level of surveillance was quite high, but active persecution low. Most visitors to China came away with the impression that life, if not exactly the same as that in the west, was certainly tolerable. To pursue one's own interests (with the important exception of politics), discover various interesting alternative publications, listen to foreign broadcasts, even attend somewhat dissident gatherings of art or pop-music, would not normally provoke a reaction from the authorities. And China is far from a bleak, alienated, depressed society. On the contrary, there are many aspects of life – the warmth of family relationships, for example, or the generally easy-going pace of life – that compare very favourably with the west. In a way this generally positive picture made events on and after 4 June 1989 even more distressing.

We will not dwell on the fact that several thousand unarmed civilians were shot by soldiers in the capital city, presumably under direct orders from the leading politicians and military commanders. This is unacceptable from any government, and Chinese citizens, especially those of Beijing, were disgusted. Perhaps less well known is the level of repression which was instituted after the crackdown. Amnesty International expressed the following concerns in particular: arbitrary detention and imprisonment of political prisoners including prisoners of conscience; human rights violations in ethnic minority regions; unfair trials; executions and summary trial procedures; torture and ill-treatment of prisoners.[28]

Given these serious allegations, many of which are substantiated with documentary evidence, the west is justified in raising human rights as an issue in the process of developing relationships with the PRC. But we would again point out some factors to be borne in mind. First, the Chinese leadership is also justified in highlighting the enormous hypocrisy practised by the USA, Britain and others in this respect. For many years, the powerful western states have supported regimes with appalling human rights records, which are probably worse in most respects than that of China – one thinks immediately of South Africa, Chile, Morocco, Bolivia or Indonesia. Condemnation of human rights

---

[28] Torture is most commonly practised on prisoners under detention before trial, either as punishment or to obtain confessions. Numerous Christians are known to have suffered in this respect. See the report *Violations of Human Rights in China: A Summary of Amnesty International's Concerns in 1991*, London, 1991.

abuses is often a matter of political expediency, not of the moral high ground. Moreover the Chinese government does not respond well to criticisms which are presented in a confrontational way, whether by the USA or the UN, which they may perceive as part of a package to undermine its own authority, a ploy to increase foreign influence in China.

Finally, as noted by Geor Hintzen, the main thrust of the Chinese government's position on human rights is 'that a developing country first has to create the necessary wealth and security before it can guarantee the kind of individual rights valued in the west. As such the Neo-Darwinian right to survival is regarded as fundamental. From it, such collective rights as the right to sovereignty, food and clothing are derived'.[29] Chinese leaders perhaps have some right to say that in comparison to most third world client states of the USA, like some of those mentioned above, or in comparison to India which is rarely singled out for criticism, the average standard of living for the vast majority of Chinese citizens, including factors such as public health, access to education and social stability has not been at all bad in the 1980s. Serious abuses do still exist, but in the overall socio-economic context they are only an exception to a decade that was in many respects successful. The long term well-being of the Chinese people will depend as much on revitalization of the agricultural and industrial base, as on increased personal freedoms. Nevertheless, progress in democracy and the rule of law is certainly a key demand for the immediate future.

How does all this affect our assessment of the control over religion? The situation for the individual believer in the 1980s was not too difficult. People were free to attend church, and could even attend home meetings with little danger of arrest. However, such attendance would almost certainly be noted in the personal dossier, and although it would not lead to punishment in the liberal 1980s, there was always the risk that it could be brought to light in the future. It was also widely thought that membership of a church would limit one's chances of promotion at work, and many Christians preferred to wait

[29] Geor Hintzen, book review, *China Information*, vol. 6 no. 3, Winter 1991, p. 67.

until retirement before making a public confession of faith. On the other hand there was careful supervision of religious organizations. Official church groups were strictly controlled in terms of personnel, publications and activities. While individual house churches could survive relatively easily, the security apparatus would crack down on larger groups, and on itinerant evangelists who became too influential. Similarly, publications were available for the committed who made some effort to obtain them, but they had to be sought from specialized, sometimes underground sources: there was not a wide range of publicly available material.[30]

The situation in these respects perhaps conformed to national norms. They are entirely comprehensible in the light of the traditions of the Chinese state and the agenda of the CCP. On the positive side, we could say that they tended to prevent friction and factionalism, and to maintain a coherent national state under one dominant ideology. In a largely peasant society, where there is constant risk of secret, possibly criminal societies, this is not necessarily a bad thing. It was also surely reasonable to limit the sudden influx of western ideology, which might well threaten the stability of an unprepared society. As it was, Chinese society was shaken by the re-emergence of rampant materialism and commercialism in the 1980s, accompanied by phenomena that had hardly been seen for thirty years: drugs, prostitution, begging, violent crime and massive corruption. Had foreign influences been totally unrestrained, the social strain might have been even greater. But China's human rights record will certainly play a role in foreign relations in the coming years and the area of religious freedom, to which we now turn, will be a key issue.

THE LEGAL FRAMEWORK AND RELIGIOUS POLICY

The religious policy of the CCP has been analysed by several writers.[31] Historically, the CCP has had a contradictory attitude

---

[30] The total number of Protestants arrested and formally charged could probably be numbered in dozens rather than hundreds through the 1980s. However many people, perhaps several thousand, suffered detention and probably beatings or torture in semi-official actions by security personnel.

[31] For detailed treatment of particular aspects we recommend: historical perspective:

towards religion. Party ideology is resolutely atheist and materialist. Following classical Leninist principles it regards religions as a form of false consciousness, a misapprehension of reality resulting in passive acceptance of the *status quo* which is exploited by the ruling classes in a feudal and capitalist society. At various periods since the 1920s, the most serious of which was the Cultural Revolution, this hostile attitude to religion has been translated into practical political measures.

However, the Party has adopted a more conciliatory approach at other times. Pragmatically it has had to admit that religion is deeply rooted among the Chinese people and that persecution is likely to alienate many of the masses which form its power base. This attitude found expression in the Revised Constitution of the People's Republic of China, announced by the New China News Agency on 27 April 1982. Article 36 on religious belief stated:

Citizens of the PRC enjoy freedom of religious belief.
No organ of state, mass organization or person is allowed to force any citizen to believe or not believe in religion. It is impermissible to discriminate against any citizen who believes or does not believe in religion.
The state protects legitimate religious activities. No person is permitted to use religion to conduct counter-revolutionary activities or activities which disrupt social order, harm people's health, or obstruct the educational system of the country.
Religion is not subject to the control of foreign countries.[32]

The theoretical basis for CCP co-operation with, or tolerance of, religious groups is the concept of the 'united front', the underlying intention of which is to ally with a broad spectrum of

Chan Kim-Kwong, 'A Chinese Perspective on the Interpretation of the Chinese Government's Religious Policy' in *All Under Heaven: Chinese Tradition and Christian Life in the People's Republic of China*, edited by Alan Hunter and D. Rimmington, Kampen, Holland: J. H. Kok, 1992, pp. 38–44; early years of PRC: Holmes Welch, *Buddhism Under Mao*, Cambridge, MA: Harvard University Press, 1972; overview of CCP policy and ideology: Chan Kim-Kwong *Contextual Ecclesiology*; official policy in the 1980s: MacInnis, *Religion in China Today*, which includes a translation of 'Document 19'; special reference to Protestant church in 1980s: Lambert, *Resurrection*, which also provides excellent discussion of provincial and internal documentation.
[32] Reprinted in MacInnis, *Religion in China Today*, p. 34.

the population at any one time in order to isolate the most dangerous enemy.[33] After a period of disuse in the Cultural Revolution, the concept was revived in the 1980s. In the context of the economic reforms, ideological conflicts were de-emphasized: provided that groups did not oppose Party rule, they were welcome to participate in the modernization effort. This offer was extended in particular to overseas Chinese from Hong Kong and Taiwan, who were encouraged to return to the mainland to visit relatives and especially to make investments. The United Front Work Department (UFWD), the CCP organ charged with implementing this policy, gained a new importance during the 1980s.

From 1978, the Party leadership allowed considerable religious freedom *de facto*, although it took several years to make a formal statement of policy. In 1982 a thirty-page circular on religion, supposedly confidential, was sent to leading cadres throughout the country. The circular, known as 'Document 19' was soon leaked to Hong Kong, and an edited version was published in the CCP theoretical journal *Red Flag* in June 1982.[34] It proved to be an authoritative document since its guidelines remained in force through the 1980s, even during the political crackdown of 1989. In 1991 a new policy document was issued, which reflected a heightened concern to oppose the influence of foreign organizations in religious circles; this is reviewed in the next chapter. However, it is essentially only a modification of the existing provisions, and unless there are major upheavals in China it seems that these directives will determine the basis of religious policy for years to come. 'Document 19' therefore serves as a useful starting point for understanding the legal position of religions in China today. The theoretical background to the document is explicitly that of the united front: 'Marxism is incompatible with any theistic worldview. But in terms of political action, Marxists and patriotic believers can, indeed must, form a united front in the

[33] Lyman P. van Slyke, *Enemies and Friends: The United Front in Chinese Communist History*, Stanford University Press, 1967, is the standard work on the earlier history of the United Front.
[34] An English translation can be consulted in MacInnis, *Religion in China Today*, p. 8.

common effort for Socialist modernization.'[35] The previous policy was repudiated, and freedom of belief asserted:

They [the leaders of the Cultural Revolution] forcibly forbade normal religious activities by the mass of religious believers. They treated patriotic religious personages, as well as the mass of ordinary religious believers as 'targets for dictatorship' and fabricated a host of wrongs and injustices which they pinned upon these religious personages . . . They used violent measures against religion which forced religious movements underground.

It should be emphasized that the crux of the policy of freedom of religious belief is to make the question of religious belief a private matter, one of individual free choice for citizens.[36]

The essential feature of the new policy was that religious activities should be tolerated, but that they should be carefully controlled, while activities that fall outside defined limits should be suppressed. The definition of what is permitted remains in the hands of senior Party officials. In the jargon used most frequently, permitted activities are called 'normal' and those of which the Party disapproves may be called 'illegal'. Among the latter, two sorts are targeted in the document: criminal and counter-revolutionary activities hiding behind the facade of religion; and infiltration by hostile foreign forces.

All anti-revolutionary or other criminal elements who hide behind the facade of religion will be severely punished according to the law. All banned reactionary secret societies, sorcerers and witches, without exception, are forbidden to resume their activities.

We must be vigilant and pay close attention to hostile religious forces from abroad who set up underground churches and other illegal organizations. We must resolutely attack those organizations that carry out destructive espionage under the guise of religion.[37]

Finally, several sections of the document give information concerning the administrative apparatus used to implement the policy:

There are a total of eight national patriotic religious organizations . . . besides these there are a number of social groups and local organizations having a religious character. The basic task of these patriotic

[35] *Ibid.*, p. 17.   [36] *Ibid.*, pp. 13–15.   [37] *Ibid.*, pp. 22–4.

religious organizations is to assist the Party and the government to implement the policy of freedom of religious belief, to help the broad mass of religious believers and persons in religious circles to continually raise their patriotic and socialist consciousness, to represent the lawful rights and interests of religious circles, to organize normal religious activities and to manage religious affairs well. All patriotic religious organizations should follow the Party's and government's leadership.

The basic guarantee for the successful handling of the religious question is the strengthening of the Party's leadership.[38]

To conclude this account of religious policy, it is important to note the existence of another layer of regulations. These are measures adopted by local government agencies, for example at city or provincial level, to control religious affairs in their region. As can be seen from the above, the national guidelines are very general and leave many issues open to interpretation. Most local regulations are stricter than those promulgated nationally, but there are also examples of liberal interpretation. This is where the complexity arises, since the level of tolerance changes according to the political situation and local conditions. Local directives are for the internal use of government agencies and have not been made public, with the exception of some that were leaked to Hong Kong, such as the 'Regulation Concerning the Protection of Normal Religious Activities in Hunan Christian Church', which was first adopted in 1981 and revised in October 1990.[39] Its clauses indicate the restrictive interpretation of 'Document 19' that is possible:

4. Evangelists begin their church activities only after the said church (meeting-point) administrative committee has reported to and got the approval of the *liang hui*,[40] and with the support of the local department concerned [i.e. the Religious Affairs Bureau, discussed in the next section] . . . To have any other meeting than the normal worship services and meetings, the church must inform the local *liang hui* and the local department concerned. Only after it is approved can it be held.

7. No meeting and sermon should run counter to the four cardinal principles, engage in propaganda which opposes Marxism,

---

[38] *Ibid.*, pp. 19–24.
[39] The full text can be consulted in *Bridge* no. 45, January–February 1991, pp. 10–11.
[40] A term used to refer to the official church leadership.

Leninism or Mao Zedong thought, or interfere in politics, education or marriage.
8. All illegal activities which are conducted in the name of evangelization . . . must be resolutely prevented.
9. The evangelization of China is the jurisdiction and duty of the
Chinese church. We do not approve any person from abroad . . . to
carry on religious activities within our boundaries.

A number of such regulations are surveyed by Lambert, who
concludes:

Although varying in detail, in broad outline these documents are very
similar in content. The main stipulations are generally as follows:
1. No unauthorized religious activities outside officially designated
churches or meeting-points, especially itinerant evangelism;
2. No proselytism of young people under 18 years of age;
3. Ministerial and evangelistic activities to be restricted to church
workers ordained under TSPM/CCC[41] auspices;
4. Prohibition of unauthorized Christian literature, whether unoffi-
cally produced inside China or received from Hong Kong or
overseas;
5. Prohibition of exorcism and prayer for healing which discourages
people from seeking medical advice.
These regulations lay down the boundaries of what is considered to be
'normal' religious activity.[42]

In practice it seems that high-level agencies, such as the
central UFWD, modify policy in response to political guidelines
from the Party's Central Committee, which in turn receives
detailed reports about new problems. Instructions are then
filtered down to lower level organs responsible for religious
control, and eventually translated into particular administrative decisions. Instructions operate on a complex grapevine
which includes Party statements, directives from the UFWD,
internal agreements with local church officials, and personal
networking. In China, policy documents and regulations are
certainly important, but perhaps even more so are the countless
informal comments, pressures and hints that emanate from the
bureaucracy and circulate through society. People in almost
any profession must be alert to the subtle changes that are
signalled by these means, and tailor their activities accordingly.

---

[41] Also refers to the official church.   [42] Lambert, *Resurrection*, pp. 82–3.

As in many areas of Chinese life, regulations concerning religion are not specific, can often be ambiguous or contradictory, and are ultimately subject to interpretation by local officials: Christian leaders have to be aware of the prevailing atmosphere in a particular location and time.

To summarize, Christianity and other religions are legally protected according to the constitution and authoritative Party directives. This represents a great advance compared to the situation in the Cultural Revolution. As regards the Protestant church, much religious activity is conducted openly and freely. The sacraments of adult baptism and communion; preaching, prayer and hymn-singing; Bible study and training courses; celebration of festivals; private devotion; and distribution of religious literature; all these take place in thousands of churches throughout China. On the other hand this is only one side of a rather complex picture, and there is considerable dispute concerning what should or should not be permitted.

INSTITUTIONS

The most important organization in the administration of religious affairs is the UFWD, mentioned above. It is a Party organ with numerous branches from provincial level down to individual institutions such as universities; its central office in Beijing is under the direct control of the CCP Central Committee. Its major task is to promote economic modernization by soliciting the co-operation of all sectors of Chinese society, including prominent non-communists, members of the non-Han nationalities, overseas Chinese and religious believers. By the nature of its work it adopts a liberal rather than hard-line approach to non-Party groups, as can be seen in the following report from a provincial conference on united front work held in Henan in March 1991:

It is necessary to give full rein to the superiority of the united front and enable it to serve economic construction. Vigorous efforts should be made to carry out united front work in economic fields as well as in overseas areas. The united front work in the economic field should centre on the work of some non-party influential and representative figures in economic circles. Through making friendly contacts and enhancing unity, their roles in the economic field can be brought into full play . . . It is necessary to strengthen contacts with overseas individuals and groups . . . Special attention should be given to work with personnel who are politically influential and financially powerful with great academic attainments and high social reputation.[43]

United Front officials are usually key speakers at conferences on religious work, both those organized by the government for supervisory purposes, and those run by religious groups themselves. The department maintains a special central research unit which advises the Central Committee and Politburo on religious questions, and in turn receives instructions from them concerning formulation of regulations. In the 1980s it essentially adhered to the policies outlined in 'Document 19', i.e. facilitating the development of permitted religious activities within defined guidelines and attempting to curb illegal activities.

The other important agency is the Religious Affairs Bureau (RAB), which was established as a government organ in the early 1950s. It is formally responsible to the State Council instead of the CCP Central Committee. This indicates that it is of lower status than the UFWD and responsible for implementing decisions taken by higher level Party organs rather than formulating policy. It is a smaller and less influential organization, having branches at provincial level, in the major cities and in some areas of high religious activity. However it has few local branches, and in some provinces may only have one or two small offices with a few dozen cadres. Its personnel are appointed by the Party and the great majority are Party members. Work in the Bureau is considered of low prestige with little opportunity for making extra income through graft, and is not a popular appointment for cadres.

The function of the RAB is to ensure the effective implementation of religious policy. In the first thirty years of communist government the role was one of repression. A major task of the Bureau was to identify and manipulate religious personnel who would fully support Party policy, and to expel or arrest leaders

---

[43] Henan Provincial Radio Service, 17 March 1991, reported in BBC Summary of World Broadcasts (FE1027) and reprinted in *China Study Journal*, vol. 6 no. 2, August 1991, pp. 46–7.

who opposed it.[44] In the more liberal 1980s some churches reported better relations with the RAB. One area of co-operation was the return of church property. In 1979 it was decided that all property which had been illegally confiscated from the churches, often occupied by work-units such as factories or schools, should be returned. The church has no authority to recover property directly, but would refer such matters to the RAB and where appropriate the UFWD who would then undertake negotiations. In many circumstances the RAB has been responsible for recovering property and allowing the revival of religious activities, and it has maintained good relations with official church leaders.

On the other hand it still functions as a restrictive bureaucracy, imposing unnecessary regulations and interfering in church affairs. Its areas of responsibility are not clearly defined. 'Document 19' states: 'All places of worship are under the administrative control of the RAB, but the religious organizations themselves are responsible for their management'.[45] The distinction between 'administrative control' and 'management' is rather hazy. In 1983 Bishop Ting denied that there was undue interference in religious affairs:

There are some people overseas who, consciously or not, have created confusion by saying that the RAB of the State Council supervises us and that Chinese Christian churches and organizations are parts of the RAB. This would be totally at odds with our social and political system. The bulk of the work of the RAB is to represent the state and government in implementing the policy of religious freedom . . . The RAB only handles the religious affairs of the State. As to the development of the Chinese Christian TSPM and the administration of the Chinese church, these are our own concerns.[46]

Some years later Bishop Ting had apparently changed his mind, and repeatedly complained of illegitimate interference in church affairs by Party cadres, for example in a letter to the National People's Congress: 'The cadres themselves do not

---

[44] Good accounts of the RAB are in Bush, *Religion in Communist China*; Eric O. Hanson, *Catholic Politics in China and Korea*, Maryknoll: Orbis Books, 1980; Patterson, *Christianity in Communist China*; Welch, *Buddhism Under Mao*.

[45] MacInnis, *Religion in China Today*, p. 18.

[46] *Ibid.*, pp. 63–4.

believe in religion, nor do they understand religion or the religious feelings of the believers. Often they are antagonistic toward religion, tend to suppress religious activities and are motivated to bring about the elimination of religion.'[47]

The third state agency which should be mentioned is the security forces, primarily the Public Security Bureau. We have identified five areas where the police are active in religious matters: arrests for illegal religious activities; surveillance; monitoring of foreign influence; arrests for ransom or extortion; and violent attacks on some 'subversive' groups.

In the 1980s the number of arrests for religious activities was far lower than in previous decades. Nevertheless the authorities at times detained believers who opposed the Party or its official structures, especially those who had achieved some kind of local prominence. Such individuals were usually first warned by members of the official church or the RAB to refrain from their activities; if they persisted, the Public Security Bureau were called on to make the arrests. The most famous cases in the late 1980s were those of Xu Yongzhe, a house church leader from Henan, and Lin Xian'gao in Guangzhou. There have been numerous allegations of torture in police custody, notably in Henan.[48] A Hong Kong evangelical publication suggests the most common causes for arrest in the 1980s were distributing Bibles or Christian literature from outside China; itinerant evangelism; association with foreigners; opposing the official church and membership of illegal sects.[49]

Religious believers suspected of deviancy, like most dissidents in China, can expect to be the object of police surveillance, although naturally it is difficult to find documentary evidence of

[47] The letter, written in spring 1988, was translated and published in *Bridge* no. 33, January–February 1989, pp. 7–8.

[48] For example in a letter received in Hong Kong from a house-church leader in 1984: 'During interrogation a brother was bound with ropes for a long time. Now neither of his arms can move. Another brother was beaten and injured with a pistol by them. He could not bear the suffering when he was being tortured and said things he should not have said.' (Copy of letter dated 3 January 1984, authenticity not established.)

[49] China Ministry Department, *Gurou zhi qin* (*My Kinsmen According to the Flesh*) Hong Kong: China Christian Communications Ltd., 1989, pp. 58–9. They provide no documentation for the above statements, but the list does summarize information received in Hong Kong by evangelical groups.

this. Especially following 4 June 1989, the control of foreign influence in China became a central theme of government policy, which was strongly emphasized in the sphere of religion. Party leaders appeared to fear both an active involvement by religious believers in politics, and a longer term ideological threat to Marxism.

The infiltration of foreign religious forces into our country has become more serious in the past few years. We should take note that some of the activities have also included obvious political ends: some are interfering with our independence and autonomy in managing religious affairs, while others are using religious activities as a pretext to build up anti-motherland, anti-government forces. We should therefore heighten our vigilance.[50]

Such statements border on allegations of espionage and it seems likely that the security forces would be instructed to monitor the situation. According to a Hong Kong newspaper report in June 1991, the government was concerned about its lack of information with regard to religion, especially the underground groups. The Ministry of State Security allegedly assigned agents to disguise themselves as believers and infiltrate Catholic and Protestant churches to collect information. Police surveillance of foreign teachers has also been reported.[51]

Another reason for police intervention is related to the low level of official salaries, which through the 1980s failed to keep pace with inflation. This produced some resentment, especially since peasant incomes rose sharply due to the free market reforms. Some police and other officials were tempted to arrest peasants and in effect hold them to ransom until their release was procured by payment of a fine. Christians have been a common target for this practice since they have a reputation for not making trouble and are partly marginalized because of their belief. Fees demanded range from about fifty yuan to several thousand yuan for influential leaders. These sums are often raised by congregations.[52]

[50] From an article in *Propaganda Monthly*, October 1990, translated by CNCR and reprinted in *China Study Journal*, vol. 6 no. 2, August 1991, pp. 44–6.
[51] CNCR 1827, 19 July 1991; CNCR 1805, 28 June 1991.
[52] Reports on this phenomenon include CNCR 1820, 12 July 1991; CNCR 1856, 20 September 1991.

Finally there have been cases of violent attacks by security forces to assert control over religious groups. The worst excesses appear to be in the province of Hebei where there have been serious conflicts between armed police and recalcitrant Catholic villagers. There have also been reports of violent assault on seminarians.[53]

In general, however, supervision of church affairs is conducted without resort to the security agencies. The great majority of functions are performed by the organizations which mediate between the state and the grass-roots believers: the official church structures. In the 1950s the new communist government formulated its policy on religion and created politically reliable national associations for each of the major religions in China: Buddhism, Catholicism, Islam, Protestantism and Daoism. For the Protestants it co-opted the services of a number of people who had been active in Christian circles in the 1930s and 1940s, mostly in the YMCA and YWCA. They formed the leadership of a new organization known as the Three Self Patriotic Movement[54] (TSPM) which was given the task of ending foreign influence in the Chinese church and bringing all congregations under government control. This was done by a series of denunciation meetings and thought reform programmes in the 1950s, a process which still leaves scars today. The activities of the TSPM were suspended in the Cultural Revolution and most of its leaders sent to work in factories.[55]

In 1979 the TSPM was reconstituted and shortly afterwards a parallel organization called the China Christian Council (CCC) was formed. The two together are commonly known as the 'two committees' (*liang hui*) and form the leadership structure of the official church. The TSPM is an overtly political organization which oversees church policy and monitors foreign

[53] Reported in *China Study Journal*, vol. 6 no. 2, August 1991, p. 57. See below, chapter 6.
[54] The term 'Three Self' is discussed in chapter 3, section 2.
[55] See below, chapter 3, for further details. Ths history of the movement is best documented in Wickeri, *Common Ground*, but Wickeri gives a far more positive assessment of the CCP and its religious policies than most analysts. More critical appraisals and useful historical accounts are provided by Bush, *Religion in Communist China* and Patterson, *Christianity in Communist China*.

relations in particular. The CCC is more pastoral and ecclesiastical in function. Many leading figures hold positions in both organizations concurrently, and K. H. Ting, Bishop of Nanjing, is President of both. For the sake of convenience we also use the term 'the official church' when discussing this structure and the churches that it supervises.

Although the TSPM/CCC is a far from transparent organization we can offer the following analysis, based on statements in its official journal *Tianfeng* and elsewhere, with additional information from leaked documents and private interviews. In 1986 the Standing Committees of the TSPM and the CCC each had around forty members who formed the senior leadership. Most of them had been TSPM leaders already prior to the Cultural Revolution, and by the mid-1980s were elderly men with a record of solid support for CCP policy. Most members of the national committees are also leaders of the provincial committees that effectively supervise local church affairs. These leaders, deputy leaders and secretaries are nominally elected by the organizations themselves, but in practice they must have the support of the UFWD. According to a recent study of the *nomenclatura* system, the senior members are directly appointed by the Central Committee of the CCP.[56]

Other members of provincial and municipal committees are appointed by the RAB in consultation with local government organs. Most of the members are chosen from the Christian community but some are simply CCP members assigned to work in the church. For example, in a city from which we received reliable information, the UFWD ordered the local pastor to ordain a person who was then appointed head of the city's TSPM/CCC committee and became minister-in-charge of the local church. Such appointees have considerable influence over ecclesial affairs and closely supervise the activities of pastors and of committees at county and district level. This frequently leads to resentment among the Christian community, who feel they are under constant surveillance and that church services are

[56] *The CCP's Nomenklatura System: A Documentary Study of Party Control of Leadership Selection, 1979–1984*, edited by John P. Burns, Armonk and London: M. E. Sharpe Ltd, 1989, p. 39.

conducted by non-believers. The level of supervision is much higher in urban areas than in the countryside, because the apparatus is far from sufficient to be effective in remoter regions.

Thus the people responsible for implementing government policies are usually the TSPM/CCC secretaries or vice-chairmen, who hold the real political power in church organizations at all levels, including in congregations. Many of them are believed to be Party members or at least Party appointees. Pastors, on the other hand, generally have a less political background. Most received their training before 1949 but by the mid-1950s were obliged to leave church work. They spent many years as ordinary workers and were recalled to the church in the early 1980s. Some of them have reservations concerning the hierarchy, but generally welcome the opportunity to work in their calling.

As pastors rise in the hierarchy they have to demonstrate political loyalty, while some senior pastors are thought to be Party members sent to work inside the church to maintain CCP influence there. This provides an incidental insight into CCP regulations. Ordinary Party members are forbidden to belong to any religious organization, since belief in God is held to be incompatible with Marxism;[57] however the so-called 'Red Pastors' are actually sent to work in the church. Presumably it is felt that their Marxist convictions will not be shaken if they only pretend to be religious! One of the more notorious 'Red Pastors' was Li Chuwen, who became a senior churchman and leader of the TSPM in the 1950s and 1960s, and whose duties included representing Chinese Christians abroad. He turned out to be an important CCP figure who later held posts related to economic and military intelligence in Hong Kong and Shanghai.[58]

The original purpose of the TSPM was to eliminate foreign influence, unite Protestants in one organization and promote CCP policies within the church, and this remains an important

---

[57] Exception is made for cadres from national minorities.
[58] A brief biography of Li Chuwen appears in *China and the Church Today*, vol. 5 no. 6, November–December 1983, p. 9.

part of its work. A good example can be seen in the September 1990 issue of *Tianfeng* where a senior TSPM leader states that the task ahead for the movement is to 'educate the new believers to guard themselves against the pollution and infiltration of western bourgeois liberalization, as seriously as against AIDS'.[59] At the same time the committees have the difficult task of representing Christians in society and in relation to the government, and they perform the vital roles of negotiating the return of church property, organizing seminaries and training programmes, opening churches and producing literature.

In common with most churches throughout the world, the leadership of the official church in China is dominated by men, although women play a more prominent role in grass-roots religion. Approximately 10 per cent of the members of the 1986 Standing Committees of the TSPM/CCC were women; however there are no restrictions on female ordination and a few women, for example Cao Shengjie, hold important posts. A particular feature of the hierarchy is its extreme age. In a recent TSPM/CCC provincial meeting in Guangdong it was reported that the average age of delegates was seventy-four. Since delegates included a few recent seminary graduates, the main body of participants were probably in their eighties. Attempts are being made to improve the situation, but progress is slow. One of the major causes of the age problem and generational disagreements is that so few church workers were educated between 1949 and 1979: most personnel now are either very old or very young.[60]

The official church thus has a complex nature. One cannot brush aside the legacy of history: memories of its leaders' participation in accusation meetings in the 1950s and the Cultural Revolution are still fresh, and it is thought to contain

---

[59] *Tianfeng*, September 1990, translated in *Bridge*, no. 44, November–December 1990, p. 3.
[60] Further discussion on the problem of a generation gap can be found in the *China Study Journal*, vol. 6 no. 2, August 1991, pp. 77–9. According to Bishop Ting: 'Leaders at various levels are mostly church people of the 1940s, with some people of the 1950s'; see *Bridge*, no. 44, November–December 1990, p. 2.

many Party agents. The organization itself is not greatly respected among Chinese intellectuals; those with whom we have spoken regard it as timid and ineffectual in the political arena. In some respects the 'two committees' differ little from government departments, functioning as supervisory and administrative organs. At times this extends to collaboration with security forces to control non-registered believers. However, there are many individuals who work within the official structures whose personal sympathies lie outside it. They may privately long for a strong and independent church, and simply view the TSPM as an expedient for survival in a hostile political environment. Their standpoint has some justification. Had the TSPM not existed, the church could hardly have survived in China in any form at all. It is a reasonable argument that in the circumstances, compromise was the only possible course of action.

The TSPM/CCC is a typical example of a nominally autonomous organization that is co-opted and utilized by the state. It legitimizes CCP leadership by promoting its policies, submits to Party vetting of its leadership and attempts to present a good image of the Chinese government, especially when dealing with foreigners. On the other hand, it has some capacity to represent its own constituency. A delicate balance is needed. If the movement is perceived as totally subservient to the state, it will lose all credibility. But if it were to develop a nationally coherent power base it might become a focus for discontent. At best, from the CCP point of view, the top leadership should be influential but ultimately reliable, while the lower level organs should be atomized and carefully controlled by the Party apparatus.[61]

In the late 1980s there were rumours that the TSPM might be dissolved, and it seems likely that some leaders, including Bishop Ting, would prefer to see more power invested in the CCC, representing a shift of emphasis from political to ecclesiastical functions. The move in this direction was strongest at the end of

---

[61] For discussion of these points see Alan Hunter and D. Rimmington, 'Religion and Social Change in Contemporary China' in Hunter and Rimmington (eds.), *All Under Heaven*, pp. 11–37. Further details of the TSPM in politics, especially following June 1989, are given in chapters 2 and 7 below.

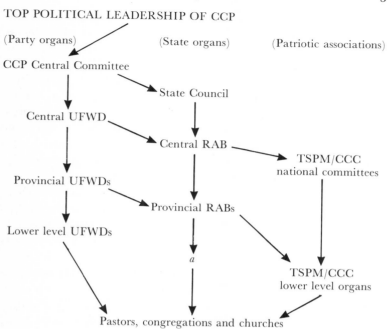

TOP POLITICAL LEADERSHIP OF CCP

(Party organs)   (State organs)   (Patriotic associations)

CCP Central Committee

State Council

Central UFWD

Central RAB

TSPM/CCC
national committees

Provincial UFWDs

Provincial RABs

Lower level UFWDs

a

TSPM/CCC
lower level organs

Pastors, congregations and churches

a Only counties with a high level of religious activities have their own RABs. In most counties decisions are referred up to provincial level or handled locally by United Front officials. The municipalities of Beijing, Tianjin and Shanghai have their own municipal RABs and branch offices in districts of the cities.

Figure 1. Administrative structure of the Chinese Protestant church

1988 when Ting proposed a 'rationalization' of roles in the organization, stating that the church should be in tune with socialism, but should not be a government department. However when the political atmosphere changed after June 1989 these proposals were dropped and the role of the TSPM in maintaining control over the church was again emphasized. The Chinese Protestant movement has not yet evolved an independent organizational form and one can anticipate quite radical changes when CCP control over society is weakened.

The formal relations between the above organizations are summarized in figure 1. The TSPM/CCC national leadership is answerable to the RAB, an administrative organ of the State Council, and the UFWD, a Party organization. Provincial, municipal and sometimes district and county RABs monitor TSPM/CCC organizations at their respective levels, and also deal directly with the pastors of individual churches. However the State Council itself and the central RAB receive their guidelines from Party organizations, the Central Committee and ultimately the Politburo. At a lower level the UFWDs issue directives to local RABs. The Public Security Bureau is also active in monitoring religions and will be called on, usually by the RAB, to make arrests where appropriate.

The house church movement, which operates outside these structures, has generated considerable emotion. Some groups abroad have given a rather romantic gloss to the situation, while TSPM sources tend to claim that the movement barely exists and that only insignificant groups of isolated eccentrics meet outside its own purview. It is difficult to describe these meetings in terms of institutions. They are diffuse, spread through cities but more particularly through the countryside. Temporary local leadership structures and informal networks seem to rise, fall and be replaced. They are subject to somewhat erratic outbursts of persecution from the security apparatus and try to keep a low profile, although in most places they are not underground. They publish very little. Those leaders who do arise are dedicated to their calling as evangelists and invest no effort in sociological studies or collection of statistics. Their education is often not sufficiently sophisticated to undertake such studies even if they felt it important. Thus the sources for even preliminary estimates of numbers and institutions are scanty, mostly letters received in Hong Kong, interviews with individuals who may themselves be poorly informed, and occasional leaked documents from Chinese government agencies, who again may be misinformed.

Most house churches have no defined hierarchy, but their informal networking is at times quite efficient and can arrange for personal travel and transport of written materials throughout China. Leadership is local and particular, often focusing for a short time on an individual with preaching, healing or other gifts.[62] Partly because of their enforced clandestine status, some house churches have tended to a rather authoritarian leadership. To date, few accounts of house-church structures have been published, although a Hong Kong research group claimed that in 1982 house-church leaders from several provinces in central China held a meeting which they termed a 'Jerusalem Conference', in order to establish effective clandestine leadership, combat heresy, oppose the TSPM, conduct mission work and provide training. They reportedly created a formal hierarchy including pastoral districts, regional conferences and a general conference.[63]

How many people are members of these various Christian communities? What kind of Christianity do they espouse? How have they responded to recent political events? We now turn our attention to such questions.

---

[62] An exception to this model of informal leadership was a house church movement in Henan led by Xu Yongzhe, who was arrested in 1989. Xu and other leaders of his group were Red Guards in the Cultural Revolution who had converted to Christianity. They had an efficient clandestine organization, received financial assistance from Hong Kong and printed their own material. See also our reports in chapter 5.

[63] Article in *China Prayer Letter* no. 82, June 1987, pp. 1–3, adapted from a paper by Dr Jonathan Chao.

CHAPTER 2

A survey of the Protestant community

REPORTING STATISTICS

There are Protestants in every province of China. The total number is impossible to determine accurately, and there is a great discrepancy in estimates. The official church claims that there are five or six million registered church members and few unregistered Christians, while unofficial sources suggest that there may be fifty million or even more, most of whom are not affiliated to official organizations.[1] But even if we cannot provide an accurate assessment, we can at least examine this discrepancy and gain some idea of the dimensions of the Protestant community.

There are several major difficulties involved. First is the question of definition. Should one count the baptized, those who call on Jesus when sick, those who attend meetings occasionally or those formally registered with a church? The numbers may be radically different, and many estimates fail to distinguish between such groups. Congregations are constantly fluctuating and new members may be only temporary. With official sources at least this problem is avoided: 'Christian' refers to an individual who has been baptized and is registered with a TSPM/CCC church. Another factor is the size of China, the remoteness of some of its regions and the lack of sociological studies, issues discussed in our introduction. A third point is that many believers are not registered with any authority. Government agencies may have some idea of the extent of house

---

[1] Statistics concerning other aspects of church life, for example studies by age, gender or social class, are even harder to come by than overall numbers.

churches in particular districts or cities, but many such meetings remain unknown, especially in rural areas.

Another kind of problem relates to the dissemination of information. In 1990 we were informed by a senior church official that there are instructions, supposedly secret, emanating from the CCP leadership that published assessments of Christian numbers must be kept low. The two main reasons for this are to avoid loss of face by the Party, which has long asserted that religion is dying out, and to avoid adding to the church's prestige and self-confidence. In a similar vein, we were told by a responsible house-church leader that close to 50 per cent of the population of his county in a southern province had become Christian, but the TSPM refused to acknowledge their existence.[2]

Provincial figures published by official sources between 1988 and 1991 are summarized in table 1. The top five provinces thus account for around three million Christians, about half the official total. Christianity is also concentrated in certain cities, the most important probably being Kaifeng, Shanghai, Wenzhou and Xiaoshan. The total compares with around one million Protestants in 1949. Growth has been faster than for Catholics, who were estimated at three million in 1949 and ten million at the most in the late 1980s.[3]

Despite doubts about the accuracy of figures, we believe that at least the indication of geographical distribution is fairly accurate. The relatively high concentrations in Zhejiang and Fujian are easy to explain. The southeastern coastal provinces have a long history of Christian activity. Areas such as the hinterland of Wenzhou in Zhejiang province and Fuqing in Fujian probably have the highest proportions of Christians in China. Both areas were important centres for indigenous churches such as the Local Assemblies and the True Jesus

[2] Discussion on the problems of statistics can be found in Tony Lambert 'Counting Christians in China: Who's Right?', *News Network International*, 14 April 1989, pp. 28–36; and 'Difficulties with Statistics', *Bridge*, no. 41, May–June 1990, pp. 11–12 (no author given).
[3] An estimate by unofficial observers. The official Chinese Catholic organizations admit to around three and a half million.

Table 1. *Official estimates of Christian numbers in selected provinces, late 1980s*

	No. of Christians	Population	Percentage of population
Henan	830,000	78 million	1.06
Zhejiang	800,000	41	1.95
Fujian	600,000	27	2.2
Anhui	550,000	52	1.06
Sichuan	500,000	103	*
Yunnan	370,000	35	1.05
Guizhou	300,000	30	*
Jiangsu	300,000	63	*
Shandong	250,000	78	*
Guangdong	130,000	63	*

*less than 1 per cent

Numbers of Christians are taken from the compilation by Lambert, 'Counting Christians', p. 34. Provincial populations are based on the *Zhongguo tongji nianjian* (*China Yearbook of Statistics*) 1987, edited and published by the State Statistical Bureau, Beijing and Hong Kong, 1987 (in Chinese). Figures are given to the nearest million.

Church before 1949, and the two provinces were among the most accessible to foreign missionaries.

Reasons for the rapid growth in some inland provinces, particularly Henan and Anhui, are less obvious. It was the unexplained growth here in the mid-1980s that first led to the use of the term 'Christianity fever'. There are unofficial claims that 5 to 10 per cent of the population in many counties of these provinces have converted to Christianity since 1979, reaching more than 30 per cent in some places. Most converts attend unregistered meetings that appear to be new formations since the Cultural Revolution, rather than revivals among traditional Christian communities. Church growth in these areas may be to some extent a resurgence of traditional folk practices or a form of syncretism rather than an orthodox form of Christianity.

Few people we met in China who take a serious interest in

church affairs, whether as believer or observer, attached much credence to official statistics. For example the church official mentioned above maintained that statistics made public were on average around 25 per cent of known figures. He stated that senior figures in the church, RAB and UFWD use private statistics which differ radically from those presented to outsiders. Particularly between 1949 and 1979, the publication of statistics known to be false was common practice, for example concerning agricultural production, and the reporting of data on religions would be subject to similar political constraints; the extent of any improvement over the past decade is uncertain. A problem that these contortions produce is that statistics may change radically from year to year. For example official spokesmen gave the number of Christians in Jiangsu as 250,000 in 1985, 300,000 in 1987 and 400,000 in 1990. Do these figures truly reflect a growth of 60 per cent in five years, or are they the result of various pressures?

Unofficial estimates tend to be of two kinds: leaks from official Chinese sources, and extrapolations from local statistics, usually provided by house church leaders. As an example of the former, we were informed by the above-mentioned official that the real number of Protestants in China known to the TSPM/CCC is twenty million but, as stated, they were only allowed to announce the existence of five million in 1990. Another leak was published by a Hong Kong China-watching journal in April 1990. It claimed that according to an internal report by an official organization in Beijing, the National Religious Committee, there were over ten million Protestants, 45 per cent of whom were students or intellectuals. It also gave a growth rate of 200 per cent to 600 per cent in major cities over the past few years.[4] Two academics in Shanghai also confirmed that the number of Christians was far higher than officially admitted, but that they were not permitted to publish this fact.

The two main sources of unofficial figures in Hong Kong have been the Chinese Church Research Centre and the writer Tony Lambert. The former frequently state their belief that there are

---

[4] *Cheng Ming*, April 1990, p. 20.

up to fifty million Protestants in China.[5] No methodology for arriving at these figures has been forthcoming, except to claim that they are based on reports from underground leaders that cannot be made public for security reasons. They are thus not open to confirmation or disproof. An unfortunate consequence is that such figures are then quoted by other writers as if they had been established by sound methods: 'After as close an investigation as it is possible to make in the existing circumstances, the reputable Christian research groups conclude that *there are now 40–50 million Christians in China*. Some other church organizations put the figure much higher.'[6] However observers inside China who were openly sceptical of official figures were equally sceptical about these: they thought it impossible that so many believers could remain undetected or that the government would allow such a vast network to exist. Occasional claims made by foreign evangelicals that there are up to 100 million Christians, 95 per cent of whom are underground, are regarded as ludicrous.

The most consistent attempt to collate figures from all sources has been that of Tony Lambert. He produces some evidence that TSPM and other official statistics 'do tend to grossly underestimate the numbers of Christians . . . the true number of Christians could be about four times those officially counted, or in the region of 20 million'.[7] The underestimate is both because unregistered believers are not counted, and in order to present an acceptable public face for the CCP. To suggest some figures of his own, Lambert uses information from house church leaders collated from letters and interviews, which he admits should be viewed with some caution. Regarding the two most important provinces, he concludes that there may be around three to five million Protestants in Henan and two and a half million in Zhejiang. For Henan, he quotes many letters from local leaders stating, for example: 'since 1982 there has been a revival, and

[5] For example in *China Prayer Letter* no. 82, June 1987, p. 1 and in CNCR 1562, 6 April 1990.
[6] George N. Patterson, *The China Paradox: Christ versus Marx*, Milton Keynes: Word Books, 1990, p. 250. [7] Lambert, 'Counting Christians', p. 30.

our church has grown from 7 to 700 people' (Shangqiu County, 1987); 'in 1978 we had 30 Christians, now there are over 1,000' (Huaiyang, 1983). Lambert believes that the highest concentrations of Christians are in coastal Zhejiang and Fujian and certain districts of Henan, which coincides with most other information.

Major problems with unofficial estimates are that there is no sound methodology for data-collection, overall scarcity of data and no opportunity for checking. Thus one finds uncorroborated assessments for particular counties, which may indeed be based on good local knowledge. But it is impossible to extrapolate from them with any confidence even to neighbouring counties, let alone whole provinces. Reports by house-church leaders may be exaggerated, and they rarely specify their definition of 'Christian'. Summarizing the available evidence we conclude:

1. Official figures are extremely conservative.
2. No estimates by other observers can claim satisfactory methodology: they are guesses rather than proven.
3. The greatest numbers of Protestants are to be found in Henan, Zhejiang and Fujian where they also from a higher proportion of the population than in other provinces.
4. The growth of Christianity has been far more rapid than overall population increase since 1949. According to the most conservative estimates Christians have increased around sixfold, while population has slightly more than doubled.
5. The increase in Protestants' numbers appears to have been greater in the 1980s than in previous decades. Even according to conservative, official figures, Protestants grew from one to five million in this period.
6. If unofficial estimates are anywhere near correct, Christians form a substantial percentage of the population in some areas. A community of some twenty million would also represent a relatively large body in terms of world Protestantism. On the other hand, compared to the total population of China the proportion is small, less than 2 per cent.

THE OFFICIAL CHURCH

A legacy from missionary days was a large number of church buildings, some of which were imposing and architecturally important, like the famous Catholic basilica at Sheshan. After 1949 the great majority were taken over for secular purposes, being used as schools, factories or warehouses. By the Cultural Revolution almost all churches were occupied by work-units, which usually entailed destruction of internal fittings and works of art, and ceased to function as places of worship. After the change in religious policy in 1979, several buildings in each city were returned to the official church committees, renovated and opened again for services, and new churches were also constructed throughout the 1980s. Those we have seen adopt the Anglo–American style of ecclesial architecture rather than attempting any indigenous design. It is worth noting that as a consequence of clandestine evangelism during the Cultural Revolution, many new churches were built in the 1980s in areas where there had previously been no Christian presence.

The return of previously confiscated church property is an urgent priority since existing churches are in many places too small to accommodate the growth in church attendance. The recovery of property has been a difficult issue to be negotiated by church leaders, the RAB, local government and Party officials and other interested parties such as current occupants. The church derives a considerable part of its income from rent, paid by work-units that occupy property to which the church has a claim. However it is also in acute need of more space. This problem is of course shared by most other works-units in big cities, so it is not an easy situation to resolve. Even the usually discreet *Tianfeng* has published letters and articles describing the frustrations incurred in attempting to regain confiscated property or to establish a more than nominal rent, which sometimes requires years of difficult negotiations.

By 1988 there were around 6,500 open churches in China, of which some 2,700 were built in the 1980s. There were also more than 15,000 registered 'meeting points' some of which are substantial, purpose-built halls able to accommodate several hundred people. Many of these are integrated in the official organizations. In some cases, however, they are registered merely for formalistic reasons, and the meetings themselves are conducted independently of TSPM supervision. Cities are far better provided with church buildings than rural areas, which still rely heavily on informal meeting places. City churches, particularly those which receive most foreign visitors, are usually in good repair and have sufficient stocks of Bibles, hymnals and musical instruments. A large city church may have several pastors and employees; country churches are generally poorly equipped and acutely understaffed.

Little information is available on the social composition of congregations, and we can only report occasional observations. In the suburbs of Shanghai we were informed that a typical congregation comprises a majority of women, a majority of people over the age of sixty and a majority with a low educational level. Most women had no opportunity to attend school before 1949 and consequently a large proportion of believers are illiterate or almost so. According to the pastor of one country church only fifty kilometres from Shanghai city, 50 per cent of the congregation were unable to read the Bible or hymn-book. Many rural churches are desperately poor, their congregations having a low standard of education and living at little above subsistence level. However, some churches and meetings attract a large number of young people. Reports from Henan and Shanxi indicate that 80 per cent of certain congregations were under the age of eighteen, although these are probably atypical. City churches are attended by many with low educational attainments, but they also attract intellectuals with high school or university education, in some cases highly qualified professionals. The majority of city congregations appears able to read, and many churches organize evening classes in literacy and Bible study. In Xiamen, for example, congregational members on the whole appear well educated and relatively affluent, but this is probably an exception to the national trend.

The question of church order has caused some disagreement. In the 1950s churches were in theory subsumed into one 'post-denominational' church. Several senior pastors worked hard over the years to develop a style of worship that would be acceptable to all. Here there seems to be considerable freedom of discussion between pastors and congregations, and consequently a measure of difference between individual churches. For example many churches retain a large cross above their altar, while others do not; some pastors wear more formal clothing than others. In places where the official church leadership is most influential there have been steps towards a unified liturgy and church order.[8]

Elsewhere the situation is more complex. Before 1949 missionary groups operated in geographical sectors, especially in rural areas, under the so-called 'comity agreements': consequently one county might be predominantly Lutheran and its neighbour might be Anglican. Chinese believers tend to value their traditions very strongly, and those who were members of a particular denomination before 1949 are often still reluctant to accept a pastor from a different tradition. This has led to some logistical problems in assigning pastors to particular congregations. In urban areas there was less division of territory and more competition among denominations, with the result that several were represented in each city, creating tension in some places. One solution has been to hold different services at different times, for example having an Anglican style of worship in the morning, Methodist in the afternoon, Local Assembly in the evening and Seventh Day Adventist on a Saturday. The shortage of church buildings does not permit each group to have its own premises except in a very few towns. The tension between denominations has been a secondary issue since 1949 in the face of more serious problems, but it is still important and was not resolved by the proclamation of a 'post-denominational era'. The differences may be only residual ones in groups happy to work within the official structures, and of significance primarily to older believers who were accustomed to particular denominations before 1949. More serious divergences exist between groups which only reluctantly accept official leader-

---

[8] In 1991 a provisional 'Church Order' was adopted by the TSPM/CCC which states guidelines for ecclesial practices; it is discussed below in chapter 7.

ship, such as the Local Assemblies. These churches sometimes adopt radically different liturgies based on their own traditions and circumstances.[9]

Official churches in the cities tend to have similar programmes. Typically they may hold two services on Sunday and on weekday evenings have several meetings such as Bible study or choir practice. The services are familiar to one brought up in a mainstream American or British tradition, and the Anglo–American influence is easy to explain: the great majority of Protestant missionaries came from these two countries, which have also been among the most active in promoting links since 1979. Congregational participation is rather restrained, and ordinances and sacraments are performed but not emphasized. The church has suffered from a progressively more severe shortage of clergy since 1979. Membership has increased far more rapidly than the number of pastors, with the result that baptism and communion can only be performed at infrequent intervals in many places.

The most important elements of the service are hymns, prayers and sermons. The favourite hymns in cities are translations of well-known British and American classics, sung to the original melodies. Perhaps surprisingly, given the emphasis on eliminating foreign influence from church affairs, little success has been achieved in promoting Chinese songs of worship. However, many rural churches use indigenous folk songs and have few hymn-books other than hand-copied manuscripts. Prayers are usually read by a pastor with the congregation concluding with the 'amen', although this pattern is not universal. Some congregations, those derived from indigenous churches, pray together with the pastor, sometimes in a loud and emotional manner; in others, especially in rural meeting points, individuals pray independently but at the same time, usually joining together for a concluding statement.

Sermons are frequently expositions of biblical texts, doctrinal and moralistic in tone, emphasizing personal piety, good conduct and salvation. By the late 1980s it had become unusual

[9] The best article on denominationalism in the contemporary church is by Deng Zhaoming, 'Church Unity in Shanghai', *Bridge*, no. 48, July–August 1991, pp. 3–7.

for sermons to be used for political statements on behalf of government policy. It would certainly be impossible to use the pulpit to criticize the CCP, but also we very seldom heard of pro-government views being promoted in church, although this was reportedly the case some years earlier. Several collections of sermons by Chinese pastors have been published. They are essentially in accordance with conservative neo-evangelical teaching, although with some interesting points of divergence. In particular, pastors are strongly discouraged from preaching on aspects of faith such as eschatology and spiritual healing. The government disapproves of laying on of hands, exorcism and miracles as evidence of a superstitious and reactionary world-view that can be attractive to the gullible. It also objects to Dispensationalist teachings which might create a mentality of escape from present reality and indifference, if not hostility, towards the temporal power.[10]

The atmosphere of official churches tends to be orderly and low-key. One senses deep currents of emotion but they are expressed in subtle ways: a rise of emphasis on certain words in hymns, facial expressions of pain or joy. The Christian community has suffered much and one can see the deep feeling with which congregations respond to the theme of suffering in hymns and prayers. There are few public gatherings outside CCP control in China, and church offers a rare opportunity for participation in a community and an outlet for emotional pressures built up during the turbulence of the past decades.

A major achievement of the 1980s was the opening of seminaries, of which there were thirteen by 1989, the largest in Nanjing, with a total of 734 seminarians. Courses range from a four-year programme for high-school graduates to two-year pastoral training courses. In Nanjing there is also a three-year post-graduate course, equivalent to a Master of Divinity programme. High-school graduates enter by examination and

---

[10] These comments are based on works such as *Zaojiu* (*Education*) edited by Shanghai Committee for Christian Education, 1989, a collection of sermons by various Shanghai pastors; and the *Jiangdaoji* (*Collections of sermons*) published by Zhejiang Christian Council, of which nineteen had appeared by April 1990. Additional information was obtained through conversation with pastors.

with the recommendation of their local churches and the RAB. According to a visitor to the seminary in Chengdu in April 1989, the students were genuinely enthusiastic and appeared to have strong motivation, perhaps because they knew that congregation members were contributing to their support. There was a strong sense of group solidarity, a close association with tutors and much use of a small library. In addition, many seminaries have a one-year training programme at a lower level, often attended by junior high-school graduates.

The TSPM/CCC has published a successful series of text-books for a correspondence course and organized many short-term training programmes. In most of these courses the emphasis is on biblical studies and conservative systemic theology; the seminaries also teach music, art and political classes, the latter being mandatory for all tertiary educational institutions in China. Young graduates usually return to their home churches and may receive ordination after two or three years' church work.[11]

As regards doctrinal issues, pastors in both official and house churches generally adopt a conservative theology, probably as a result of traditionalism, and of isolation after 1949. Their teaching materials in the 1980s, and also material received through Gospel radios, tended towards fundamentalism and biblical literalism. Older pastors in particular often have an exclusive attitude with regard to other religions, to be politically passive and have little interest in social Gospel or inter-faith dialogue. On the other hand, a few centres like the Nanjing seminary have produced more sophisticated theological work that reflects some liberal developments in twentieth-century Christian thought and also Chinese Marxism, for example relating positively to the concept of socialism and stressing the importance of a satisfactory material provision for all. Important themes are church and society, the nation and patriotism,

---

[11] See Sha Guangyi, 'A Survey of the Situation of Seminary Graduates in Jiangsu Province', *China Study Journal*, vol. 6 no. 2, August 1991, pp. 75–80; short articles in *Bridge*, e.g. 'The Problems of Theological Graduates in China', *Bridge* no. 34, March–April 1989, pp. 3–7 and 'Yunnan Theological Seminary', *Bridge* no. 45, January–February 1991, pp. 14–15. We are grateful for further information from Sybille Van Der Sprenkel in personal correspondence dated 14.6.91.

nature and grace. A 'new theological awakening and fermenta-
tion', including an interest in feminist theology, is now evident
in the Chinese church, according to Chen Zemin, the Dean of
Nanjing Seminary.[12] A contradictory note is introduced because liberal theology normally encompasses social and political
criticism, which would be unacceptable to the Chinese government. The TSPM has resolved this problem by reserving its
political criticism for foreign governments and the capitalist
economic system, while fully endorsing CCP policies.[13]

The lack of exchange with the outside world and the
restrictions on freedom of expression have contributed to the
widespread traditionalism. Another serious obstacle to the
development of a more intellectual form of Christianity is the
lack of publications. After many years of difficulty there is a
successful printing press in Nanjing that has published over two
million Bibles and one million hymnals. At least in cities and
towns these are relatively easy to obtain. A handful of TSPM/
CCC publications, such as collections of sermons and the
journals *Tianfeng* and *Nanjing Theological Review* are also available to the general public. However it is very difficult to obtain
any serious literature on theology, Christian spirituality or
church history, although a few academics have published works
on Christianity in the past ten years. Apart from problems of
permission, the distribution network for books in China is
haphazard, and most publishers demand substantial subsidies
before they produce a book. The situation is somewhat al-
leviated by the radio broadcasts described below.

The international aspect of the church has been controversial
throughout the century. Missionaries were able to offer privileges to converts, who were for decades viewed with contempt
by many of their compatriots. The church was a visible symbol
of foreign influence in China and was attacked by the rising
forces of nationalism after 1919. The CCP emphasized the close
ties of Christianity and imperialism, at times singling churches

[12] Chen Zemin, 'These Ten Years', *China Study Journal*, vol. 7 no. 1, April 1992, pp. 8–13.
[13] *The China Theological Review* is the most convenient source. See also *No Longer Strangers:
      Selected Writings of K. H. Ting*, edited by Raymond L. Whitehead, Maryknoll: Orbis
      Books, 1989.

out for special attack, and at times adopting a more conciliatory stand to avoid antagonizing foreign powers. After 1949, changes in CCP religious policy tended to reflect changes in foreign policy, both ultimately deriving from shifts in internal politics. For example, the persecution of believers in the early 1950s coincided with the Korean war and campaigns against counter-revolutionaries. Similarly the Cultural Revolution attacked religious believers along with other 'rightists' at a time of international isolation. The church in China is now to a great extent protected by the open door policy initiated in the 1980s to attract foreign investment: the harshly repressive policies of the 1950s could not be repeated without provoking a massive international response. Nevertheless it can still be a dangerous thing to have 'foreign friends', as foreign influence can provide a pretext for harassment. In religion as in many other areas of Chinese life, the government feels a tension between gaining economic or political advantages and preserving ideological purity.

Church leaders make great efforts to represent their movement overseas and receive numerous foreign delegations. They have met some success in establishing friendly relations with ecumenical churches, most notably in gaining readmission to the World Council of Churches in 1991. In the mid-1980s they also persuaded a number of previously critical evangelical leaders, for example some American Baptists, to adopt a more positive stance. Billy Graham accepted an invitation to visit China in 1989, which would have been impossible some years previously. The Chinese government appears to believe that churches play an important role in US political life, and sent several Chinese scholars and officials to study church affairs in the USA. These efforts at cultivating foreign connections can be understood in the context of the CCP's diplomatic tradition. The young People's Republic tried to enhance its image in Asia by presenting itself as a protector of the Buddhist faith in the 1950s: likewise the present government regards the church as an ally in maintaining harmonious relations with western countries.

As well as contacts between church hierarchies, the 1980s

allowed an upsurge of personal visits, inter-church, student and academic exchanges with many different countries. Consequently, although there are grey areas, the Chinese church is more transparent than at any time since 1949. News travels, even if sometimes it takes circuitous routes. An important factor has been the large number of Taiwanese and Hong Kong visitors who have virtually unlimited access and considerable influence in southeast China. But direct foreign influence in church affairs seems small. In the official churches it is probably non-existent, since all committees are vigilant against foreign intervention of any kind, limiting themselves to inviting occasional guest speakers. Some house churches have more regular contact with visitors, often family members, and the receipt of financial help from abroad can be a controversial issue. In northern provinces overseas help is minimal. Foreign involvement is one of the factors that will bring a house church to the attention of the police and therefore has to be discreet.

A good example of the official church's liaison with the outside world is the Amity Foundation, a charity based in Nanjing with both Christians and non-Christians in leading positions. It runs a number of projects including rural development, health care, education and a modern printing press in Nanjing. Its office in Hong Kong also serves in effect as the overseas information department of the church hierarchy. Amity provides an acceptable way for foreigners to donate funds for social welfare projects, and it was a useful initiative for the official church: it was good publicity at home and abroad, and politically irreproachable. Individual church groups have undertaken social welfare projects in collaboration with foreign organizations but at the time of writing most are only in initial stages. In larger cities some churches operate projects such as clinics and old peoples' homes.[14]

---

[14] For example a 'Home for the Aged and Disabled' and a 'Rehabilitation Center for the Hearing and Speech Impaired' were set up in 1988 in Changsha, Hunan Province, by local churches. 'Christian Social Service in Hunan', *Bridge* no. 45, January–February 1991, pp. 11–12.

HOUSE CHURCHES AND AUTONOMOUS COMMUNITIES

Before introducing this topic, we would like to propose a change in terminology, from 'house church movement' to 'autonomous Christian communities', especially to designate the house churches that have expanded since the early 1980s. Some of the larger groups have now grown to a point where the term 'house church' is inadequate: the 'Apostolic Church' described in chapter 5 is an example. In several provinces they have constructed large church buildings that rival those of the official church. Some meet in the open or in large halls, particularly in the countryside, and quite commonly attract congregations of several hundred people. Others have established theological training procedures, independent of the official church, that can be quite sophisticated and may be taught by highly qualified staff from Hong Kong, Taiwan, Korea and other countries. Such groups may have extensive contacts with Christians in other parts of China and also abroad. Moreover, the term 'movement' may be misleading. The groups do not form a coherent structure with a single leadership, purpose or ideology; it would be particularly misleading to envisage them as some kind of anti-communist clandestine organization.

In our view, the term 'autonomous' is appropriate since the groups do not accept the authority of the TSPM, the Chinese government, nor of any foreign denomination; and 'communities' is preferable to 'house churches' since their size and complexity has now outgrown the confines of any individual household. This formulation also avoids the confusion that might arise from the term 'movement'. An alternative term, 'home meeting', to describe the very intimate, family-centred prayer groups, is quite acceptable, as is the term 'meeting point' which is widely used in China to refer to individual gatherings, official or otherwise.

The Protestant church in China has a long tradition of lay leadership and has always had a shortage of trained professional staff relative to the number of believers. One cause was the reluctance of missionaries to grant ordination to Chinese church workers. Another is the ecclesiastical tradition of the Chinese independent churches, which tend to reject professional staff: the Local Assemblies, for example, refer to all church members as brothers or sisters, and are opposed to paid clergy. Few of the important Christian leaders of the pre-1949 era were ordained: John Sung (Song Shangjie), Wang Mingdao and Watchman Nee (Ni Tuosheng), three of the most influential figures, were lay persons, and also opposed ordination as a practice of the denominational churches that carried a foreign stigma. The sentiment against it often derived from nationalistic pride, and non-ordained leaders were seen as more spiritual and independent.

Instead, lay leaders, including many female evangelists known as 'Bible-women', formed the majority of church workers and are of great importance now in the autonomous communities. This pattern has become more pronounced in the 1980s. According to official figures there are now around 15,000 clergy associated with the TSPM/CCC, approximately the same number given by missionary estimates in 1949; since then the number of believers has grown many times over. Congregational self-supervision is inevitable.

A long-standing custom of Chinese Christians, particularly in rural areas, has been meetings held in homes. Interaction with popular culture has created an indigenous flavour in some of these meetings, for example praying for material rewards, and there are reports of syncretism with local cults in some areas. The extended family network is the social base for many groups, again emphasizing how this ecclesial model corresponds with deep patterns in Chinese culture. The meetings generally have a tendency to conservatism and fundamentalism in theology. In some provinces a Pentecostalist style of worship has been practised since around 1910. Phenomena such as speaking in tongues and spiritual healing have been noted, particularly in rural Shandong and Henan. However, other indigenous movements such as the Local Assemblies were opposed to charismatic displays and emphasized literal belief in the Bible, sober behaviour and what they interpreted as Apostolic traditions. Many of these unregistered, unsupervised meetings maintained some kind of continuity through the first three decades of communist rule, when the institutional church collapsed.

Ironically it was the attempt to eliminate religion during the Cultural Revolution that promoted the growth of the house churches. The only option for believers who were determined to practise their faith was to do so in secret meetings, usually in individual homes. Numerous testimonies agree that this was a period of great growth for the church, and that underground networks flourished despite the persecution. Another important factor was the movement of Christians from cities to remote rural areas. In the 1950s it was common practice for an urban family to send one child to work in frontier regions. This was taken as evidence of patriotism and provided the family with a measure of protection during political campaigns. Many more urbanities were sent to the countryside during the Cultural Revolution. An unintended consequence of these population displacements was that Christians from cities such as Shanghai settled in Xinjiang, in particular, and formed groups that are now flourishing. By 1979 when open religious activities were again permitted, the house church groups were well established, both in traditional areas of Christian activity and in regions where evangelization had hitherto not taken place.

Survival, even growth, in times of persecution has long been a proud tradition of the church and one may, of course, seek theological explanations for this phenomenon. We must leave it to the reader to determine whether there are useful parallels to be drawn between the Chinese church and the early church in the Roman Empire, or with a dissenting tradition such as Puritanism. For now, one can state with some certainty that the first vital element of the Chinese 'resurrection' was the relatively small community of Christians who showed remarkable perseverance in their faith, in the face of almost overwhelming psychological and physical pressures. The second was that in the social upheavals of the early communist decades, and in particular the Cultural Revolution, many more people turned to Protestantism as an alternative ideology and organizational structure, as their confidence in the state was shaken. Thus persecution was unsuccessful in two respects at least: it neither broke the existing community, nor prevented the spread of Christian influence among non-believers. Moreover, by driving religion underground, it possibly encouraged a relatively un-compromising form of Protestantism that was effective and attractive in the social crisis; and we may see the house churches and autonomous communities as classic examples of spiritual dissent from a prevailing orthodoxy.

Some leaders, perhaps a minority, but a committed and important one, have specific objections to TSPM leadership. They feel that the official church has compromised too much with an atheist state and has abandoned the essence of Christianity. In their view, given the present government, the only honest recourse for Christians is to operate outside the TSPM network, practising their religion without political or religious compromise. Some of these critics are elderly pastors, ordained in conservative traditions, who suffered greatly in the campaigns of the 1950s. Their theological stance is for separation of church and state, and they regard the temporal power as secular and unspiritual, perhaps a tool of Satan. They usually adopt a Dispensationalist view of eschatology. Small groups of such persons can be found in most cities with a Christian community, and their views are occasionally reported by CCRC and other agencies.[15]

Many who participate in the autonomous communities, however, do so for a different reason: either official churches do not exist in their locality or they do not provide the spiritual satisfaction that is sought. The six thousand TSPM churches are a very small number given the huge size of China. Even in Shanghai, which is exceptionally well served, there are only fifteen churches in the urban area, an enormous city of seven million people. A journey to the closest church can easily take forty-five minutes on an unreliable and overcrowded bus. This might be a daunting prospect for anyone, and particularly for the elderly and infirm who form a large proportion of congregations. In rural areas it could take a day or more for believers to travel to the nearest church.

---

[15] For example in the *China Prayer Letter* no. 82, June 1987.

A related issue is frequency of worship. Many believers are retired people with few demands on their time who like to attend services almost daily rather than the once or twice a week offered by most churches. For practical reasons the obvious solution is to organize small circles for prayer or study in private homes. Many people also find a significant difference in spiritual and emotional impact between these home meetings and organized churches. Home meetings are the ideal environment for healing, miracles and a charismatic form of worship with a strong emotional charge, compared to the relatively austere public services. Fellow believers are often neighbours or close acquaintances speaking the same dialect and with similar interests and way of life, whereas the larger urban churches cater to a broad spectrum of the city and often use Mandarin.

Similar reasons for the existence of house churches were given by Bishop K. H. Ting: 'There are objective reasons for the existence of these home gatherings: (1) The number of open churches is insufficient or their locations are too far away for people to attend, or they are too crowded. (2) The TSPM and its pastors are thought by some not only not to "love the church" but even to betray the Church.'[16] Other reasons given by Bishop Ting are differences of opinion concerning doctrines and liturgy, the unsuitable behaviour of some pastors and leaders, and infrequency of services.

In our experience the home meetings are not politicized. Those who attend seek a satisfying spiritual life and tend to favour a strict separation of religion and politics, often typical of theologically conservative, quietistic traditions; engagement in politics may be seen as liberalism and unspiritual. They are often apolitical, poorly educated, devout believers following a long tradition of lay leadership and indigenous patterns of religious organization. A few have objections to particular TSPM pastors, but usually on personal rather than political grounds. One of the doubts that could be raised about the autonomous communities is that they may be rigidly exclusive and not wish to associate with non-Christians. They may also be

[16] *Bridge* no. 33, January–February 1989, p. 4.

too ready to accept doctrines from local leaders and form groups around charismatic personalities, sometimes leading to antinomian behaviour and beliefs. Occasionally there have been scandals concerning money or sex, which may be well grounded or may be artifices: it is common practice in Confucian culture to denounce a leader by questioning his morality in these areas.

Radio broadcasts from abroad are also extremely important in the education of leaders at all levels. About six Christian broadcasting companies operate from Hong Kong and other locations, transmitting in Mandarin and some dialects, which are received all over China. One station broadcasts a 'Seminary of the Air', with courses on church history, New and Old Testament studies, theology and evangelism. Much of the material is of a high academic standard and is an important service for both ordinary Christians and leaders. Foreign radio was perhaps the most influential single training resource in the 1980s. Many pastors in the official church also listen to it, despite disapproval by the TSPM hierarchy and the RAB. The content of the programmes reinforces the conservative tendency of Chinese Christianity, since more liberal denominations are not involved in these efforts. The stations avoid references to politics and seldom even broadcast news, to lessen potential conflicts with the Chinese authorities. It is not feasible for the government to jam all radio transmissions, but they do make efforts to control their impact: according to one report, a directive was issued in Beijing in June 1989 forbidding Chinese citizens to listen to the Voice of America and gospel broadcasts.[17] Local TSPM regulations also often prohibit listening to the broadcasts.

Customs regulations forbidding the import of religious literature likewise attempt to limit foreign influence. The broadcasting companies receive tens of thousands of letters from China expressing interest in their programmes. They try to respond by personal correspondence and also send Christian literature to enquirers. According to an official report, 240,000 religious books and over 3,000 audio-visual aids were seized by customs in 1989 alone, which indicates the scale of imports.[18]

[17] *News Network International*, 14 August 1989.
[18] For statements forbidding listening to radio, see the regulations for Hunan province

Relations between Christians from official and unofficial circles are highly complex. It is relatively easy to characterize the extremes. Senior TSPM/CCC leaders strongly downplay the importance of the autonomous communities, and some officials have co-operated with the police in repressive measures. *Tianfeng* occasionally prints statements condemning those who try to split the church by refusing to acknowledge the official leadership, and particularly criticizes those with foreign connections. Some officials are also jealous of the popular support gained by house churches and their financial resources, often gifts from relatives abroad.

Moreover, the TSPM/CCC claims to be the true representative of all Protestants in China; it is embarrassed to admit to the existence of a large body of Christians outside its control, which moreover is beginning to find a voice outside China. Assertions by the TSPM that it should monopolize inter-ecclesial communion inside China, and that it has exclusive rights to represent Chinese Christians overseas, constitute one of the most unpleasant features of the official church.[19] At the other extreme, some house church members regard TSPM/CCC officials as hypocrites, collaborators with the 'Anti-Christ' or even as the 'Anti-Christ' himself, and criticize both their theology and practical work.

Between these extremes is the grey area where the majority are situated. For example, many TSPM pastors have more sympathy for the autonomous leaders than for their own hierarchy, and take opportunities to protect them. On the other hand, many house church members have no particular objection to the official church, but either have practical difficulty in attending services there, or seek something more or something different. At a local level the two groups co-exist and many people participate in both. One observer commented that the pastors of the official church actually have a more stressful and

quoted in *Bridge* no. 45, January–February 1991, p. 11. A report on customs operations forms part of 'An Internal Circular on Vigilance against Infiltration', see chapter 1, note 50.

[19] See for example the controversy between Han Wenzao and Jonathan Chao which appeared in *China Talk*, vol. 13 no. 1, pp. 2–8, and *China Prayer Letter*, no. 89, February–March 1988.

demanding role than independent leaders: they must reassure their supervisors that they are politically reliable, and they also have to persuade their congregations that they are not compromised. The leaders of autonomous communities, by contrast, have the benefit of a simple, clear-cut standpoint.

The situation reflects the ambiguity of religious policy as stated in 'Document 19': 'As for Protestants gathering in homes for worship services, in principle this should not be allowed, yet this prohibition should not be too rigidly enforced. Rather, persons in the patriotic religious organizations should make special efforts to persuade the mass of religious believers to make more appropriate arrangements.'[20] In accordance with this principle, house churches and the larger autonomous communities were generally tolerated through the 1980s, albeit grudgingly and with occasional lapses. The use of force to prohibit religious activities, specifically repudiated by the present leadership, became exceptional rather than widespread.

REPRESENTATIVE LEADERS

The outstanding leader of the official church in the 1980s, and indeed since about 1960, has been K. H. Ting, Bishop of Nanjing, who holds numerous senior positions in the church hierarchy and in national political organizations. He was ordained in the Anglican tradition, having attended the famous missionary St John's University in Shanghai, and the Union Theological Seminary and Columbia University in New York. Ting became a staff member of the World Student Christian Federation in Geneva before returning to China in the early 1950s. He rose rapidly to a high position in the Chinese church in the 1950s and was one of the few church personnel allowed to meet foreign visitors during the Cultural Revolution.[21] In 1979 he emerged as the undisputed leader of the official church. Besides being President of the TSPM and the CCC through the

---

[20] MacInnis, *Religion in China Today*, p. 18.
[21] Ting disappeared from public view in 1966 and was rehabilitated in 1972, after which he began to receive foreign visitors. Lambert, *Resurrection*, p. 23. For a selection of his works in translation see Whitehead (ed.), *No Longer Strangers*.

1980s, he was also Principal of the Nanjing Theological Seminary, Director of Religious Studies at Nanjing University and member of the Standing Committee of the National People's Congress. He has been extraordinarily influential inside China and has also made numerous visits abroad. He has generally made a favourable impression on foreign visitors, perhaps aided by his impeccable command of English.

As leader of an essentially pro-government organization, Bishop Ting has naturally received criticism from some quarters, notably conservative evangelicals. First it has been said that he is a member of the *'bimidang'*, a secret section of the CCP which recruits supposedly non-communist members of the intelligentsia in order to increase its influence in literary, academic and religious circles. One eyewitness account, denied by Ting himself, maintains that he worked for a time at the CCP base in Yenan in 1937, which, if true, would lend credence to this allegation.[22] Second, critics believe that his rise to power has been at the expense of personal integrity, and that he cannot be considered Christian in a meaningful way. They point to his collusion with repression in the 1950s and his support for Maoism and the policies of the Cultural Revolution.[23]

This may have been personal opportunism, but it may also have been a long-term strategy of accommodation that has eventually paid off. It is our impression that many Chinese believers have confidence in him and feel that he has helped the church as much as was possible. He could be acceptable to the CCP only by following orders, exercising tight control over the church and refusing to intervene in controversial issues. On the other hand, if he became regarded as merely a communist lackey he would quickly lose prestige at home and abroad. Apart from hard-line anti-TSPM elements, most people appear to regard him with some measure of respect. This was considerably enhanced by his stands during and after the democracy

[22] A letter from an elderly Chinese pastor alleging Ting's connections with the CCP, and communist infiltration of the church in general, was circulated in Hong Kong in 1989. Copy in possession of the authors. See below, chapter 3, section one, for further discussion of the secret section of the CCP.
[23] Lambert, *Resurrection*, p. 23.

movement of spring 1989. Ting issued statements supporting the student protests, and was ambiguous in his acceptance of government policies. At the same time he argued for reform inside the official church and for ending political control over religion.[24] Ting's liberal position since 1989 provoked a strong reaction from the conservative old guard of the TSPM, which is reviewed in the following section.

A less cautious assessment would give him credit for some remarkable achievements. He has kept the church alive in difficult times and presided over a large increase in membership, organized the printing and distribution of several million Bibles and hymnals, helped to found Amity, established the basis for Protestant academic institutions, trained a new generation of pastors, recovered much church property that seemed irrevocably lost and maintained links with foreign churches without succumbing to foreign control. He has probably done as much as any person to promote freedom of religion in China and has argued far more vigorously for the rights of house churches than have any of his colleagues. It is doubtful that anyone could have done more.

Most other TSPM leaders are now old men, known disparagingly as 'old Three-Selfers', who still have close connections with the Party apparatus. They appear to have their power base in Shanghai. Many of them emerged from a group of Christians who became close to the CCP in the years before 1949, often after education at St John's University in Shanghai and participation in YM/YWCA activities. Two senior figures in the official church in the late 1980s, for example, were Bishops Shen Yifan and Sun Yanli. Shen is the son of T. K. Shen, formerly Bishop of Shanxi, an Anglican minister and a graduate of Central Theological College in 1951. In 1986 he was Vice-President of the CCC with special responsibility for domestic affairs of the church.[25] Sun studied at the Jinling Theological Seminary from 1934 to 1944, during which time it was obliged to move from Nanjing to Chengdu. He returned to Shanghai in 1946 and was a prominent activist in the Three Self Movement

---

[24] *China Study Journal*, vol. 6 no. 1, April 1991, pp. 54–5.
[25] *China Talk*, vol. 11 no. 5/6, November 1986, p. 7.

through the 1950s. He was apparently rescued from Red Guards by intervention of the Religious Affairs Bureau in 1966 and returned to church work in 1979.[26] As in most Chinese institutions, it is very difficult to dislodge old men from positions of power.

Leaders of house churches have generally not achieved national prominence: they have no access to media at the best of times and have had to operate clandestinely at others. Nevertheless a few have become household names among Christians in China and also known abroad, such as Wang Mingdao and Lin Xian'gao (Samuel Lam). Wang was perhaps the best known outside China, and his career forms an interesting contrast to that of K. H. Ting. From the 1920s until the 1950s he was an independent preacher, running his own small church in Beijing and travelling widely in China to address meetings. He was long known for an uncompromising conservative theological stance and Biblical literalism, and also for his insistence on independence, which meant that he did not accept posts in any missionary organization. He was also famous for outstanding moral rectitude. His confrontation with Japanese occupying forces in the 1940s foreshadowed his refusal in the 1950s to have any dealings with the TSPM, which organized a series of denunciation meetings against him in 1954/5. The charges against him were that he was not in sympathy with the government, that he refused to participate in the TSPM and that his preaching was individualistic. He was arrested, subjected to considerable ordeals and spent most of the subsequent twenty-three years in prisons and labour camps. He emerged in 1979 and lived in Shanghai until his death in 1991 aged ninety-one. Through the 1980s he was feeble, almost deaf and inactive, but still regarded by anti-TSPM Christians as a symbol of resistance and independence. He continued to write, receive visitors and conduct home meetings weekly until he died. He was still being criticized for his stand by TSPM leaders in 1989.[27]

[26] *China Talk*, vol. 13 no. 4, October 1988, pp. 1–7.
[27] For example see Wang Weifan, 'Wu Yaozong yu Wang Mingdao' ('Wu Yaozong and Wang Mingdao'), *Tianfeng*, September 1989, pp. 12–13.

Wang's opposition to the official church was theological rather than political: 'Wang insisted the essence of Christianity was the preaching of regeneration to all people who were lost in sin. Regeneration came solely by the grace of God through faith. This was invisible to the human eye. Yet once regenerated, a Christian would always display this internal faith . . . The kingdom of God came only with the personal second coming of Christ. The social gospel of an earthly kingdom of God was thus a forgery from the devil.'[28] Even before 1949 he had strongly criticized Chinese liberal theologians such as Wu Yaozong, the future leader of the TSPM, for his disbelief in the Virgin birth, resurrection, ascension and second coming. The issue was not the political stance of the TSPM, but that Wang could not accept the leadership of those who betrayed the true faith as he saw it. In this he is probably representative of the older generation of house church leaders.[29]

Finally, Lin Xian'gao (Samuel Lam) has been the most prominent house church leader since 1978. A young associate of Wang Mingdao in the 1940s, he was arrested in 1958 and served a twenty-year sentence. Released in 1978, he founded the most famous autonomous Christian community in China, Damazhan in Canton. The local government reluctantly tolerated Lin's activities through the 1980s, and he built up a congregation of around one thousand, with regular worship services, baptisms, evangelism and other forms of activity. He also met many foreigners, including journalists, and was a channel for information about house churches. After the events of 1989 Lin was thoroughly investigated by the police for alleged links with the democracy movement, but was cleared: like Wang he always maintained that the church should restrict itself to spiritual matters. After refusing, despite strong pressure, to register with

[28] Lee Chun-kwan, 'The Theology of Revival in the Chinese Christian Church, 1900–1949: Its Emergence and Impact', Ph.D. thesis, Westminster Theological Seminary, 1988, p. 249.

[29] See CNCR 1839, 23 August 1991. For critiques of Wang's theology see Wickeri, *Common Ground* and Ralph Covell, *Confucius, the Buddha and Christ: A History of the Gospel in Chinese*, Maryknoll: Orbis Books, 1986. There are several studies of Wang in Chinese, for example Lam Wing-hung *Wang Mingdao yu Zhongguo jiaohui* (*Wang Mingdao and the Chinese Church*), Hong Kong: China Graduate School of Theology, 1982.

the TSPM, he was arrested in February 1990 for failing to comply with local regulations on religion. *Tianfeng* fully supported the arrest.[30] Lin was released shortly afterwards with strict restrictions on his activities, but remained unrepentant and doubtless committed to resuming his work at the first opportunity. Many local leaders operate under similar conditions, thriving in more liberal periods and coping with repression at others.

THE POLITICS OF THE CHURCH

The years 1988 to 1991 provide an excellent opportunity to analyse the political life of the Protestant community. By 1986 there were rumours that both Zhao Ziyang and Hu Yaobang, General Secretary of the CCP, were interested in working towards a more liberal religious policy that would have coincided with the other reforms of the mid-1980s. Lambert cites unconfirmed reports that Bishop Ting had met Hu Yaobang and Yan Mingfu (then head of the UFWD), who had both appeared to favour reforms.[31] Both Ting and Zhao Puchu, the President of the Chinese Buddhist Association, used their positions on national political bodies to argue for greater religious freedom.[32] It seems likely that, had other events not intervened, there would have been progress, and in 1988 it became apparent that the call for reform had spread to the internal organization of the TSPM itself. A Christian leader in Fujian made an outspoken public attack:

For thirty years the Chinese Christian Three Self Patriotic Movement, under the leadership of the Religious Affairs Bureau, has truly had its achievements! Under their tight supervision, 99 per cent of the churches in the entire country were closed down; 99 per cent of the pastors were attacked – some were labeled rightists, some were sentenced as counter-revolutionaries, some died, some were im-

---

[30] CNCR 1541, 2 March 1990. The article in *Tianfeng*, April 1990, is summarized in CNCR 1568, 27 April 1990.   [31] Lambert, *Resurrection*, p. 205.
[32] See for example Zhao Puchu's speech to the CPPCC in 1988 'Call for a New Look at an Outdated Policy', translated in MacInnis, *Religion in China Today*, pp. 71–6, and 'Statement by Bishop Ting to the National CPPCC (March 1989)', translated in *China Study Project Journal*, vol. 4 no. 2, August 1989, pp. 72–3.

prisoned, some were exiled to the remote border regions, some were remoulded.[33]

A letter written to the RAB by Bishop Ting in September 1988 states the position of the reformers within the official church at this time. He maintained that the home meetings of Christians should not be subject to interference by the authorities and admitted that 'quite a number of patriotic Christians do not support or associate with the TSPM. This being the case I think we can only respect their position.' In other respects he implicitly admitted the criticisms that had long been made by opponents of the TSPM, namely that many of its officials were government appointees, often hostile to religion, and that the TSPM had failed to respect other Christian groups: 'The TSPM organizations do not respect the special worship practices of certain believers . . . Beginning from the 1950s the TSPM organizations have done some things which Christians find despicable. Indeed, similar things are still being done in some places today.'[34] Two points emphasized in the letter are that the authorities should cease their harassment of home meetings and end the practice of appointing non-Christian cadres to administrative positions in the church.

The culmination of this trend was a call for the abolition or radical reform of the TSPM itself. There were rumours from Christian sources that Ting and his liberal supporters were proposing the abolition of the TSPM, while hard-liners in the organization, particularly those based in Shanghai, were strongly opposed to these plans. In February 1989, in an interview with a Christian news agency in the USA, Ting announced categorically that the TSPM would be phased out by 1991; it was now an anachronism, too authoritarian and should be replaced by a church.[35] On his return to China, Ting issued a more cautious statement, but it was openly admitted that radical reform of the TSPM was on the agenda.

We cannot precisely assess Ting's personal motivation in this

---

[33] Zhang Shengcai, 'Huyu quanguo renda, zhengxie' ('Appeal to the NPC and CPPCC'), 24 March 1988, translated by Tony Lambert in *Resurrection*, p. 202.
[34] The letter can be consulted in *Bridge* no. 33, January–February 1989, pp. 3–8.
[35] See Lambert, *Resurrection*, p. 210, and *News Network International*, 20 March 1989.

process. Lambert wonders 'whether Ting was speaking from heart-felt religious convictions or as a consummate diplomat, concerned to smooth relations between the CCP and the church', and tends to the latter explanation.[36] However one source who knows Ting personally suggested that he became far more aware of the real situation in China through the 1980s, partly because of the extensive network of seminary graduates who often visited him. Previously he had been somewhat in a gilded cage in Nanjing, but he increasingly visited grass-roots churches and talked with pastors. When he felt there was a chance of support from high-level political figures he was keen to grasp the opportunity for the church. Whatever Ting's personal motives, we agree with Lambert that a convergence of factors led to the calls for reform: the overall climate of political and social change, grass-roots dissatisfaction with the TSPM and RAB, a desire by many Christian leaders for greater independence, and finally a sense of *real-politik* that only a more liberal policy would ultimately be effective in regulating church life.[37]

Ting's pro-reformist stance was again apparent during the demonstrations of spring 1989. On May 18 he issued a statement wholeheartedly supporting the 'patriotic activities' of the students, and called on the State Council to enter into dialogue with them. Staff and students of the Nanjing seminary marched in support of the democracy movement. Even after martial law had been declared and a crackdown was inevitable, he stated: 'I am glad that Christians are making their presence felt in these demonstrations. I am very glad that the students in the Nanjing Theological Seminary are taking an active part.' He also signed letters calling for emergency meetings of the NPC.[38]

Considering the level of repression and the return to hardline policies in society as a whole in 1990 and 1991, Ting and his colleague Zhao Puchu maintained a surprisingly vigorous defence of religious rights. On 1 July 1989, Ting was obliged to make a statement in the NPC, but he studiously avoided voicing support for the government, and instead called for a fight against corruption – which had been one of the main demands of

---

[36] Lambert, *Resurrection*, p. 206. [37] *Ibid.*, p. 212.
[38] See *Bridge*, no. 36, July–August 1989 for documentation.

the student movement. The following year he made an outspoken speech at the Standing Committee Meeting of the NPC:

There are various signs which are worrying us: whether we are going back on Document 19 and whether we have embarked on another reversal of policy . . . There are those who say that Chinese religions should justly be run by the Government, or that Government control is the expression of the leadership of the Party. This kind of opinion is very alien to most people and cannot be accepted by the masses. I hope this will not be seen as a mandate for speech or action.[39]

In the same speech he firmly rejected the idea that religion could play a role in overthrowing communist rule in China, as the church had done in East Europe, and insisted on the continuation of the policy of religious freedom. In another statement, made on the occasion of a meeting with Party General Secretary Jiang Zemin in January 1991, he again castigated repressive measures adopted by administrators within and outside the church:

They try to use administrative measures to restrict religion, to weaken it, to strip religious believers of their legal rights, and to confiscate places of religious activities. They make all kinds of excuses for not permitting the carrying out of lawful religious activities. They use the method of withholding registration to cause many places of religious activity to become illegal. Such places cannot but turn underground . . . Some cadres at the grass-roots scolded and struck persons who attended such meeting points. They put them in prison and fined them.[40]

After June 1989 the main objective of the central Party leadership was to reassert stricter control over society in the field of politics and ideology. A typical statement appeared in the *People's Daily* in October 1989: 'We must strengthen the people's democratic dictatorship, thoroughly quell the counter-revolutionary rebellion, create a stable political situation and social environment for the sake of continuing the socialist modernization, work to extend democracy, strengthen supervision, and punish and tackle corruption in order to win the trust of the people.'[41] Such sentiments continued to inspire the top leader-

[39] *China Study Journal*, vol. 6 no. 1, April 1991, pp. 53–5.
[40] *Bridge*, no. 46, March–April 1991, pp. 3–5.
[41] *Renmin ribao*, 9 October 1989, translation in *China Study Project Journal*, vol. 4 no. 3, December 1989, p. 33.

ship in the following years. For example, in August 1991 high-ranking military leaders and political officers held a meeting in Guangzhou to step up ideological work, to ensure the armed forces' 'absolute obedience' to the Party.[42] The cult of Mao was reinstated as a symbol for Party supremacy and government statements again emphasized socialism, rather than mere material prosperity, as the nation's goal. The *People's Daily* announced that: 'There is not a power in the world that can shake the determination and faith of 1.1 billion Chinese people in taking the socialist road.'[43]

Senior personnel were reshuffled to ensure that supporters of the new line were in leading positions in institutions of all kinds across the country as orthodoxy was reimposed. One senior casualty, whose replacement had direct consequences for religious affairs, was Yan Mingfu, the reformist head of the UFWD, who was replaced by Ding Guan'gen, a hard-liner with few qualifications for the job other than a close personal relationship with Deng Xiaoping.

By 1990 the government was seriously concerned by religion for two main reasons. First it assumed that since the churches had played an important role in the politics of East Europe, they might do the same in China; second they were disturbed about the allegedly fast growth rate of religions, for example Islam in the western provinces, popular sects in various parts of China, and Protestant Christianity in the southeastern provinces. There were further difficulties with the underground Catholic Church which at the same time mounted what was almost a campaign of disobedience in some areas where it was relatively powerful.

Inside the Protestant movement, the expression of these changes was a campaign against Bishop Ting himself. According to reports in Hong Kong in February 1991, there was considerable antagonism towards the Bishop on the part of more conservative members of his organizations, who were even considering bringing charges against him. They had two main

[42] Hong Kong *Mingbao*, 1 September 1991.
[43] *Renmin ribao*, front page editorial, 1 October 1991.

points of criticism: first that he was too independent of the CCP; and second that he was in collusion with foreign powers. It was to some extent a generational conflict also, since most of the hard-liners were old men who had a record of solid Party support since the 1950s, while Ting represented the opinions of many younger Christians. It appears, however, that Ting's position was unassailable, and he emerged unscathed. Presumably either his considerable international prestige or very high-level political protection was to thank for this.

Although this personal campaign did not get very far, the tone of official Protestant publications did change. Two targets for attack were brought up time and again: home meetings and foreign influence. A speech that perfectly illustrates the new tone was made by Bishop Shen Yifan to a joint meeting of the TSPM/CCC leadership in August 1990. It is especially significant because Bishop Shen was thought by many to be the favoured replacement for Ting:

International hostile forces are constantly changing their strategies to use Christianity to carry out subversion and sabotage . . . International anti-China forces use Christianity to undertake every kind of subversive activity. This is an important part of the strategy of 'peaceful evolution' undertaken by overseas hostile forces. They vainly want to split our church and destroy the unity between Christians and the great mass of the people, and fan enmity against the People's Government and the CCP. We must be on the alert, and resolutely unmask them and prevent them . . .

[House church leaders] steal money, rape women, destroy life and health, spread rumours and destroy social order. Some even foment believers to oppose the leadership of the Party, and seek to destroy the Three Self Movement . . . Self-appointed evangelists worm themselves everywhere and form reactionary organizations. Some have formed links with overseas hostile forces, and gained their financial support.[44]

Such sentiments were echoed at meetings of the TSPM, which seemed desperately to wish to reassert its credentials as an anti-imperialist, pro-CCP body, in a return to the rhetoric of the 1950s. In an article in *Tianfeng* an old Three-Selfer stated: 'The

[44] Full reports of the meeting, including this speech, were published in *Tianfeng*, November 1990. These extracts were translated by Tony Lambert, *Resurrection*, pp. 225–7.

TSPM is a powerful weapon . . . to oppose the division created by hostile forces outside China which use denominationalism as a lure, and to resist the infiltration of all kinds of bourgeois liberalization from abroad . . . In our patriotic study of the 1950s, we criticized bourgeois individualism as the key point. We have therefore been inoculated against the infectious disease of western bourgeois liberalization.'[45]

This new 'inoculated' orientation was neither spontaneous nor limited to the Three Self movement. Between autumn 1989 and summer 1991, state organs concerned with religion held numerous meetings.[46] The most important were three in Beijing: a seminar organized by CASS in November 1990; a national meeting on religious policy in December of the same year; and a 'frank, heart-to-heart talk' between Jiang Zemin and five senior religious leaders in January 1991. They illustrate the various attitudes to religion among the Party élite at this time.

The CASS meeting was restrained in tone. For example it noted that the label 'underground forces' is inaccurate; the majority of believers outside 'patriotic' associations were not necessarily anti-government, nor did they operate in secret. Probably only a small minority were actually hostile to the CCP. The conference recommended that a religious law be drafted after consultation with all parties to clarify the situation and place the administration of religion on a sound footing.[47]

The first national conference on religious policy, convened by the State Council and attended by over 200 senior cadres, was held in December 1990. The conference was opened by Premier Li Peng, probably the first time that such a senior figure had addressed religious questions since Zhou Enlai in the early 1950s. The topics of the conference have not been made public,

---

[45] *Tianfeng*, September 1990, translated in *Bridge* no. 44, November–December 1990, p. 3.

[46] For example at provincial level, in February 1991 the Shandong Party Secretary addressed religious leaders; Fujian provincial officials held a work meeting on religion; the Shaanxi Party Secretary addressed a forum for religious leaders; Xinjiang CCP officials addressed meetings concerned with religion and a religious work conference was held in Liaoning in early March. Details in *China Study Journal*, vol. 6 no. 1, April 1991, pp. 31–4.

[47] *Wushenlun, zongjiao (Atheism, Religion)* no. 2, 1991, pp. 16–19. Extracts in translation can be found in CNCR 1860, 27 September 1991.

but it is thought that the main outcome was to reaffirm strict Party control over religion without resorting to overtly repressive measures such as mass arrests. A similar message was relayed to the most senior religious leaders in China by Jiang Zemin:

> It is necessary to strengthen, according to the law, administrative management and supervision in the implementation of laws, regulations and policies related to religious work . . . [This] will help prevent and check undesirable elements from using religion and religious activities to create chaos, violate laws and commit crimes, as well as resist infiltration by outside hostile forces who exploit religious activities.[48]

The meetings resulted in a new series of practical measures and policy decisions, some of which were publicized. Others, such as new security operations, were initiated quietly. The most important document to emerge so far is known as 'Document 6', entitled 'Notice on Further Tackling Certain Problems of Religious Work', issued by the CCP Central Committee and the State Council in February 1991. It is a formulation in policy terms of the concerns which were expressed at the December work meeting on religion, and again focuses on the need for vigilance against 'hostile foreign forces' and illegal activities under the cloak of religion.

The content and style of the Document is similar to that of 'Document 19' analysed earlier, and it does not repudiate the provisions of the latter. The essential difference is the emphasis on control – 'penalizing according to law and strengthening the management' – of religious groups. Public security bureaux are instructed to join in the fight against illegal religious organizations, which must be eliminated. Ideological political indoctrination should be strengthened; the patriotic organizations should serve as a bridge for educating religious personnel. The underlying theme of the document is anti-infiltration, anti-subversion and anti-peaceful evolution.[49] Whereas the thrust of 'Document 19' was towards increased tolerance, the trend of 'Document 6' was to impose stricter controls, especially in the

[48] *Xinhua*, Beijing, 30 January 1991, translation in *China Study Journal*, vol. 6 no. 1, April 1991, pp. 25–6.   [49] CNCR 1872, 1 November 1991.

question of unregistered religious activities. This change of attitude at the centre resulted in new regulations at local level, congruent with the trend mentioned above, i.e. tighter controls and strong warnings against contact with foreigners.[50]

Finally, policy and regulations have been translated into action, the most common forms of which have been closer monitoring of foreigners, arrest and harassment of house churches and increased political training for official church members. The attitude of the current Chinese administration with regard to foreigners is rather complex. On the level of rhetoric, it appears that 'hostile foreign forces' are a serious problem. Almost all the hard-line statements cited above, and many others, refer to these forces as the prime target, pinpointing the following subversive activities: radio broadcasts, evangelization through academic channels, using social work or tourism as cover for religious activities, subverting local clergy, fomenting dissatisfaction among minority peoples close to national frontiers, and interfering with the patriotic religious organizations.

The claims seem to fall into two categories. First is the problem of evangelization, not necessarily with any political intent. A typical example is the radio broadcasts, which focus almost exclusively on religious questions. It seems that the official objection is not that the foreign forces are particularly 'hostile' in a concrete political sense, but more that the spread of Christianity itself is seen as a threat. Presumably the more serious charge is using religious activities as a cloak for anti-government subversive organization. The most explicit condemnation is for the underground Catholic movement which according to the Propaganda Monthly, 'is emerging as a political power to oppose our government'. No similar accusations have been made against Protestants to date.

Is there in fact a conspiracy to overthrow the Chinese government, operating under the cover of religious organizations? So far we have seen no evidence that this may be happening, and the only persons known to have been arrested,

---

[50] For Hunan, see *Bridge* no. 45, January–February 1991, pp. 10–11. Lambert, *Resurrection*, pp. 232 ff., also discusses these regulations.

and later executed, on such a charge were two Taiwanese agents in 1983.[51] In reality the emphasis on foreign subversion is probably a face-saving device adopted by the current leadership. They appear to be profoundly embarrassed by the revival of religions and disturbed by the potential power of religious organizations. Rather than admit that these have their roots in a China that has been communist since 1949, it is more acceptable to blame the situation on outsiders. Thus control over foreigners is perhaps more important at the level of rhetoric than reality, although it is true that visitors – church people, journalists or academics – are more closely monitored than before 1989.[52]

In distinct contrast, the pressure on both official and unofficial church groups is a reality, although not so widely advertised. In official groups, the main technique has been the reintroduction of the 'study sessions' which were a favourite tool of the Party between 1950 and 1979. On these occasions, held once a week or more frequently, responsible persons explain new aspects of Party policy and the audience is expected to indicate its approval. Failure to attend the meetings, and also failure to register sufficient enthusiasm, is ground for criticism and discipline. A fine example of study sessions was reported from Chaozhou, when after the 4 June incident in 1989 the TSPM pastor Reverend Guo 'put great emphasis on teaching his flock the spirit of patriotism':

He called all members of the church affairs committees as well as theological students and office assistants together to study statements and notices issued by the government. From June 6 to September 28 they conscientiously studied the report delivered by the Beijing mayor Chen Xitong on 'Checking the Turmoil and quelling the counter-revolutionary rebellion', and a series of articles compiled by the Chaozhou Municipal Party Committee such as 'Upholding the Four Cardinal Principles and Combating Bourgeois Liberalization'.[53]

The tightening of the official church seems to have been

[51] For a résumé of the affair see 'Spies or Missionaries?', *Bridge* no. 2, November 1983, p. 19.
[52] See for example the difficulties experienced by journalist Deng Zhaoming, *Bridge*, no. 46, March–April 1991, p. 2.
[53] *Bridge*, no. 44, November–December 1990, pp. 4–5.

confined to relatively small changes at the margin: more study sessions, closer observation, tighter regulations on new membership, less chance to argue for reform of the administration. But on the whole, with Bishop Ting's survival as a symbol, it seems fair to say that the official church has emerged from the turmoil of 1989 relatively unscathed – and that may mean that in real terms its influence has increased.

The major *locus* of confrontation has shifted to the unregistered churches. At the time of writing it was difficult to obtain reliable documentation of the level of repression. Reports appeared in Hong Kong about the imprisonment of house church leaders and breaking up of Christian meetings by public security personnel, but it is hard to assess their accuracy.

The Chinese Government has started another wave of repression against churches in China . . . Three provinces, namely Henan, Zhejiang and Fujian, have been particularly mentioned because of the high level of religious activities . . . There was also news of arrests in other provinces. In a northern province where eight Christians have been detained since last year, several have already been sentenced to three years' imprisonment in a labour camp, the stiffest possible penalty, another Chinese source said. The atmosphere in northern China is rather tense and Christians are forced to meet in smaller groups following the government crackdown in recent months. The repression is due to information given to the authorities by 'Judas's' who appear to be devout believers.[54]

It seems likely that in the early 1990s the authorities renewed efforts to restrict, control and punish unregistered church groups. This would be in line with policy decisions from the centre, is confirmed by Bishop Ting, and has been related by several unofficial sources.

Despite some uncertainty about details, and the fact that much evidence is unavailable, we can draw general conclusions concerning the church in politics in the early 1990s. The TSPM retains its role as a 'patriotic religious association', still charged with supervising church affairs and in particular relaying Party policies to the congregations and pastors. It has considerable

[54] CNCR 1856, 20 September 1991. A similar report appeared in CNCR 1869, 25 October 1991.

influence in appointments and control over publications. Many officials are closely aligned with state organs including the security apparatus, and appear to approve the current policy of a crackdown on foreign contacts and house churches in particular. Personnel appointments are vetted by CCP organization departments.

On the other hand, the late 1980s saw changes in attitudes which are probably irreversible. There was widespread criticism of the TSPM which was regarded as out-of-date, obstructive and repressive. The dissatisfaction was voiced at the very top of the organization and could easily have led to its dissolution. The events of 4 June produced a temporary reprieve for the present structure of the Chinese church: the form of administration has been retained, but its authority is based only on state power, and probably will not survive the next political swing. More liberal groups in the church have been relatively successful in holding their positions, and will doubtless resume a more active campaign when the national situation changes; under present circumstances they are probably quite content if they can maintain the *status quo*.

Thus far we have surveyed the state of the Protestant community in the context of China since 1979. We now move on to pose some questions which will hopefully lead to a deeper understanding of the movement. In later chapters we will discuss some relevant cultural and sociological issues. How does modern Chinese Protestantism relate to traditional beliefs? Who becomes Christian and why? What is the life of a Christian community? Before addressing these questions, we will clarify the historical background: the development of the Protestant movement before 1949 may help us to understand the current situation.

CHAPTER 3

The historical legacy

PROTESTANTS, POLITICS AND THE CHINESE COMMUNIST PARTY

From 1911 to 1927, the provinces of China fell under the domination of various warlords, the central government was ineffective and there was no national religious policy. Even when the nationalists consolidated their control, the ruling GMD itself held an ambiguous attitude towards religion. On the one hand it regarded religious freedom as an expression of modernism and democracy, which it espoused in theory at least. Thus in the GMD First National Congress in 1924 a resolution was adopted offering 'absolute freedom of association, of speech, of publication, of domicile and belief'. Again in 1931 a draft for a provisional constitution stated 'There shall be freedom of religious belief' and in 1935 the new criminal code gave protection to all kinds of religious services.[1]

However there was also a strong tendency towards authoritarianism in the GMD, and many of its officials regarded religion as superstitious, an expression of backwardness, or as a potential source of rebellion. In the case of Christianity, the conceptual critique was largely borrowed from mid-nineteenth-century European materialists such as Haeckel. A more graphic illustration was provided by an immense poster on the gate of the Jiangsu GMD headquarters which stated: 'Jesus Christ is an obstacle to human progress and an evil spirit incompatible with the spirit of this generation.' In 1936 all civil societies, including

[1] Quoted in Arne Sovik, 'Church and State in Republican China: A Survey History of the Relations between the Christian Churches and the Chinese Government, 1911–1945', Ph.D. thesis, Yale University, 1952, p. 282.

religious organizations, were required to register under new regulations that stated:

1. No word or act against the Three People's Principles [the official political slogan of the GMD] is permitted.
2. The organization shall receive guidance from the GMD.
3. The organization shall observe the laws of the nation and obey the mandates of the government.
4. Membership shall be limited to those permitted by law.
5. Counter-revolutionaries and those deprived of their civil rights are not permitted to be members.
6. Any extraordinary meeting must secure the consent of the highest local Party and government officials.

Thus there was legal ground for considerable government influence in religious affairs, and officials were frequently unsympathetic to religious organizations.[2] For example, the Buddhist Association of Hangzhou appealed unsuccessfully to the government to restore Buddhist property that had been occupied by civilian and military officials. Buddhists also objected without avail to proposals presented at a Conference on Civil Affairs in 1931 that aimed to convert certain temples to governmental uses, train monks in 'useful' occupations, curb political activities by religious organizations and restrict the number of religious schools.[3]

The two major studies of church–state relations in the Republic show that Protestants experienced an ambivalent situation. Legally and constitutionally there were positive steps towards guaranteeing religious freedom. But in accordance with many centuries of tradition, the government also felt entitled to demand registration, and it had legal powers to control religious organizations.[4] In practical terms, abuses could occur at local level and there were certainly examples of illegal occupation of property. Much of the blame for this lay with the prevailing social turmoil: localized violence was frequently out of control.

---

[2] *Ibid.*, p. 270.
[3] Miner Searle Bates, 'The Chinese State and Religion, with Particular Reference to Christianity, 1840–1949', Columbia University Seminar on East Asia, 29 November 1967, p. 30.
[4] See the works listed in chapter 1, note 31 for discussion of religious policies in China.

The main areas of official disagreement with Christians concerned registration, taxation, and control of education, but they
were generally settled by compromise. The presence of Chinese
Christians in the highest echelons of the GMD was a helpful
factor in this.

Arne Sovik concludes that by 1937 'China's legal structure
was still not adapted to the existence of free religious institutions
parallel with, not subject to, the state.'[5] Miner Searle Bates
agrees with this assessment, noting that there was a 'serious
failure of the Chinese state to provide a reasonable legal status
for Chinese church bodies'; but he also concludes that the
situation was quite tolerable in practice 'because the administration was generally lax and usually tolerant . . . to Christians'.[6] Relations between the state and religious organizations
were not ideal, but neither were they too difficult. This tolerable
situation was interrupted by the Japanese invasion which led to
twelve years of chaos and war, when religious issues inevitably
stayed in the background.

Protestant denominations, with their different orientations,
brought a variety of approaches into the political sphere. Since
Chinese society was and is highly politicized, it is worth
examining the political culture that the Protestant groups
evolved in the Republic, which also allows us to consider the
continuities after 1949. In general, the Protestant movement
played a reactive rather than pro-active role in Chinese politics,
not surprisingly considering its numerical weakness and fragmentation. When it did become involved it was usually in
response to attacks. Foreign organizations and individuals
tended to stage retreats, allowing more powerful forces to
temporarily, at least, dominate the scene. Foreigners relied on
their nationality for some measure of protection. At times of
physical danger they often returned to the relative security of
the treaty ports or even their home countries. There were some
fatalities and incarcerations, but these were limited in number
(twenty-nine missionaries were killed between 1924 and 1934,
according to the *Chinese Recorder*, the majority by bandits). Even

[5] Sovik, 'Church and State', p. 217.
[6] Bates, 'The Chinese State and Religion', p. 44.

dedicated enemies of the missionaries, such as the CCP in the late 1920s, had to acknowledge the protection afforded to the missionaries by the foreign powers that then held *de facto* power in many areas of Chinese life.

The problems were far more acute for their Chinese co-workers. The latter found it harder to withdraw behind foreign protection and they were less insulated from the realities of Chinese social life. Chinese Christian students in particular had to face critical onslaughts from their anti-imperialist colleagues. A dominant political theme of the era was the question of nationalism: how to gain national independence from the hated foreigners, at first the British and other Europeans, later the Japanese. Perhaps missionaries failed to recognize the pressures that were directed against Chinese Christians, especially when political tensions were high, for being traitors to their culture and their country.

The 'Nanking Road Incident' of May 1925, when soldiers under British command shot dead seven unarmed students, contributed to tension between Chinese Christians and foreign missionaries. Dr Yu Rizhang (David Z. T. Yui), a politician, educator and the chairman of the National Christian Council, subsequently called on Chinese Christians to join the nationalist movement, abrogate the unequal treaties and free China from foreign oppression. His principal argument, which became a major theme for Chinese Christian leaders, was that the church like any other institution must reflect the rising tide of nationalism in the country, or else fail. These demands were felt most acutely by youth groups: the YMCA, for example, was the most radical of all Christian organizations, yet even it was denounced as a tool of imperialism by the National Student Union in 1925.[7] In the years that followed several Chinese Christian leaders stated publicly that the Christian movement must somehow identify with the revolution if it were to survive. At the extreme, a few Chinese Christians, aware of the challenge posed by the revolutionary movements, adopted a radical anti-imperialist political stance, some going so far as to support the CCP. They

---

[7] Miner Searle Bates, *Gleanings from the Manuscripts of M. S. Bates: The Protestant Endeavour in Chinese Society*, New York: The China Programme, NCCCUSA, 1984, p. 69.

were a small minority, since the mainstream position among Chinese Christians, especially those connected with the independent churches and revival movements that we examine later, was the rejection of politics. However, we will consider their position in some detail, since the patterns established in the 1920s are useful for assessing later events.

The CCP was founded in 1921 at a secret meeting in Shanghai under the leadership of Chen Duxiu, and under the guidance of a Comintern agent, Maring. Among its first tasks was the organization of youth groups to gain influence among students, and one of the tactics was to attack Christianity. Inflammatory articles began to appear in CCP front journals such as *Vanguard*, and a successful campaign was sustained for several years. The main point of attack was that Christianity saps the will to fight, is inevitably bound to imperialism and is a vanguard of capitalist penetration. Until 1937, the CCP maintained a vigorous anti-Christian orientation. In the field of ideology, conflict seemed inevitable. For its first fifteen years at least, the Party adopted the rigid stance, imported from the Soviet Union, that religion is the opium of the masses, a tool in the hands of the ruling classes, a symbol of imperialism and oppression by foreigners. This critique coincided with the rationalistic and anti-feudal intellectual trends of the period; it received broad approval among the GMD as well as CCP and proved to be an effective tool for winning popular support. One of the most widely distributed anti-Christian tracts, by Chu Zhixin, was in fact written in 1919, before the foundation of the CCP and published in the GMD organ *Jianshe* (*Reconstruction*). It was reissued several times and used by the Anti-Christian Federation in many campaigns in the 1920s. Its spirit is rationalist, pointing out historical implausibilities in the gospels, characterizing Christian figures as selfish and narrow-minded, and the religion itself as an obstacle to China's liberation.[8]

The CCP promoted its anti-Christian campaign throughout the 1920s. For example in the Cantonese Peasants Delegations in 1925 and 1926, delegates were told that: 'promoters of

[8] Jessie G. Lutz, *Chinese Politics and Christian Mission: The Anti-Christian Movements of 1920–1928*, Notre Dame, IN: Cross Cultural Publications Inc., 1988, p. 20.

religion like priests, pastors etc. are all under imperialist
influence and cannot become members of peasant associations'.
Practical measures were rather restrained, however, and the
attack was limited to debate rather than physical confrontation
– one document explicitly states that this was to avoid armed
conflict with the foreign powers who were so strong in China.
The only outbreak of violence was the 'Nanking Incident' of 24
March 1927. Soldiers of the Northern Expedition, apparently
under communist command, burst into the British and US
consulates in Nanjing, killing several officials and pastors. They
later attacked many pastors' houses in the city. The reason for
this exceptional incident is not clear, but it may have been an
attempt to damage GMD/western relations, or an attempt to
split foreign solidarity, since Japanese property was left alone.

   The policy of hostility but non-violence was maintained until
1937, except for the kidnapping and occasional deaths of
missionaries in rural areas. It is not clear if these were ordered by
CCP authorities, who were leading a difficult clandestine
existence, or if they were mere bandit operations. However,
events in the Jiangxi soviet area between 1932 and 1936 gave an
indication of what policy might be when the Party was in a
stronger position: religion was virtually outlawed and church
property confiscated. Throughout these years there was little
contact between Christians and the CCP with the exception of a
few individuals like Pu Huaren, a pastor of the 'Christian
General' Feng Yuxiang. Pu, one of the first Christians to support
the CCP, later became a Party member and served in the
post-1949 government at a high level. Most missionaries
regarded the communists as just another bandit nuisance which
added to the dangers of China as a mission field. Only a few
more careful observers began to analyse their programme and
wonder if they held the key to the future development of China.
Until the mid-1930s the CCP had little impact on national
political life and it was understandable that the Christian
movement should pay them relatively little attention.

   Based on the experience of these years, then, the CCP was
unremittingly hostile to religion, and Christianity in particular.
However the years 1937 to 1949 saw a quite different orienta-

tion, which laid the basis for the more sophisticated policies
adopted in the 1980s. This was the time of the United Front
strategy, according to which enemies were not determined by
ideological differences; rather, a pragmatic accommodation was
sought with diverse interest groups. From 1937, emphasis was
laid on uniting all patriotic Chinese against the Japanese
aggressor, and later the communists adopted the same strategy
against the GMD. After the Japanese invasion, Zhou Enlai and
other communist leaders insisted that they had a genuine wish to
join in a common national struggle. Many thousands of young
intellectuals made their way to the CCP base area in Yenan,
which became a focus for radical resistance to the Japanese. In
1936 the party began to call on the church explicitly to help the
anti-Japanese struggle, and in 1939 religious freedom was
allowed in areas under communist control.[9] Many missionaries
immediately noted an improvement in communist attitudes
towards them in rural areas, and Christians began to reevaluate
the Party. In particular they appreciated its potential for rural
reconstruction, its patriotic policy and its apparent probity in
contrast to the perceived corruption of the GMD.

Interaction between Christians and communists grew rapidly: Sovik reports that there were enough Christians in Yenan to
fill a church. There were two main reasons for this. First, as the
CCP halted its overt confrontation with the nationalist government, it used its new prestige to recruit members and sympath-
izers in cultural circles. The policy was spelt out in a speech by
Mao Zedong: 'When any of our Party members are forced to
join the GMD let them join it . . . Our members should infiltrate
extensively into the *pao* and *chia* organizations,[10] educational
organizations, economic organizations and military organizations, and they should extensively develop the work for the
united front.'[11]

The communists spread their influence among academics,

[9] Fox Butterfield, 'A Missionary View of the Chinese Communists (1936–1939)' in
American Missionaries in China, Papers from the Harvard Seminars, edited by Liu Kwang-
Ching, Harvard East Asian Monographs, 1966, pp. 249–301 (p. 267).
[10] These were local security organizations.
[11] From 'Questions of Tactics in the Present Anti-Japanese United Front', *Selected Works
of Mao Tse-tung*, London: Lawrence and Wishart, 1954, vol. 3, p. 203.

journalists, artists and writers, and were especially active in the
student movement from which many new members were
recruited.[12] To conduct this work the Party set up a special
section known as the *bimidang* (secret party) or *dixiadang*
(underground party): its membership and history are secret
since the organization is still operative today. Typical members
are leading scholars and artists, and the main purpose is to have
secret Party members in a wide range of organizations. In the
Christian movement this programme was most successfully
implemented in the YM/YWCA and the various relief committees that operated after 1945, all of which became virtual CCP
front organizations. Important individuals from this background among the Chinese Christians were Wu Yaozong, Liu
Liangmo and Li Chuwen.

Secondly, some Christians began to revise their opinions of
the CCP, as did other sections of both the urban and rural
population. The communists never achieved mass support in
the cities, but many people regarded them more favourably as
GMD rule degenerated into chaos and corruption. Increased
contacts between the 'United Front' CCP and Christians, for
example in relief work efforts at the end of the war, also created
an improvement in relations, as did a mutual interest in rural
reform. Some missionaries regarded them as reformist socialists
rather than hard-line soviet-style communists, while in liberated
areas the communists were quite accommodating to Christians
and co-operated on rural reconstruction programmes.

Thus as 1949 approached, church/CCP relations were not too
tense. On one level the Party regarded the church as a target of
United Front policy, to be won over against the common
enemy. Christians were permitted to work in the CCP controlled areas, and others were recruited or infiltrated to maintain a
communist presence inside the church and para-church groups.
However, the cruder version of anti-religious Leninism had
never been repudiated, and events would soon show how close to
the surface it was. On the church side many still viewed the CCP
with suspicion. Conservative missionaries and church leaders

---

[12] The best-known examples were the 'Leagues' of progressive artists, such as the
'League of Left-wing Writers' in Shanghai.

openly supported the GMD and aligned themselves explicitly
against the CCP, which naturally did not escape the latter's
notice. But there was also a groundswell of opinion in the
Christian community that there was room for productive
co-operation with the communists. The Protestant movement
was never a united anti-communist force, unlike the Roman
Catholic church.[13]

THE DENOMINATIONAL CHURCHES

The pattern of early mission work was decisive in forming the
character of the Chinese Protestant movement. The customary
mode of operation was for a missionary board in the home
country to provide funds for a new project. In the nineteenth
century, the initial stage was to open mission compounds in the
treaty ports of Guangzhou, Xiamen, Fuzhou, Ningbo, Shanghai and Tianjin. In these coastal cities were established
administrative headquarters, language schools for new arrivals,
housing and other facilities.[14] These arrangements reinforced
the sense of separation between missionaries and the local
population. At times missionaries were advised by British and
American government officials to refrain from close contact with
the Chinese to avoid unnecessary disturbances; Pearl Buck
recalled: 'the small white clean Presbyterian American world of
my parents and the big loving merry not-too-clean Chinese
world, and there was no communication between them'.[15]

In the following decades, missionaries tended to adopt a
similar approach in new areas. They would start with the
purchase of land and buildings in a town, followed by the
establishment of a church and other institutional work, such as a
school or hospital. The degree of emphasis on para-church

[13] The attitudes of missionaries and church leaders during the last years of the
revolution constitute too large a question to examine here. Readers will find relevant
material in Wickeri, *Common Ground* and George Hood, *Neither Bang Nor Whimper: The
End of a Missionary Era in China*, Singapore: Presbyterian Church in Singapore, 1991.
[14] For details of daily life in such a mission station see Sidney A. Forsythe, *An American
Missionary Community in China, 1895–1905*, Cambridge, MA: Harvard University Press,
1971.
[15] Jerome Ch'en, *China and the West: A Study of Social and Cultural Change*, London:
Hutchinson, 1979, p. 149.

welfare institutions varied, but even the most evangelical society, the China Inland Mission, recognized the value of schools as an aid to attract converts. Evangelistic work would be conducted by preaching in public places, distribution of tracts, personal conversations and revival meetings. After the nucleus of a congregation had been gathered, the missionary worked towards financial self-sufficiency and hand-over to a Chinese pastor. This process of 'transplanting' took on average twenty to twenty-five years and was rather limited in a cultural sense: the new church was basically a western ecclesiastical model built on Chinese soil. Chinese pastors usually relied on missionaries both for their understanding of Christian faith and the practical arrangements of church organization.[16]

These large denominational churches, often located in coastal cities, were known as 'Mother Churches'. Even in the 1930s many were still run by missionaries with substantial financial support from abroad, surrounded by schools, clinics and foreign residences. The churches were supervised by senior clergy and well furnished with personnel. The congregations had a long training in western forms of worship and behaviour, and included foreign residents together with well-educated and westernized Chinese. Music, liturgy and regularity of attendance approximated to European or American standards. Thus in one respect they were the most overtly western of the Protestant institutions. But at the same time, most of the intellectual discourse concerning the indigenization of Christianity and most of the social experiments were also made in these city churches and their institutions. They were the channels for new modes of Christian thought to enter China.

All denominations attempted to establish churches in the countryside.[17] Compared to city churches, those in rural areas were smaller and poorer. Urban churches had an average

---

[16] Jonathan Chao Ti'en-en, 'The Chinese Indigenous Church Movement, 1919–1927: A Protestant Response to the Anti-Christian Movements in Modern China', Ph.D. thesis, University of Pennsylvania, 1986, p. 276.

[17] Some reports on the rural church are summarized in Orville A. Petty, *China. Laymen's Foreign Missions Inquiry. Vol. 2, Supplementary Series, Part One*, New York: Harper and Brothers, 1933. Frank Price, *The Rural Church in China: A Survey*, New York: Agricultural Missions Inc., 1948 is the most comprehensive study.

membership of seventy to eighty with paid staff and a variety of ministries; a rural church typically had a membership of less than fifty, with far fewer staff, less variety of activities, and fewer young people and women among the congregation. Rural pastors generally had less theological education than their urban colleagues, and their income was lower. City churches were closer to self-support and had better ties with other Christian institutions. They were also more likely to compete with each other, since rural churches benefited from the comity agreements, whereby denominations arranged to work in different parts of the country. A rural church was usually the only Christian institution serving a large area 'like tiny islands in a vast surrounding sea'.[18]

The social composition of rural church membership created difficulties. According to surveys by the Rural Church Department of the Nanjing Seminary in the mid-1930s, the average ratio of Christians to the general population was 1 : 400 even in the eastern provinces, and distances between churches were so great as to make attendance difficult for women and young people.[19] The average church had around only forty members, who were widely dispersed, often over a ten mile radius and thus unable to form a cohesive body. Home meeting-points were more numerous than churches, and open-air preaching was also common. Factors which limited conversion were the prohibitions against gambling, smoking, ancestor worship, concubinage, participation in local religious activities and support of temples which some churches ordered. Only about 10 per cent of church members kept the Sabbath, which was difficult to observe in the context of the rural economy, and one of the major weaknesses of the whole system was the lack of financial support for the churches and pastors.

Altogether, the rural churches did not appear healthy in the late 1930s, although one report pointed out that improvements were at least underway. More church leaders were aware of the problems and willing to acknowledge the cultural environment in which they operated. There was a trend towards broader

[18] Petty, *China*, p. 93.   [19] Bates, *Gleanings*, p. 100.

programmes which would benefit the entire community, and serious pioneering attempts were made in undertakings such as agricultural co-operatives.[20] But these new initiatives were insignificant in number, and the state of the rural church overall seemed extremely precarious as it underwent the years of war. A quarter of all churches suffered serious property damage in the war years, and congregations were scattered in the migrations from Japanese occupation. The only bright spot in this was some benefit to the church in west China from the influx of displaced pastors and church members.

The pattern of church growth in rural areas showed some distinctive features. For example, of the eighty missionaries of the London Missionary Society in 1905, almost all were based in twenty mission stations. But the majority of Chinese converts were serviced by 320 'outstations' staffed by 287 Chinese preachers, only a handful of whom were ordained and working full time. A similar pattern is reported for the American Board of Commissioners for Foreign Missions in 1904. Most outstations had more than one meeting point in the countryside, which were rarely if ever visited by missionaries.[21] Thus the distinctive form of organization was the congregation, centred around local lay leaders. These congregations often clustered around particular villages and kinship groups. Other reports noted similar patterns for the 1930s: 'About one third of [rural] churches have resident pastors or preachers, over one third are supervised by circuit or itinerant preachers or evangelists, and nearly one fourth have lay leaders . . . The proportion of churches which have a responsible layman in charge is surprisingly large and indicates a definite move in the direction of a more lay leadership.'[22]

Finance and the devolution of control from missionaries to Chinese nationals were two important issues of the period. Money was a controversial element of the Christian movement, not least because it was a focus for anti-Christian resentment.

[20] *Ibid.*, pp. 100–1.
[21] Daniel H. Bays, 'Christianity and the Chinese Sectarian Tradition', *Ch'ing Shih Went'i*, vol. 4 no. 7, June 1982, pp. 33–55 (p. 34).
[22] Price, *The Rural Church*, p. 19.

The rural churches still depended on foreign funds and personnel: less than half of their budget was covered by income from local sources, and in nearly two-thirds of churches the chief supervisor was a missionary, even if *in absentia*. Although much mission money was put to philanthropic uses, there was nevertheless a strong popular hatred of western power, coupled with bitterness at the unequal treaties, foreign exploitation and the scornful superiority assumed by the imperial powers. A particular contempt was reserved for Chinese converts. They were popularly perceived as 'rice-bowl' believers, fawning on the rich foreigners to obtain lucrative employment and protection. Even inside the Christian movement there was some resentment of those who took paid employment as pastors, and Chinese Christians responded warmly to the ideas of indigenous churches such as the Local Assemblies partly because of their non-clerical organization. The satirical writing of the novelist Xiao Qian reflects popular sentiment:

Standing outside the church entrance are slaves who are even more despicable and contemptible than those high-stepping, arrogant Westerners. Carrying their greasy moneybags, they deal in Chinese souls at the beck and call of the Westerners . . . These Pharisees are the equivalent of traitors to the Chinese people . . . Their trick lies in getting on the good side of the Westerners and the elders in the church – the rest follows naturally.[23]

Devolution of Christian activity from missionary to Chinese control was a significant trend of the period. The process started in earnest around 1920 and was well underway by the outbreak of war in 1937. It would presumably have been completed in due course whatever the outcome of the civil war, but was brought to an abrupt and thorough conclusion after the communist victory in 1949. Several of the major mission boards, especially Methodist and Presbyterian ones, adopted an explicit policy that leadership should be handed over to Chinese nationals at the earliest possible opportunity. Factors which hastened this course were the anti-foreign movements of the mid-1920s and the world recession of 1929 which sharply

[23] From the short story 'P'eng cheng', quoted in Lewis S. Robinson, *Double-Edged Sword: Christianity and 20th Century Chinese Fiction*, Hong Kong: Tao Fong Shan, 1986, p. 131.

reduced financial support from abroad. World war and the Japanese invasion further weakened the missionary enterprise and prepared the Chinese church for complete independence.

The slogan under which devolution of control took place was 'Three Self', a term originally proposed by an Anglican clergyman, Thomas Venn, in the nineteenth century, according to which the church should be self-supporting, self-governing and self-propagating. The practical details of implementing this idea varied according to denomination and locale, and the process required adjustment on all sides. Missionaries had to learn to be advisers and to relinquish their paternalistic role; Chinese pastors had to work more independently, without mission protection and assistance. There were changes in administration, personnel, property rights and financial arrangements to be undertaken. The issue of the 'indigenous church' and its precise content and form became a central topic in the 1920s and 1930s as can be seen from articles in the *Chinese Recorder* and other journals. For example, in 1926 a major conference was held on 'The Church in China Today' which focused on these themes. An Anglican educator, Dr Francis Cho-min Wei, argued that a truly Chinese church would have Chinese leadership and would be funded from Chinese sources. Architecture, liturgy, music, social organizations and other aspects of church life should all be transformed away from western models. This movement accorded with the rising tide of nationalism: as we will see, some Chinese Christians began to work towards a wholly indigenous church, not merely Chinese control of a western model.

By 1949, there were an estimated 625,000 communicant members of the mainline denominational churches, and around 1,400,000 Chinese had been baptized. They were served by about 10,000 pastors and evangelists, and could make use of some 20,000 church buildings. As we have mentioned, they were concentrated in the southeastern provinces, with the greatest numbers being in rural areas. Church institutions, however, and missionary personnel, were firmly urban based. The Church of Christ in China, which included most Presbyterian and Reformed congregations, was the largest denomination. Other denominations with large memberships were the Methodists, Baptists, Anglicans and Lutherans. The China Inland Mission was very influential in rural districts.[24] The missionary enterprise was rather notorious for its sectarianism, and denominational rivalries aroused criticism from Chinese Christians. Before 1949, the Chinese church certainly displayed the ecclesiastical diversity that is an essential feature of Protestantism.

THE INDEPENDENT CHURCHES

Another strand to Protestant life in China from the early years of the century was formed by a number of indigenous Christian movements that were institutionally independent of all foreign organizations. The first was the Independent Church of Shanghai, founded in 1906. Its constitution gives three fundamental reasons why autonomy was necessary. First, to eliminate the 'foreign colouring' of Christianity and the charge of being foreigners' slaves. Second, to reconcile believers with their fellow Chinese. Third, to conduct more effective evangelism in China than foreigners could. After being subjected to bitter criticism by missionaries, the church broke relations with foreign missions. Complete separation became characteristic of most independent Chinese churches.[25]

Many new churches were formed in the same spirit and by 1920 a National Conference of Chinese Independent Churches was organized, with 120 delegates representing 189 churches and 10,000 members. Estimates until 1949, however, suggest that these independent churches did not maintain rapid growth. Over six hundred affiliated churches were opened before 1931, but most of them were short-lived and closed after political unrest. The great majority were in two provinces, Zhejiang and Henan. A similar movement also appeared in the cities of North China, particularly Hebei and Shandong. The first church was opened in Tianjin in 1910, and there were forty-two altogether by 1936.[26]

---

[24] Denominational membership is given in Whyte, *Unfinished Encounter*, p. 200.
[25] Chao, 'Chinese Indigenous Church' is the best study of this movement.
[26] The churches in the south and east were generally called *Zhongguo Yesujiao Zilihui*

Chao's study of the movement explains the key differences between the development of missionary and independent churches. As noted above, the former usually began by purchasing buildings and starting educational or medical work as a base for evangelism, hiring Chinese workers where necessary. As congregations were formed, more money was sought locally, ideally leading to self-sufficiency. After this a Chinese pastor might take over responsibility for the church and for further propagation. The independent model was almost the opposite: leaders emerged who wished to establish an independent, non-denominational church, and they started teaching at prayer meetings. If sufficient interest was aroused, a church was formed. The search began for finances to support a full-time pastor, and later to erect a building. Finally there might be expansion into social work or related activities.

The above churches, although entirely Chinese in leadership, institutions and funding sources, nevertheless retained strong western influences in theology, ecclesiology and other matters. They aimed towards the same goals as missionaries, except that they formed their own churches rather than inherited existing ones. A more radical break with the foreign tradition came from a number of movements that not only were Chinese in personnel and funding, but also in significant cultural aspects, representing a deeper level of integration with Chinese customs and religiosity. The most significant were The True Jesus Church, the Jesus Family and the Local Assemblies, all of which survive in the 1990s.

The True Jesus church had its origins in the Pentecostal mission movement which emanated from Los Angeles in 1907. Three Chinese believers, Zhang Lingshen, Paul Wei (Wei Enbo) and Barnabas Zhang after experiences of spiritual healing and glossolalia decided to form a Pentecostal church in China. Paul Wei was convinced that most doctrines taught as orthodox by the mainstream churches were false, and that only a new church could revive the Apostolic period and establish the true faith. Their first church was founded in Tianjin in 1917,

(Chinese Independent Churches of Jesus), and the northern ones *Zhonghua Jidu Jiaohui* (Chinese Christian Churches).

and emphasized faith healing, speaking in tongues and a communal living style. From 1917 until 1929 the two Zhangs (Wei having died in 1919) carried out a highly successful programme of church formation in Shandong, Hebei, Henan, Zhejiang and other provinces. Barnabas then formed a schismatic section based in Hong Kong and was excommunicated. The following years were unstable as the headquarters moved to Chongqing and back to Nanjing in 1945, but the church registered very fast growth, particularly in Hunan, Fujian and Henan. Estimated membership was at least 120,000 by 1949, with 700 churches all over China.[27]

The Jesus Family was founded by Jing Dianying at Mazhuang, Shandong, in 1921. It also was characterized by a Pentecostalist style of religion, with emphasis on healing, glossalalia and other 'spiritual gifts'. The distinctive feature of the Jesus Family was a communal style of living in which everything was shared. The community was strongest in a desperately poor part of China and provided, as a present-day believer put it: 'a love fellowship, a meeting-place for the weary and a place of comfort for the broken-hearted . . . wherever you are, there is your home, and your home is everywhere'.[28] Although it did not spread as widely as the True Jesus Church, it counted a total of some 6,000 members in its heyday.[29]

The other major indigenous church is properly known as the Local Assemblies, although it is usually called 'Little Flock' by outsiders. Founded in 1928, and with no support at all from missions, it had some 70,000 members by 1949 and is still influential today. Its founder was a dynamic and controversial Fujianese called Ni Tuosheng, better known in English as Watchman Nee. While still a student at the Anglican Trinity College at Fuzhou, Nee rebelled against the formalism and rituals of the Anglican tradition. He became an ardent evangelist who led bands of students through towns and villages

---

[27] See Rubinstein, *Protestant Community*, pp. 117–25 for an account of the True Jesus Church.
[28] *Bridge* no. 34, March–April 1989, p. 17.
[29] A first-hand if rather romanticized report is Dr D. Vaughan Rees, *The Jesus Family in Communist China*, Exeter: Paternoster Press, 1959.

attempting to win converts. Early in the 1920s he joined a few friends in home meetings where they established the practice of 'breaking bread', performing a kind of lay communion without the assistance of a pastor. By intense personal evangelism they attracted large numbers of Christians to follow their example, especially in Jiangsu, Zhejiang and Fujian. They ignored previous church customs, had little contact with foreigners and established new ecclesiastical traditions of their own, which they maintained were those of the first apostles. In 1928 Nee founded his own central church in Shanghai and became recognized leader of the movement. In the 1930s he had contact with the Plymouth Brethren, but eventually found it impossible to co-operate with them. The early 1930s saw a rapid spread of the Local Assemblies: a missionary was forced to admit in 1935 that the movement was growing very fast, especially in Zhejiang, attracting many church members and even leaders.[30] Despite confrontations with the Japanese and war devastations the church continued to spread until 1949. Nee was arrested in the 1950s, accused of being a GMD agent as well as opposing the TSPM, and died in jail. The movement was ordered to merge with the TSPM in the drive towards unification in 1958, but the impact of the 'Little Flock' tradition is still very strong among house churches, especially in southeast China.

The movement suited the Chinese environment in terms of practice, ecclesiology, nationalism, worship and theology. Church leaders were unpaid, and supported by contributions from the congregation. In fact many of them lived in poverty and literally did not know where the next day's food would come from. The church was independent from missionaries and had no foreign stigma, although it is true that much of its theology derived ultimately from western sources, notably the Plymouth Brethren. The teaching was simple, based on reiterated statements of doctrine that led to an intense loyalty and sense of belonging. It was pietist and spiritual in orientation with

---

[30] C. Stanley Smith, 'Modern Religious Movements', *China Christian Yearbook*, 1935, pp. 97–110 (p. 104).

minimum emphasis on social welfare. Liturgy was rejected in the interests of solidarity and egalitarianism.[31]

Thus already by the 1920s there were vigorous movements towards Chinese control of church institutions. Among the mechanisms tending towards this were devolution of control inside the denominational churches; the widespread network of unsupervised Christian groups in rural areas; the foundation of neo-western churches by separate Chinese groups; and the creation of Chinese churches that were to some extent Chinese in cultural content as well as personnel.

THE SOCIAL GOSPEL

A crucial difference between conservative and liberal theology concerned the relative importance of social service as compared to individual salvation. The liberals maintained that the ultimate goal of the Christian enterprise was to transform the whole of society so that every person could lead a dignified, secure existence, and that Christian witness by deeds would be far more meaningful in the long term than preaching. Their theological stance was for building the Kingdom of Heaven on earth rather than hoping to gain it after death; their pragmatic critique of fundamentalists pointed out that it was relatively easy to convert individuals in the short term, but that such individuals often did not continue to practise an alien faith in a hostile environment and with the absence of social support.

Their great concern in the 1930s was that the church was irrelevant to the political and social needs of the Chinese masses. They believed that the sorry state of the rural church in particular was the result of a mistaken strategy, based on lack of understanding. The old style of mission, according to them, was 'foreign in character, isolated from the larger life of the community, standing apart from the life of the majority, and ministering only to a single aspect of the human need and only to

---

[31] Angus Kinnear, *Against the Tide*, Wheaton: Tyndale, 1978, is a useful biography of Nee. A critical assessment of his theology is given by Covell, *Confucius, the Buddha and Christ*, pp. 196–200; a more positive one by Lee, *Theology of Revival*, pp. 253–9.

a small fraction of the community'.[32] The well-known educator Dr Y. C. James Yen made a similar point: rural China suffered from poverty, ignorance, disease and selfishness, and Christianity could not succeed unless it provided a remedy for all four. The older methods of evangelization tended to ignore the social and economic conditions of life. The preacher came with the message of salvation for the individual, but left the village and the 'iron conditions of life' pretty much as they were before. Isolated churches were unlikely to survive unless they made positive contributions to local welfare, but the trend was for short bursts of enthusiasm rather than long-term commitment.[33] A survey made by the Nanjing Seminary noted that preachers gained more prestige from new conversions than from nurture of old ones, which did not encourage steady pastoral or teaching work.[34]

According to this analysis it was a mistake to start evangelization by preaching, seeking converts, building a church and employing a pastor, all with foreign financial assistance. Rather, Christians should go to the villages with programmes of literacy, health education or agricultural aid: 'When the community sees that an unmistakable contribution is being made to its life, when a new spirit of neighbourhood co-operation has been created . . . a church which embodies these traits and qualities will naturally emerge and will be welcomed by almost everybody'.[35]

Equally disturbing to liberal missionaries was the limited value of most sermons, reflecting the poverty and lack of education of many rural pastors. The emphasis of preaching was on doctrinal phrases rather than on issues relevant to everyday life. Christianity was presented as a static, remote and abstract tradition, with an obsessive repetition of the theme of man's fall and need for salvation. 'Far too often one gets the impression that Christianity is a religion of talk, and that it moves round and round within an ingrown system of doctrines.' Many such missionaries were dismayed by the evolution of the rural church: in 1930 one Methodist thought the best thing to do in his

[32] Petty, *China*, p. 81. The whole report is a good example of this kind of analysis.
[33] *Ibid.*, p. 79.   [34] Bates, *Gleanings*, p. 100.   [35] Petty, *China*, p. 83.

province would be to close all the churches and start again from scratch.[36]

Although the more conservative mission boards never forgot their prime interest in evangelization, the reforms in theology in the west, especially the social gospel in the USA, contributed to a large investment in social welfare efforts in China. Schools and hospitals were among the most visible results. By 1930 Protestant organizations ran over 6,000 primary and almost 300 secondary schools with over 200,000 pupils; by the 1940s there were fourteen Protestant colleges and universities, including some of the most prestigious in the country, which educated about one-seventh of all students in China. It was an important component of the national educational system, especially for the urban élite, although Christian schools were criticized for inefficiency and failure to meet Chinese needs.[37] Mention should also be made of the YM and YWCAs which made some impact among young people in the major cities.[38] In particular the Student Relief Committees associated with them were to play an important role in the future of Chinese Christianity because many leaders of the official church, including Bishop K. H. Ting, were to emerge from these organizations.[39]

Protestants were also responsible to a great extent for the establishment of a modern medical system in China, having founded six major medical colleges and a network of hospitals that greatly outnumbered Chinese ones. Two other areas in which foreign Christians engaged were programmes for rural development, especially in the 1930s; and relief work during and after the Japanese war, which earned them, apparently, considerable reputation among the population.

These endeavours had mixed motives. Some were purely welfare efforts, undertaken out of compassion or concern. Others were conceived within a framework of Christian witness, with the idea that a more modern and healthy environment was

[36] *Ibid.*, p. 77. See also Paul A. Varg, *Missionaries, Chinese and Diplomats: The American Protestant Missionary Movement in China, 1890–1952*, Princeton University Press, 1958, p. 215.   [37] Varg, *Missionaries*, p. 216.
[38] Shirley Garrett, *Social Reformers in Urban China: The Chinese YMCA 1895–1926*, Cambridge, MA: Harvard University Press, 1970, gives a full account of the earlier years.   [39] See Wickeri, *Common Ground*, p. 125.

the only long-term salvation for China, material as well as spiritual. Yet others were a rather more calculating attempt to spread Christian influence and attract converts.[40] Nevertheless an important consequence was that the influence of Christianity was rather broader than can be assumed from the number of communicants in churches. One of the great missionary educators, Miner Searle Bates, gave a thoughtful summary of the varying emphases between evangelical and social work, doctrinal witness and servant witness. Looking back in 1968, when the various Christian welfare institutions had long since been closed or absorbed into the state, Bates asked: 'Would it have been better, then, to have done *less* in education and in medicine, *more* specifically in strengthening the church?' A superficial answer would be yes, but he points out also that the enterprise had at least some impact on the millions of people who were in contact with it, not least for a whole generation of young women who would otherwise probably have received no education.[41] Attempts to revive social welfare in the church began to reappear in the 1980s, as we have seen. Thus this dimension, like much else, was suspended but not forgotten in the intervening years.

REVIVALS, EVANGELISM AND CHARISMATIC TRENDS

An important current of Christian life was an emotional form of religiosity generated in numerous revivalist meetings, through the agency of itinerant evangelists or special groups within churches. This was not tied to any one denomination, but was rather a religious trend which affected them all from time to time.[42] The Manchurian revival appears to have been the first in China, and its pattern was repeated in later revivals. The main protagonist was a Canadian Presbyterian missionary, Jonathan Goforth, who was invited to address a series of meetings in Manchuria in 1908. He gave discourses about sin and repent-

---

[40] This kind of conversion by external inducements is considered further in chapter 4.
[41] Miner Searle Bates, 'The Church in China in the Twentieth Century' in *China and Christian Responsibility*, edited by William J. Richardson, New York: Maryknoll Publications, 1968, pp. 46–72 (p. 61).
[42] An excellent study is Lee, *Theology of Revival*.

ance, and led the audiences, who were mostly Christians, in prayers. In an intense emotional atmosphere, according to a sympathetic eyewitness, men would confess their sins with sobs, shrieks and groans; there were experiences of strange bodily sensations; some had ecstasies and visions. An important aspect was the public confession of sin, the need for which was constantly repeated in the talks.[43] The revival was powerful for around two years and then subsided.

In the late 1920s revivalism regained importance. This time the theological background is more explicit. Conservatives were alarmed by the implications of the social gospel and liberal Protestantism in general. In particular they disagreed with the presentation of Christianity as essentially an ethical system: in their view, the uniqueness of Christianity was not in its ethics or social philosophy, but in salvation through Jesus Christ. Spiritual power was available only through the 'apostolic preaching' of the New Testament. Institutional work should be secondary, with prime stress laid on individual salvation from sin, an awakening through the supernatural power of the Holy Spirit. Signs of true revival were love and holiness in inward life, and bearing witness to others by preaching that took the atoning death of Christ as the centre: the true heart of the gospel was the cross and the resurrection of Jesus. Social service was important, but only as a consequence of the work of the Holy Spirit in the new life.

John Sung, probably the most influential evangelist of his time, exemplifies the trend of emotional revivalism. The son of a pastor, he studied chemistry in the United States, gaining a Ph.D. in 1926. Overcome by faith in Jesus he decided to pursue a religious career and enrolled in the Union Theological Seminary in New York the following year. He soon found the atmosphere there too liberal, could not accept the interpretations of Christianity that were being offered, and suffered a nervous breakdown that led to a period in a psychiatric institution. He recovered and later found his spiritual home in a

---

[43] A good review of the movement is Daniel H. Bays, *Christian Revivalism in China, 1900–1937*, a paper presented at the Institute for the Study of American Evangelicals, Wheaton College, March 30–April 1, 1989.

radical revivalist environment. Sung returned to China, throwing his diplomas overboard on the return journey, and started the most successful campaigns for conversion ever undertaken in China. He first gained experience as an evangelist in the 'Bethel Worldwide Evangelistic Band', a group of five young men from the Bethel Mission in Shanghai who would address congregations in any church that invited them.[44] They visited towns and villages, preaching to huge meetings on the theme of repentance and salvation: it was estimated that by 1935 they had held 3,400 revival meetings in over 133 cities.

In contrast to the reformers described in the previous section, Sung focused only on spiritual matters, showing little interest in intellectual pursuits or social welfare. He did not try to start his own church but rather led people to Christianity and then let local organizations take over the care of converts. His work was comparable to that of Goforth, producing similar psychological dynamics by calling for repentance, cleansing by making restitution for sins and making much use of predictions of imminent apocalypse. The individual Christian should surrender to Jesus and the Holy Spirit, when revived living would be shown by constant confession, Bible study, prayer, preaching and service. Suffering and death would always be present in this world, but would eventually vanish in the new heaven and new earth promised by God.[45] Sung consistently opposed the programmes of the National Christian Council and other liberal institutions: he felt that efforts such as rural reconstruction were futile. His views were shared by many other evangelists.

Missionaries from all denominations were naturally interested, sometime dismayed, by such developments, and the *China Christian Yearbook* published several papers that provide a good account of contemporary perceptions.[46] Abbott notes that the

[44] The Bethel Mission was an independent Holiness enterprise founded by three women, two Chinese and one American. Its primary purpose was to train enthusiastic young Chinese evangelists.
[45] Lee, 'Theology of Revival', pp. 194–201, gives an account of the ideas of Sung and his fellows.
[46] Paul R. Abbott, 'Revival Movements', *China Christian Yearbook*, 1934, pp. 175–92; Smith, 'Modern Religious Movements'. Further attitudes are reported by Bates, *Gleanings*, pp. 78–80.

Chinese Church was experiencing important revivals in many regions, often associated with some ten Chinese evangelists who were nationally known: Wang Mingdao, John Sung, Watchman Nee and others. They were well educated, some of them having degrees from American universities, they were well versed in the scriptures and all held a conservative theological position. According to Abbott: 'These men are making a profound impression on the Christian community. Their work cannot be ignored in any estimate of present day religious trends in China.'[47] The basic technique of evangelism was to stage large meetings. Some were calm, peaceful and serious, with an intense spiritual atmosphere. Others were more lively, addressed by fiery speakers. Special stress was laid upon the deadly power of personal sin, with the result that large numbers of listeners were moved with strong conviction of guilt and the desire to repent. Public confession was emphasized and others heard hundreds of private confessions in the course of their revivals. Some preachers 'go to the extreme in noisy, dramatic, sensational and Sundayesque preaching, outdoing even their prototype in startling and unique features'. Those in need of salvation form a curious selection of humanity:

Bloodthirsty bandits, rapacious officials, overbearing soldiers, anarchistic students, dishonest servants, communists, polygamists, sedate scholars, hardheaders, businessmen, rickshaw coolies, beggars, men and women, young and old, city dwellers and country folk were moved to confess and forsake sin, and to make reparation and restitution. In Peiping a total amount of more than twenty thousand dollars conscience money was returned . . . Churches cold and careless have been reborn and filled with flaming enthusiasm for witnessing . . . Singing has become spontaneous on the streets and in homes. It represents a new freedom from self-consciousness as well as a new joyousness in religion. Christianity has no gloom with these radiant young apostles.[48]

Another aspect of revivalism was known as the 'spiritual gifts movement' because of the special emphasis laid on gifts allegedly granted by the Holy Spirit. The most influential group was called the 'Spiritual Gifts' Society', whose influence spread

[47] Abbott, 'Revival Movements', p. 177. [48] *Ibid.*, pp. 177–9.

through congregations, especially in Shandong. It was essentially an indigenous movement with an emotional and charismatic style of religious practice, started by Chinese preachers although also encouraged by some westerners. It is not possible to quantify its influence although, according to Abbott, in some counties almost the whole church accepted the movement. Among the most important elements were public confessions, swaying of the body and arms while chanting repeatedly, glossolalia, visions and dream-interpretation, faith healing and psychic phenomena. Believers also showed great evangelical fervour, 'eager to share with others, indifferent to hardship, criticism or opposition'. Abbott notes that women played an important role in the movement, providing them with an outlet for their energies often denied by Chinese conventions: 'delicate women have penetrated to the dangerous haunts of bandits and the dens of vice to preach to hardened men'. Such elements apparently influenced many church groups, notably the Jesus Family and True Jesus Church mentioned earlier, in Shandong, Henan, Anhui and Hunan.[49]

Missionaries had mixed reactions to the upsurge of revivalist evangelism and the charismatic 'spiritual gifts movement'. Some, like Abbott, approved of the new enthusiasm, the revitalizing of congregations and their increased independence and self-reliance. C. Stanley Smith, quoting a Chinese colleague, applauded them as a reaction against certain defects of the denominational churches. 'He said they indicated a revolt against: (1) authority; (2) a theological instead of a spontaneous religion; (3) over-organization; (4) over-intellectualism; (5) a dry church program with no provision for social fellowship; (6) a method of training and preaching which allows the congregation to be passive.'[50] Other positive comments were reported by Searle Bates. For example an anonymous missionary said of John Sung's visit to Xiamen in 1935: 'The church was deeply stirred and many different Christians were awakened. Backsliders were arrested and restored, nominal Christians . . . received a new vision of Christ.'[51]

---

[49] *Ibid.*, p. 180.   [50] Smith, 'Modern Religious Movements', p. 109.
[51] Bates, *Gleanings*, p. 79.

However, criticisms were often directed against these indigenous leaders by mainline missionaries: that the revival meetings preached a distorted, simplistic and ultimately detrimental form of Christianity; that the movements were divisive and sectarian; that the excessive emphasis on spiritual gifts led to confusion. John Sung's preaching, for example, attracted much negative comment from missionaries. He tended to minimize the value of education and had no interest in social welfare; instead he almost obsessively focused on the topic of sin, his favoured technique being to dwell on vivid portrayals of the sinful life, and then to call on the audience to raise their hands to renounce it. His teaching was considered obscurantist even by theological conservatives.[52] His meetings were conducted with great emotionalism, as were those of the Little Flock which also placed special emphasis on apocalyptic elements in the Gospel. Excessively confident predictions concerning the imminence of the last day were commonplace, as were assertions that only a fundamentalist view of the Bible was valid. While many missionaries were insisting on greater social involvement, the indigenous movements were far more concerned with other-worldly issues – and finding a greater response.

It was also felt that many movements were sectarian, dogmatic and separatist. They tended towards personal, charismatic and authoritarian leadership, and at the worst could scarcely be considered part of the Christian church. Sung and Nee were both subject to this criticism. Abbott maintained that some Chinese leaders' 'work has been divisive and has resulted in separatist movements, the narrowing of the lines of Christian fellowship, and the raising of barriers between disciples. These have eventually and frankly declared their purpose to be the destruction of the present Church as moribund, corrupt and apostate and the formation of a purified body called "The Little Flock".'[53] In Suzhou one Little Flock group rented a building opposite a Presbyterian church and held their meetings at the same time as church services 'doing their best to disrupt the church and to attract members to their group. In Hangzhou the

---

[52] *Ibid.*, p. 78.   [53] Abbott, 'Revival Movements', p. 180.

irrepressible John Sung denounced the American evangelist Sherwood Eddy and called for a show of hands of those who would boycott his meetings, with great success.'[54] Smith also noted: 'various sects . . . are creating division and dissension in some of the churches and are drawing many members away from regular church organizations. There seems to be no limit to the number of smaller sects into which these movements divide themselves. The sect is generally dominated by one strong personality who commands the loyalty of his followers.'[55]

The leading personality would generally possess great power in preaching or healing. Many stories circulated concerning Sung's gifts as faith healer, which more sophisticated missionaries, at least, felt were fraudulent.[56] Sung and his colleagues were generally recognized as orthodox Christians, but the period also saw religious movements that seemed to be a mixture of Christianity and popular Chinese religious traditions. Some local leaders claimed divine inspiration and rejected human aids such as education, theological training or knowledge of scripture. Personal experience and private revelation were glorified and there was 'fantastic allegorizing of scripture'. At the extreme, new deities began to appear, especially a Mother-God. In places there was also a deep commitment to certain scriptural phrases, sometimes corrupted into shorter forms, such as 'Ah-Lu' for Hallelujah, that were used as incantations. 'The expressions have been described as bullets with which to drive off the devil and so a rapid fire of them repeated vehemently is considered very efficacious.' Slogans, rhythmic singing, dancing and drumming and a violent form of exhalation were also reported as means to drive away the devil.[57]

Occasionally, psychic and antinomian elements appeared. There was talk of sexual laxity after long night meetings which were rather excitable and emotional. Swoons and trances conferred prestige, returnees telling of fabulous journeys to the

---

[54] Smith, 'Modern Religious Movements', p. 105.
[55] *Ibid.*, p. 99.   [56] *Ibid*, p. 107.
[57] Abbott, 'Revival Movements', p. 187. Such practices have been called 'Christo-paganism'. We consider the relation between Christianity and local traditions further in chapter 4.

Celestial City and glimpses of the sufferings of the damned. A catalogue of 'excesses' is eloquently recounted by Abbott: 'Dancing, jumping and unrestrained actions in church are practised without check. The meetings are pandemonium. As if to break with the past and its quiet and dignified worship, the gatherings glorify noise, "cacophonous praying" splits the ear, wild wailing and tears . . . rob the services of all reverence. Carried on often until the small hours of the morning, they degenerate into exhibitions of "emotional debauchery" as the devotees abandon themselves to the floods of emotion. The bodies strained with fasting and lack of sleep react with jerks and the vocal organs with jibbering. Hysterical laughter makes the gathering uncanny. Many go into religious swoons and remain in such for long periods, sometimes indeed for twenty-four hours. A few have died as the result of the emotional strain; not a few have lost their reason.'[58]

The increasing interest in Christianity was perhaps partly a reaction to the uncertainty of the times: national calamities and poverty, political tension and ideological emptiness. One missionary noted that particularly in Manchuria, labouring under Japanese aggression, many people: 'found in the church the only ship unwrecked in this storm. For them the Church was the only remaining means of holding themselves in touch with all that in their Chinese way of life had been most dear and familiar.'[59] Moreover, repression frequently meant that any form of political or social involvement was dangerous. A conservative spirituality was far safer.

To review the state of the Protestant movement, first there were relatively well-organized churches and institutions associated with western denominations. They accounted for approximately 75 per cent of Chinese Christians. Their organizational structures were concentrated in the major cities, where they ran numerous hospitals, colleges and other agencies as well as churches. Christianity became quite influential in the leadership of the GMD. The movement as a whole was making

[58] *Ibid.*
[59] Austin Fulton, *Through Earthquake, Wind and Fire: Church and Mission in Manchuria, 1867–1950*, Edinburgh: St Andrews Press, 1967, pp. 350–1.

considerable progress towards devolution, and Chinese Christians were taking over leadership roles. In the countryside the church was much weaker. There were more Christians, but churches and pastors were thinly spread. Money was especially short in the countryside and churches were far from self-supporting. Many Christians met in home gatherings and were served by lay persons, often women.

Second, important churches were founded entirely independent of foreign control. In numerical terms the most important were the Local Assemblies and the True Jesus Church which experienced a relatively fast growth rate, to account for some 20 per cent of all Protestants after only thirty years' work.[60] The reasons for their appeal included the sense of being truly Chinese and offering a fellowship not found in the denominational churches. They tended to be egalitarian, non-sacramental and non-clerical. They were conservative in theology, much concerned with eschatological questions and disinclined to social or political involvement. They met with particular response in areas devastated by war and occupation.

Third, the 1930s in particular gave evidence of a great release of religiosity which was channelled through Christian activities of various kinds. These sometimes aroused the animosity of missionaries, who perceived them as primitive and disruptive. Two main expressions were emotional revival meetings, with a fervent atmosphere, public confession, emphasis on sin, salvation and faith healing; and spiritual gifts such as psychic phenomena and glossolalia. Only a few westerners were involved with these movements, which appear to have swept through congregations and won new converts to existing churches rather than created new ecclesiastical structures themselves. A Pentecostalist style of worship appears to have been important in Shandong and Henan, while revival meetings took place all over China. Many new and short-lived sects were formed around local leaders.

---

[60] Membership figures for Chinese indigenous churches are less certain than for foreign ones, and there is also the problem of double membership, since many people might be registered with more than one church at once. However it is commonly estimated that there were around 200,000 members of the Chinese churches by 1949.

The missionaries perhaps failed to appreciate the significance of these expressions of popular religiosity, which they compared unfavourably to the quieter and more orderly forms of worship they advocated themselves. As we look back from the 1990s they seem a quite natural form of religious behaviour among peasant communities and recent immigrants to cities. It is easy to find analogies in African Christianity to all the phenomena described above; moreover, they all bear a close relationship to ancient patterns within popular Chinese religious culture, as we shall see below in chapter 4. It is not surprising that at a time of intense social stress they surfaced in rural China.

CONTINUITIES, 1920–1990

As we move on to the People's Republic we can find many parallels with the Republican period both in official structures and popular religiosity, despite the political and social changes that occurred. The historical legacy is an important factor in the present situation of the Chinese church. To make this more explicit, we will summarize the areas where continuities between the Republican period and the current era can be observed.[61]

The religious policies of the communist government followed on from those of its predecessors. The state reserves the absolute right to control religious organizations; the latter are obliged to register, they must follow strict guidelines and above all have no right to oppose the ruling party. The implementation could vary considerably, both with the GMD and the CCP. At times there could be relatively co-operative relations between church and state, as in the early 1980s. On the other hand the state had little hesitation in asserting its authority when necessary, as after 4 June 1989. The period from 1949 to 1979 was an extreme example of state authoritarianism, but even this extended persecution of religion had precedents in Chinese history, for

---

[61] An earlier version of this section with more statistical information is Alan Hunter, 'Continuities in Chinese Protestantism, 1920–1990', *China Study Journal* vol. 6 no. 3, December 1991, pp. 5–12.

example in the mid-Tang suppression of Buddhism, or the Qing persecution of the Catholic church.

Christians responded in a time-honoured way by retreating underground. The most characteristic theological position of Chinese Christianity is a conservative pietism, based on an evangelistic programme of saving souls, free of the 'contamination' of politics. This was, it is true, the only way the community could survive during the first three decades of communist rule, but it was also a legacy of the earlier period. The China Inland Mission, the most important agency in rural areas, was little interested in social questions. Similarly in the indigenous movements, leaders such as Wang Mingdao and Nee rejected political involvement, sometimes in heroic fashion.

The theological positions of the Chinese groups are consistent with ideas imported from pietist elements in western Christianity, but they accord well with the mainstream tradition of Chinese religiosity, whereby religion is firmly rooted in family worship and localized, well away from political concerns. It was perhaps particularly attractive to women in the home, concerned with harmonious relationships, morality, prosperity and healing. For many men too, political life was extremely limited: in most rural areas it would not extend beyond seeking favours from local gentry. Chinese peasants only became politically active under exceedingly severe social conditions, notably Japanese invasion or communist reform, and certainly were not seeking a politically sophisticated religion. Many observers have noted that the Chinese peasant avoided politics as far as possible, sometimes even in the middle of a war: 'They plainly considered their destiny was to till their own few square feet of soil, whoever ran the nation . . . The war had flowed over them for weeks and made victims of them, and they were not yet part of it.'[62]

The anti-Christian orientation of the communist government is also a product of history. In the 1920s the CCP promoted a vigorous anti-Christian campaign in line with Soviet ideology, and this readily found a response among the Chinese popula-

---

[62] Graham Peck, *Through China's Wall*, London: Collins, 1941, p. 304.

tion. The Chinese anti-Christian tradition has a long pedigree, and was vigorously promoted by Confucian officials under the Qing dynasty also.[63] The GMD did not adopt it wholeheartedly because of the presence of Christians in the top leadership, and because of their conciliatory attitude towards the western powers, but the CCP encouraged its full expression. However, the pragmatic demands of the United Front policy allowed a basis for limited tolerance, which was revived in the 1980s.

Continuity in the location of Christian communities is evident. The Protestant missionaries, and hence the main areas of church activities, were concentrated in the southern and eastern provinces such as Jiangsu, Zhejiang and Fujian; missionaries later penetrated up the Yangtze valley and into Hebei. Yunnan was also evangelized before 1949, both by a small number of pioneering missionaries earlier in the century, and then as a result of population displacements in the Sino-Japanese war. It is precisely these areas where Christianity has taken root, and where much of the 1980s revival took place. Most Christian communities are proud of their history, and older people remember the pre-1949 churches. In many cases even the church buildings themselves have been renovated. In a more personal sense there is a strong continuity, namely that many older people in congregations became Christians before 1949, and returned to public expression of their faith when it became safe to do so. The main exception to this pattern of continuity are the provinces of Henan and Anhui, which were most successfully evangelized towards the end of the Cultural Revolution and in the early 1980s. The same is true of some other interior provinces such as Xinjiang, which had almost no Christian presence before 1949.

If one compares statistics of the late 1980s and the 1930s, one is struck by the growing weakness of ecclesiastical structures. The number of officially recognized believers has increased by around tenfold since 1936, while the population of China increased threefold. But this has not been reflected in church organization. The number of pastors acknowledged by the

---

[63] See Paul A. Cohen, 'The Anti-Christian Tradition in China', *Journal of Asian Studies*, vol. 20 no. 2, February 1961, pp. 169–80.

TSPM in the late 1980s approximately equals the number of pastors, evangelists and missionaries in the 1930s. The number of churches is about the same. The precise accuracy of the figures is doubtful, but the trend is significant: Protestantism in China has a high proportion of believers to registered clergy, about 400:1. The number of churches is totally inadequate for communal worship.

In fact the situation is far more acute than the overall figures suggest: clergy and church buildings are concentrated in cities, leaving rural areas even less serviced. Recent reports indicate the following ratios of pastors to believers: 1:5,000 in a county in southern Jiangsu; 0:60,000 in Cangan county, Zhejiang; 200:800,000 for the whole of Henan; and 50:400,000 for Jiangsu province.[64] Moreover the number of Christians given here may well be a gross underestimate, while the number of churches and clergy are more likely to be correct. In any case it is significant that, despite the intense political pressure for control, the characteristic of congregational self-reliance and relatively weak hierarchical organization has become even more pronounced.

The political role of the church in the People's Republic has tended to overshadow other factors, especially in discussions comparing the official church and the unregistered home meetings. The focus on politics tends to explain differences between Christian groups in terms of support for or independence from the state. However it seems that the differences in political orientation are part of deeper divisions in Chinese Christianity. The official church of the 1990s essentially maintains a church tradition inherited from western missionaries. Urban-based, its congregations are relatively educated, and its intellectual environment increasingly modern and rationalistic. The church structure is quite centralized, liturgical and clerical in nature, and relatively affluent. The house churches are more closely related to indigenous forms of religiosity. Their members are more likely to be poor, with a lower standard of education, still strongly influenced by traditional culture. The ecclesiology of these groups is for a diffused network, with no professional clergy, and an experiential, perhaps charismatic, style of worship.

The situation has been masked by political positions adopted after 1949, since the official church leadership has presented itself as anti-western, and accused independent Christian groups of being pro-imperialist. This was quite a paradox, since official church leaders themselves tended to be western educated, comparatively modern in outlook and aligned with the reformist wing of the Communist party. The independent groups, on the contrary, were founded outside missionary organizations and were closer to traditional culture. A further point of confusion is that the official leadership inherited a tradition of social criticism and political thought that it had to abandon after 1949, except for the repetition of anti-western slogans. The unofficial groups, on the other hand, tend to an apolitical stance because of their Dispensationalist theology, but have been obliged to operate semi-clandestinely. They have therefore, unwillingly, become political deviants.

In ecclesiological terms there is an interesting contrast here between sectarian and state churches. The TSPM/CCC is in a curious position. It is a state church in the sense that the state recognizes no other Protestant organization; but the state also limits, obstructs and opposes its expansion. As Ernst Troeltsch pointed out, a church has to pay a price to achieve the comprehensive status of state-churchhood: it compromises the purity of Christian ideals. This kind of adaptation has been a dominant historical model in England and much of Continental Europe. It is perhaps no coincidence that church leaders in these countries have been relatively accommodating in their attitude towards TSPM leaders. At the opposite extreme stand those free churches and sects who can espouse whatever ideals they please: they have not the slightest chance of being widely accepted or put into practice. Christian purity can be maintained, at the expense of social realism. This kind of stance can easily be appreciated in the USA with its tradition of independent sectarianism. In terms of social organization the situation remains in some respects surprisingly similar to the 1930s. The focus of resources is on central urban churches which are relatively affluent and well staffed. On the other hand most believers are in rural areas and meet at home or in very poor church buildings. In these areas the care of believers is often in the hands of non-ordained preachers, often women.

To what extent can Christianity fulfill the religious needs of the Chinese people? In the 1930s it appears that revival meetings, a Pentecostal style of worship, healing and emotional forms of religious expression were important factors in conversions and the spread of Christianity. People were attracted to this new religion which preached good conduct, promised fellowship with divinity, afforded healing and exorcism and offered forms of worship that could be corporate or individual according to circumstances. The religious revival of the 1980s suggests that these are still deep needs among the urban and rural population of China. In some ways the home meetings or rural churches are better able to fulfill them than the closely supervised urban churches, which perhaps partly explains their great success in recent years. We now turn to consider to what extent Protestantism resonates with the Chinese religious tradition as such. Was it something totally new and strange? A revelation? Or essentially a familiar message in a new format? Who needed it and why?

CHAPTER 4

Protestantism and Chinese religious culture

PRAYER AND THE INDIGENOUS TRADITION

The Chinese people approached by the missionaries had already created a culture with richly varied religious traditions, some aspects of which were surprisingly similar to those of Protestantism itself.[1] Christianity, as it began to spread, encountered an environment imbued with religious beliefs, practices, traditions and organizations, many of which still show signs of great vitality today. Interaction with the indigenous traditions is arguably the most important single formative factor of Chinese Christianity, but to date it has attracted little scholarly attention; the present chapter is, therefore, necessarily tentative and exploratory.[2] In the first five sections we focus on key areas that call for further comparative study.

Human beings have long believed in the possibility of communication with divine or spiritual entities. This activity, 'prayer', is an essential feature of religion in every culture. A commonly found form is the recitation of a sacred text, corporately, individually or by a religious specialist. Often such a text is not comprehensible to the participants, since it may be in an archaic language, formulaic or an incantation. In this case the prayer is a kind of meta-language with ritualistic functions that may be extremely effective in creating mood, evoking a

---

[1] Unfortunately there is no space here for an account of Chinese religious traditions. Readers may refer to Laurence G. Thompson, *Chinese Religion: An Introduction*, Belmont, CA: Wadsworth, 1979; and Christian Jochim, *Chinese Religions: A Cultural Perspective*, Englewood Cliffs: Prentice Hall, 1986.

[2] One of the rare studies, with accounts of fieldwork in contemporary Fujian, is Chen Zhiping and Li Shaoming, *Jidujiao yu Fujian minjian shehui*, (*Christianity and Popular Society in Fujian*), Xiamen: Xiamen daxue chubanshe, 1992.

spiritual atmosphere and an emotional response. Alternatively, prayer may be free, spontaneous, in colloquial speech and immediately comprehensible. The intention of praying, or the nature of the communication, may also contain disparate elements even within the same tradition: some common uses of prayer are as petition, invocation, adoration, confession and intercession. The nature of prayer raises central issues in any faith since it should reveal the doctrine of God. For example, is prayer a monologue or dialogue? Is it merely emotional release? Why can one assume that any Being is 'listening'?

China has had its own rich prayer traditions dating back to antiquity. One feature, still seen today, is the reciprocity between humans and gods: if a person prays in the correct manner, gods are almost constrained to respond. Chinese religious traditions have emphasized correct ritual, and most prayers are accompanied by offerings. Complex élite ceremonies demanded sacrifice of oxen, while even the humblest homes offer incense or candles before prayer. The concept of god, however, has varied. In classical texts such as *The History* and *The Odes* one can find the concept of an all-powerful deity, known as *shen*, *tian* or *shangdi*: terms still used by Christians. He hears and sees, enjoys offerings, can be honoured and served, confers moral sense on men, and protects but may withdraw his protection. But, like the earthly realm, the spirit world was also populated by a network of lesser officials and intermediaries – local gods, spirits and souls of departed ancestors – who could be approached by the common people, aided by an assortment of shamans and other specialists. A study by the sinologist Wolfram Eberhard shows how the concept of god in China evolved in parallel to changes in human society. At first gods were arbitrary and capricious, like powerful monarchs, but they later became constrained by laws and quasi-bureaucratic procedures.[3]

Prayer to spiritual beings was given further impetus by the spread of Buddhism, specifically the influential popular schools that, in sharp contrast to the doctrines of orthodox Indian

[3] Wolfram Eberhard, *Guilt and Sin in Traditional China*, Berkeley: University of California Press, 1967, pp. 16–18.

Buddhism, emphasized devotion to Bodhisattvas, salvation by faith, and heaven and hell. Prayers and invocations were a central aspect of its religious practice, performed individually by the believer, usually after offering incense before a statue,or collectively by clerics. Following the decline of Buddhism after the Tang dynasty, Chinese popular religion further developed its syncretic character, incorporating Shamanism, animism, Buddhism, Daoism and ancestral observances. Temples all over China contained an apparently random selection of images from these traditions, and individuals were under no obligation to affiliate to one in particular; but petitionary prayer, which can still be observed in almost any temple in the Chinese world, is a unifying factor. The purposes of prayer are consistent: material security, health, family harmony, the well-being of deceased relatives and advice for the future.

Prayer in the Christian tradition has its roots in Judaism, and is seen as intimate communication between humanity and God. Christian prayer derives its particular character from the concept of a unique, personal deity and a variety of beliefs concerning the importance of Christ and the Holy Spirit. In Protestantism one can find examples of individual and corporate prayer, spontaneity and ritual, and various legitimate aims. The tradition has emphasized personal and collective acknowledgement of God and Christ as unique deity; praise and thanksgiving; repentance and requests for forgiveness. Petitionary prayer is certainly permissible, especially for safety at times of danger, although concern for spiritual development or community well-being rather than for personal enrichment would be considered more orthodox. The typical setting is the formal congregation, meeting at an appointed time in a church – a classic example of sacred time and space. Prayers here are usually led by a pastor who serves as ritual specialist following sanctioned patterns, with corporate participation by the congregation. The conceptual model is explicitly of a deity who can hear and may respond to human words and thoughts. Protestants have generally adopted a comprehensible vernacular form of language rather than ritualistic meta-language; there has been less uniformity in content, which can be either closely based on texts, such as the Book of Common Prayer, or more informal and spontaneous.

Christian prayer in itself would thus not be a strange phenomenon to one nurtured in the Chinese religious tradition, although a convert to Protestantism would have to accept important changes. Obviously the first would be acknowledgement of a new deity. However, this might not be too problematic since the Chinese are welcoming of new gods, who tend to be judged on performance rather than theological criteria. The concept of reciprocity might need more subtle modifications: in Christianity, obedience to God's will and service to others are expected, rather than tangible offerings, in return for divine favour. Petitionary prayer could remain, although with heaven or spiritual development as more appropriate requests than material wealth; likewise the use of sacred texts, familiar from Buddhist and sectarian traditions, would be retained.

Interaction between Christian and traditional approaches to prayer can indeed be seen today in China. Christians interviewed in Fujian stated that they offered money in church just as they had previously offered incense to the Buddha, believing that it was a symbol of their piety, and that the more they offered the more help they would receive. The concept of reciprocity was strongly held, and on the walls of a church in Fuzhou there were numerous letters of praise and thanks to Jesus after success in examinations, obtaining a scholarship for a Canadian university, healing of ailments, happy betrothals and finding employment. A phrase commonly used to praise a Chinese god is *youqiu biying*: 'infallibly granting requests for favours'. Almost identical terms were used in the Christian environment of the church.[4]

However, significant modifications might be necessary for practitioners of the folk religion who wished to adopt Protestant forms of personal devotion or congregational prayer. A feature of the Protestant tradition is the sense of each individual living in God's presence, the legitimacy of each person conducting

---

[4] Chen and Li, *Popular Society*, pp. 69, 88.

spiritual life and intercourse with God in private, if so desired, without reference to church hierarchies or community approval. In this area of personal spirituality there appear to be few parallels in the Chinese tradition. Perhaps the closest would be the meditation practices of some schools of Buddhism and Daoism, but they carry a flavour quite different from that of the pietist Christian.

Congregational prayer needed time to take root in China, where sacred time and space are less clearly marked off from the secular. Temples are usually open to the street throughout the daylight hours, and people wander in as they please. Sometimes the premises are bustling with hundreds of visitors, including children who play noisy games; sometimes there is a lull. The great majority of visitors pray individually, so that even when many people are gathered in front of the same icon, it is as a fortuitous combination of separate individuals, not as a corporate unit. Even with Buddhist ceremonies that have definite starting and ending points, the onlookers are separate individuals participating simultaneously rather than collectively; only the monks or nuns themselves function as a corporate entity, as do the congregations of some sects. The Chinese attitude towards time and space occasioned some irritation among missionaries, who perceived it as too casual. It was an area where many years training was invested to produce church behaviour similar to that found in the west, not because of any particular doctrinal issue, but to produce conformity to a foreign cultural model. The relatively successful integration of corporate prayer into Chinese Christian life can be witnessed in almost any church service in China today, especially in the city churches. Most use translations of well-known prayers from the Anglo–American tradition, or close approximations.

HEALING

Healing, or more accurately the widespread belief in it, is one of the most important factors in the spread of Christianity in the 1980s. We have both heard testimonies from converts who attached great significance to healing, and other researchers also concur in this judgement.[5] It is another example of tradition and change. Calling on spiritual beings for healing and exorcism has long been a core feature of Chinese religious life. Its Christian version requires a new orientation of the believer, but is not a radical innovation; on the contrary it maintains the essence of the tradition. We may also note that social changes in the 1980s made spiritual healing a popular recourse for the sick and their families.

Healing through prayer or other 'spiritual' means has been an important element of most religions. The simplest form is petitionary prayer, based on the premise of a responsive divine or spiritual being. The sick person may pray on his or her own behalf; family or friends may intercede; in many situations it is the business of a religious specialist. Besides prayer a variety of techniques may be adopted, such as laying on of hands, chanting or trance. The specialist may offer diagnosis as well as cure, for example attributing illness to past sins or spirit-possession.

Social scientists have generally been sceptical about claims that physiological illnesses can be cured by such methods. One of the most consistently vocal groups to cite such cures in a modern western society was the Pentecostal movement in its early years in the USA. Spectacular miracles of healing were claimed, including the regeneration of amputated fingers and restoration of the dead to life. However, careful research by scholars in 1925 concluded that all reports were grossly exaggerated and often fabricated. There appears to be little evidence to support claims that spiritual healing has any particular effect on the course of an illness, although patients in natural remission may, of course, attribute their cure to such intervention.[6]

There are several other issues that need to be considered.

---

[5] This was confirmed in conversation with researchers at various institutes in China, and also by Deng Zhaoming in Hong Kong. It is mentioned frequently in academic papers and the religious press.

[6] A committee of ministers, doctors, professors and a lawyer investigated 350 alleged healings in Pentecostal circles, without discovering one case they regarded as genuine. Robert M. Anderson, *The Vision of the Disinherited: The Making of American Pentecostalism*, New York: Oxford University Press, 1979, p. 93.

First, many symptoms of illness may be dysfunctions caused by nervous or psychic disorder. These are not uncommon following bereavements or other shocks. It is quite possible that such complaints could be cured, temporarily or even permanently, by intense emotional experiences such as those generated in mass meetings. Exposure to healing rituals in cultures that value them highly can also have this effect. Second, it seems that some patients with serious physiological disorders can rise above them for very short periods. As Anderson reports: 'Many Pentecostals . . . saw people rise from their sick beds and wheelchairs, or throw away their crutches at the laying on of hands and prayer. That they often returned to their former state or became worse soon after was not known to most who had witnessed the "miracles".'[7] One of the authors has personally seen a temporary remission of this kind, having met a young woman in South India who was paralyzed from the waist down after a car accident. She was 'healed' at a meeting with a famous guru, when she stood up unaided and took a few paces for the only time since the accident. She reverted immediately to her paralyzed state, but insisted that the 'healing' had given her enormous self-confidence and will to survive. For her, it was a positive experience that could not be written off as trickery in any way. Third, it is not unusual for mass meetings to be deceived, by some form of mass hysteria or manipulation. In contemporary China, for example, it is common gossip that certain *qigong* practitioners have paid assistants planted in the audience who undergo 'miraculous' cures at public demonstrations. Sceptical missionaries attributed some of John Sung's 'cures' to mistaken perceptions in emotional meetings.

By listing the above cautions we do not imply that the healing activities of prayer and intercession are useless or harmful, although they might be in some circumstances, for example if they prevented a patient from seeking competent medical help. On the contrary, there are benefits in exploring the religious dimension of suffering, illness and the approach of death. The wave of interest in holistic health in the west shows that modern

[7] *Ibid.*, p. 94.

medical science appears reductionist to many patients, and that there is a deep need for understanding the condition of the spirit at a time of disease. Contemporary theologians extend this to recognition of the need for healing in society, and repair of psychological traumas in the collective, after experiences such as the Holocaust, as well as in the individual. After an analysis of Pentecostal testimonies, Anderson concludes:

What seems to have mattered was not the real or imagined cause or cure, nor the relative merits of divine and mundane healing, but the 'moment' or experience itself. Those who experienced or witnessed the act of healing were strongly impressed that they stood in the presence of supernatural power, and what passed before or after had no effect on that impression.'[8]

One should be cautious in taking at face value any accounts of spiritual healing. So far there is no verifiable evidence of physiological illness cured by these means. But undoubtedly healing can be a profound emotional and spiritual experience, of central importance to religious life.

A study of healing in traditional Chinese culture would require a whole volume to itself. It was a respected part of every religious tradition, and examples can be found from ancient rural communities to urban Singapore. Almost every conceivable technique has been explored. Daoists experimented with naturalistic and animistic models: herbs, chemical potions, talismans and chants. Buddhists were somewhat less concerned with physical ailments, but still had many prayers for the sick and a Bodhisattva dedicated to healing. A vast array of methods was available at the popular level. At the simplest one could pray to a local or national god and offer sacrifices in return for help. On the community level there were regular ceremonies to purify a whole village or district, and special rituals to ward off epidemics of plague or smallpox. Most peasants held an animistic world view and unusual dysfunctive automatisms were generally attributed to spirit possession. Exorcism was thus

[8] *Ibid.*

a particular form of healing widely offered by religious specialists, of which there are many dramatic accounts.[9]

Turning to Christianity, healing and exorcism have played an important, albeit fluctuating, role in Protestant traditions. The synoptic gospels have accounts of exorcisms, healing of leprosy, blindness and raising from the dead. The Gospel of St John extends the significance of healing miracles (semeion = sign) as signs of God active in the world. Many incidents of healing are reported in Acts.[10]

One can discern three main developments in later Christianity. One, to be found in the medieval church and groups such as the Christian Scientists, was a form of obscurantism that opposed medical science; since its impact at present is very limited we will not pursue this here. Second was the retreat in the face of rationalist critiques. Healing is still seen as an important form of service, but claims of direct spiritual healing are rejected, and, instead, energies transferred to the promotion of modern medical services. As a consequence one can find numerous Christian initiatives in hospitals and nursing care, medical research and aid to poor countries, a development that parallels the Social Gospel. This does not necessarily imply a denial of God's healing powers, but rather a belief that humanity's energies are more fruitfully channelled through science. The third is to retain belief in the importance of an active spiritual healing ministry alongside secular medical services, enjoying the benefits of material progress but upholding the right of intervention in key areas such as emotional support, spiritual counselling and preparation for death.

Indigenous church groups in Republican China often centred on local leaders who were able to heal as well as preach: the most successful were those, like John Sung, who excelled at both. The issue of spiritual healing also surfaced after 1979 with great vigour, and it is not hard to find an explanation for this. From

[9] There is a detailed description of exorcism in Peter Goullart, *The Monastery of Jade Mountain*, London: John Murray, 1961, pp. 86–9. For a morbid account of the darker side of traditional medical beliefs, see the short story 'Medicine' by Lu Xun. Francis L. K. Hsu, *Religion, Science and Human Crises*, London: Routledge and Kegan Paul, 1952, describes community response to a cholera epidemic in southwest China.

[10] A classic statement of New Testament thought is James 5: 14–15.

1949 to 1979, although there was never a comprehensive system of medical provision, most peasants could attend basic clinics staffed by para-medics, while residents of the major cities had access to a wider range of services. Despite their shortcomings, treatment was very cheap or free, and replaced the network of traditional healers – herbalists or mediums – who had previously provided a kind of folk medical system. In the 1950s such practitioners were forced to cease their activities by CCP officials who regarded them as peddlers of superstition.

The overall trend of the 1980s market reforms obliged families to be self-reliant rather than to seek collective solutions. As regards health, they produced a down-grading of public health provision, including preventive medicine, which had made good progress in the first decades of communist rule. Many of the limited health services offered by collective institutions ceased to function, and medical care, even where available, is now expensive, not affordable by poor peasant families. Moreover, the liberal administrative policies have allowed the revival of traditional practices that were forbidden between 1949 and 1979.

A return to spiritual healing is, for many, the only recourse in times of sickness. Chinese Christians have a strong interest and belief in spiritual healing and exorcism. In Shanghai, one of the most sophisticated cities in China, we heard several reports of miraculous healing. According to a group of women in a house church, one man they knew had been close to death, suffering from inoperable cancer. He 'found the Lord', recovered and became an evangelist. The nephew of one of the women told us that they loved repeating such stories, which according to him were just gossip, always unverifiable. In the countryside such beliefs are rife, and stories circulate of mass healings and exorcisms. A craze for healing by *qigong* also spread through China in the 1980s, provoking massive popular enthusiasm and considerable scepticism from professional researchers.

A researcher at the Shanghai Academy of Social Sciences, Luo Weihong, has confirmed the attraction of this aspect of religion for elderly people in contemporary China.[11] When

[11] Luo Weihong, 'Laonianren xinjiao yuanyin shixi' ('Tentative Analysis of the Reasons for Elderly People Believing in Religion'), internal report *c.* 1986, no

people reach old age, their thoughts begin to turn to death, especially as their friends and contemporaries pass away. This may cause them to visit temples or churches to seek salvation. Many Shanghai residents who do so are illiterate or semi-illiterate and still strongly influenced by traditional beliefs. Another point is that many old people suffer from chronic illnesses that make them depressed, and they grasp any opportunity to comfort themselves, even if in illusion, by attending religious ceremonies. There is a good deal of gossip in such circles, for example among groups of old people who meet in parks for morning exercises, about alleged healing miracles. Those whose illnesses do in fact improve – by spontaneous remission or by medicine – may attribute the improvement to God and become enthusiastic evangelists. Another important factor is that old people suffer from a feeling of loneliness. Retirement from work and lack of support from families contribute to this, and then retired people may seek solace and company in religious groups.

The current upsurge of interest in healing has caused some difficulty in official church circles. One positive response has been the revival of a few clinics and similar enterprises, usually staffed by volunteers. There is at least one Christian hospital and the Amity Foundation and other groups have attracted foreign funds to promote rural health work among other projects.[12] Such projects, however, may easily run into government opposition since religion is supposed to be a private affair: the Party is keen that it does not spill over into social networks that could mean public support. Pastors in the official church are obliged to downplay spiritual healing in their sermons, and encourage people to seek medical attention where necessary. They will pray for the sick, but they are, in our experience, cautious about making claims and do not use healing to gain

---

bibliographic details. A similar study from the Shanghai Academy is 'Shanghai mou jiedao tuixiu zhigong xinyang jidujiao qingkuangde diaocha' ('An Investigation of Retired People's Belief in Christianity in a Street in Shanghai'), in Luo Zhufeng (ed.), *Religion Under Socialism*, pp. 214–32.

[12] *Bridge* no. 34, March–April 1989, pp. 14–15, reports on what it calls 'The Only Christian Hospital in China', opened by local Christians in August 1985.

popularity. This marks a significant distinction from the practice in home meetings.

This level of interest in spiritual healing suggests parallels between China and other non-industrialized societies, where the so-called 'third wave' of the charismatic movement strongly emphasizes 'signs and wonders'. This is seen again in the following section, and in the material presented in chapter 5. 'Power evangelism' has come to the PRC, and it is no surprise that Marxist officialdom should find it disquieting.

CHARISMATIC PHENOMENA

A range of phenomena, at first sight rather strange, have been an important element in some forms of religion; they are significant for us since they were an established element of the Chinese religious tradition, promoted by some missionaries, and have reappeared since 1979.

Worship is characterized by overt emotional expression and a wide range of unusual phenomena . . . a general class of motor dysfunctions that includes crying, sighing and groaning, stuttering, barking and crowing, complete muteness, and sustained automatic discourse . . . The common feature of these varied phenomena is that they are carried out in an automatic, involuntary way that convinces those who exhibit them and often onlookers as well that they are being controlled by some force beyond themselves. For this reason such behaviour has long been considered an indication of possession by some spirit, good or evil.[13]

Such phenomena were an integral part of Chinese religious practice, notably in the activities of spirit-mediums. In the earliest texts there are accounts of shamans who were responsible for invoking the descent of the gods, for such purposes as exorcism and rain making. They practised 'magic flight' in trance states, and would sometimes return with messages from the dead. Such people are still highly regarded in Chinese communities: as for example the spirit-writing sects and *tong khi* of modern Taiwan, and spirit-medium healers of Hong Kong's New Territories, many of whose activities have been described by anthropologists.

---

[13] Anderson, *American Pentecostalism*, p. 11.

A striking example in recent western Christianity was the Pentecostalist movement that following the Azusa Street Revival of 1906, where glossolalia and other manifestations featured prominently. Pentecostalists built up a missionary presence in China, and by 1933 there were 67 missionaries and 155 Chinese evangelists working in their mission stations. As mentioned in chapter 3, a number of other western missionaries, for example some Baptists and independents, also emphasized 'spiritual gifts' of various kinds. They quickly found a response in Chinese communities, both in congregations of existing churches, and in new organizational forms. The most important of these was the True Jesus Church, which still forms one of the most numerous groups outside the official church. Its characteristic forms of expression have been described by Murray Rubinstein:

> In True Jesus practice, believers pray for the Gift of the Spirit and through such prayer open themselves up to possession by the Holy Spirit. This prayer takes place at a given point during the worship service. The atmosphere has been created through the singing of hymns as well as through the recitation of short prayers . . . They begin with simple words or verses. It is about this time that many begin to shake and sway. From their mouths come strange sounds that seem to flow out. Some of these resemble formalized chanting – the davening of Jewish prayer – while others are sharp glottal sounds. This is glossolalia in its classic form.[14]

The export of Pentecostalism was extremely successful, and it forms one of the most dynamic strands of Christianity in the non-industrialized world, for example in Brazil and southern Africa. It also accounts for a third of all Protestants in Taiwan and, as far as we can tell, a large number in the People's Republic. In the latter, it is precisely the kind of 'superstition' deplored by the official church and bureaucracy. A few True Jesus congregations operate within the TSPM, but the majority lead an independent church life.[15]

[14] Murray A. Rubinstein, 'Taiwan's Churches of the Holy Spirit' in *The American Asian Review*, vol. 6 no. 3, Fall 1988, pp. 23–58 (p. 46).
[15] For Taiwan see Rubinstein, *Protestant Community*. For the PRC 'Introducing the True Jesus Church', *Bridge*, no. 41, May–June 1990, pp. 7–9.

Interpretations of such charismatic phenomena are problematic. The usual explanation provided by participants is that their unconventional behaviour is evidence of indwelling of Spirit. Critics, however, both Christians and non-Christians, raise objections to this claim. For example, they argue that glossolalia never results in genuine ability to speak foreign languages, that healing has never been proven to take place, and that groups often make dubious assertions about the history of their particular sect. Sociologists of religion have tended to argue that Pentecostalism is best understood as a 'religion of the dispossessed', an attempt to gain power and 'a voice' by regressive, symbolic means. As for the movement in Taiwan, Rubinstein suggests:

The True Jesus service is geared to envelop the participant in spiritual feelings of great power. While there is a formal structure to the service the basic objective seems to be to create within the individual a psychological state which allows one to be open and submissive to an enveloping religious presence. When one is part of such a service, one feels swept away by a vast and powerful emotional river. There is, no doubt, an enormous sense of release, a catharsis.[16]

He concludes that such release is a welcome release from the strict restraints of Confucian codes of behaviour.

Concerning the values of Black Pentecostalism in the United States, it has been suggested that it was an expression of the desire for freedom, dignity and equality. It meant freedom to be oneself, to let one's mind, body and emotions be overwhelmed. There was tremendous eschatological hope for the humiliation of the oppressor and the exaltation of the poor. It might represent a gradual process of empowerment through spiritual experiences, community solidarity and emotional release. Such feelings had necessarily to be generated outside the official church structures, since the latter were closely implicated in the structure of exploitation.[17] Other writers offer more negative assessments of this kind of religiosity, for example that it is an

---

[16] Rubinstein, *Protestant Community*, p. 142.
[17] Iain MacRobert, *The Black Roots and White Racism of Early Pentecostalism*, London: Macmillan, 1987.

extreme form of mystification, diverting energies which could be productively used in more rational pursuits.

A letter from a house church leader and itinerant evangelist in Henan indicates the kind of interest in these matters in contemporary China:

Although I am very old the Lord bestowed great grace on me and allowed me to experience glory I had never known before . . . I was even able to jump across streams I would never normally have been able to cross . . . One man had a large tumour on his face, but when I laid hands on him and prayed it disappeared. The next day he stood up and gave a thrilling testimony . . . The Holy Spirit descended in great power and everyone experienced Pentecost . . . The Holy Spirit came down like fire upon the workers in this region. They all went out having obtained power, because the Lord desires to use them to preach the gospel in every province and region of China.[18]

Within the Pentecostalist movement one can find relatively restrained as well as exuberant groups, distinguished from more mainstream churches primarily by a strong sense of congregational participation, reliance on personal experience, orality of liturgy and interest in dreams, visions and healing. This may be a fertile ground for interaction with the Chinese indigenous tradition. Emotional religiosity is not at the centre of mainstream Christianity in China, but is nevertheless influential in many congregations.

MORALITY

The striking areas of congruence between Christian and Confucian morality were noted by the earliest Jesuit missionaries. In fact moral ideals were already prominent in pre-Confucian classics. In the *Book of History*, a document from around 600 BCE, nine virtues are praised: 'To be magnanimous yet inspiring respect, gentle yet firm, honestly outspoken yet respectful, commanding yet respectful, pacific yet bold, straight yet agreeable, generous yet discriminating, resolute yet guarded, valiant yet just.'[19]

---

[18] Translated by Tony Lambert. Further extracts from the document can be found in his *Resurrection*, pp. 166–71.

[19] Cited in William E. Soothill, *The Three Religions of China*, London: Oxford University Press, second edition 1923, pp. 192–3.

In the *Analects*, Confucius stresses five virtues: kindness, justice, reverence, wisdom and good faith. A particular feature of Confucian, and almost all Chinese moral teaching, was the emphasis on filial piety and respect to seniors as the root of all human duty: 'When a youth is at home, let him be filial; when abroad respectful to his elders; let him be circumspect and sincere, and while exhibiting a comprehensive love for all men, let him ally himself with the good.' As Chinese society evolved, other moral themes emerged, including an altruistic form of universal love, compassion for animals and even the injunction to love one's enemies. Particularly after 1400 CE many books, known as *shanshu*, were written to inculcate moral values into the population. Some had a religious dimension, but others were purely ethical tracts such as those issued by emperors instructing all classes of people to be good and to follow the law.

Thus missionaries in the early twentieth century followed a long tradition when they called for 'virtues' such as honesty, sexual restraint, self-sacrifice, hard work and abstention from alcohol. Many fought against opium, slavery, concubinage, corruption, gross inequalities and apparent indifference to suffering. Some were particularly shocked, for example, by private appropriation of funds collected for famine relief. The Christianity that entered China between 1880 and 1920 and that most influenced the first generation of converts was stern and puritanical. Some missionaries were extremely critical even of smoking and refused to accept converts unless they foreswore such peccadilloes.

The rise to power of the CCP provided a distinctive new impetus to concepts of morality. Here the emphasis was on social justice and contribution to the public good, theorized as progress towards socialism. Until 1979 a certain kind of puritanism was, for better or for worse, imposed: the sex and drugs industry was eliminated, there was no flamboyant consumption and social inequalities were greatly reduced. There were constant media exhortations to work hard, to minimize personal gain and to sacrifice oneself for future generations. Religions were severely repressed, but a new spirit of puritanism and idealism was much in evidence.

Several developments shattered this idyll by the 1980s. For one thing, the population, deeply disillusioned by the violence of the Cultural Revolution, became aware of a deep lack of morality among its rulers. Resentment aroused by the rampant corruption and nepotism was one of the main causes of the discontent that led to the 1989 democracy movement. Consumption by the élite was less conspicuous than in capitalist countries, but all the more galling because of their egalitarian rhetoric, which masked grades of privileged access to material goods and power. The leadership was also blamed for leading the country into chaos and responding by state terrorism. Tiananmen marked a loss of moral authority.

Also, the social and economic results of the reforms produced deep changes in life-style. Consumer goods became ever more available, for most sectors of the population for the first time ever. Young people were fascinated by sunglasses, walkmen and Hong Kong fashions. Families saved hard to buy videos, washing machines and even pianos. A witticism current in 1990 was a pun on the phrase '*xiang qian kan*', which could either be a Maoist slogan ('look to the future') or a consumerist one ('look to money'). Money became power, often outweighing official position. Consumption conferred status. The poor but honest were considered naive, and farmers were told 'to get rich is glorious' no matter what the cost to the environment.

Meanwhile there was an equally profound change in attitudes to sexuality and gender issues. In the Maoist era, sexuality was taboo. Almost everyone wore shapeless blue clothes, make-up was never used, couples did not hold hands or kiss in public. By the late 1980s, fashionable clothes and public displays of affection were to be seen in all the cities. Surveys revealed extensive pre- and extra-marital sex; many were distressed to see the massive return of prostitution, especially in southeastern cities. Violent crime and commerce in narcotics once again became a serious problem.

Morality in modern China presents a confused picture. The Confucian tradition is undoubtedly strong, particularly in rural communities. The older generation may find the new mores distressing, and they are perhaps confusing for many younger people. There has been a dramatic loss of faith in public morality and previously accepted norms for behaviour are now in question. In this context, we have heard that the clear moral guidelines offered by Christianity are appreciated by believers. In some areas, Christianity is now known as the religion which promotes family harmony, seeking reasonable and forgiving relationships.[20] Moreover, the preaching of moral standards is quite acceptable to the government, which sees it as a positive contribution that the church can make to society. The official church frequently emphasizes morality – honesty, obedience, restraint – in sermons and publications.

Despite differences of emphasis, one could suggest that here Christianity, Chinese tradition and the present government are substantially in agreement. Whether their combined influence can form a counter-balance to consumerism is a different question. Researchers in Fujian make a strong statement about the importance of morality in contemporary Chinese Christianity: they found that their interviewees, in every location, whether Catholic or Protestant, and from whatever class, occupation or cultural background, insisted that the practice of high standards of moral behaviour was an essential part of Christian life.[21]

SIN, SUFFERING, SALVATION

Healing and charismatic phenomena are important factors in the spread of Christianity in China as in other countries of the non-industrial world. However, they are marginal to what most Christian traditions consider the essence of religion: the redemption of humanity, which involves questions such as sin, the cause of suffering, triumph over death and the possibility of salvation. Here again, the rich heritage of thought on these matters in Chinese religious traditions formed a basis for receiving the Christian teaching. The topic has particular interest with reference to the sociology of religion, since some scholars have argued that acknowledgement of 'sin' is a step on the path to

[20] Examples are in Chan and Hunter (eds.), *Prayers and Thoughts*, pp. 34 and 40.
[21] Chen and Li, *Popular Society*, p. 84.

conversion, especially when a traditional local culture is confronted by a technologically superior and evangelizing one.

The cause of suffering, the nature of sin and the possibility of salvation have exercised humanity since earliest times, as evidenced by ancient Indian and Judaic literature. Classical Chinese doctrines are too varied even to review here, since Confucianism, Daoism and Buddhism all offered accounts of suffering, sin and release. In common with most religious traditions, the Chinese from early times developed the concept that sin is the major cause of suffering. Soothill notes that the *Book of History* uses the concept of a ruler's sins to justify political revolt. A noble rebel states: 'It is not I, this child, who dare undertake the setting up of rebellion, but for the many crimes of the Hsia king, Heaven has willed his destruction. The sovereign of Hsia is an offender and as I fear God, I dare not but punish him.'[22] In a later passage, sin is recognized as an offence against morality, and also against God, which He will punish either directly or through human agency.

In the classic texts of Confucius and Mencius, sin is discussed in terms of error or transgression. The emphasis is on the need for reform: 'To err and yet not reform, this may indeed be called error'; 'If you know that a mode of action is wrong, then use all dispatch in putting an end to it. Why wait till next year?' In accord with the general temper of these philosophers, specific punishment for the sinner is not discussed, except that he will suffer in some way: 'Man is born for uprightness; without it he is lucky if he escapes with his life.'[23]

Popular religion, absorbing themes from Buddhism and Daoism, and reflecting the imperial social order, evolved a colourful and chaotic set of ideas about sin and retribution. The Celestial Emperor had a host of subordinate spirit kings and ministers, and numerous hells that resembled earthly courts (*yamens*) and prisons. As Soothill relates: 'There are numerous judges in the spirit yamens, with their secretaries, lictors, torturers, also prisoners undergoing examination for the things

---

[22] Quoted in Soothill, *Three Religions*, p. 213. The word *zui* is used here for 'crimes' and 'offender'; it is still frequently used to translate the term 'sin' in Christian scriptures.
[23] See Analects xv, 29; Mencius iii, ii, viii, 3 and Analects vi, 17 for these passages.

done in this life. Each spirit prisoner is taken before the judge appointed to try the offences of which he has been guilty . . . Whatever the facts, there is no escape from a myriad-fold retribution for his sins.'[24]

In the earlier part of this century, a theory widely held by cultural anthropologists was the distinction between 'guilt societies' and 'shame societies'. According to this, in most western societies, children are conditioned to internalize the social norms; when they fail to live up to them, there is a strong feeling of self-blame, remorse and regret. 'A guilt-oriented person feels guilt when he transgresses, even if no-one around him notices his transgression, because the agent of punishment is always in him.'[25] By contrast in other societies, notably those of East Asia, socialization is achieved with more emphasis on group approval: the most important thing is to behave correctly to avoid anger or disapproval from others. 'A person "loses face" if he does not live up to the expectations set for his role . . . he is then punished with ridicule, contempt or social ostracism.'[26]

However, Eberhard suggests that, in China at least, this emphasis on shame rather than guilt is only applicable to the educated élite. On the contrary, there was a very intense guilt culture among the lower classes of China, particularly after the spread of Buddhism. Social norms were internalized and moreover, as in Christian cultures, were reinforced by religious ideologies: certain types of behaviour were seen as crimes against God. Folk Buddhism displays remarkable similarities to popular Christianity in this respect:

The sinner knows that his actions may remain unknown to others, but they are known to the supernatural powers and will receive punishment. No bribery, no attempt to cheat, no attempt to use social status and influence will help. Punishment will come after death and it will be horrible. There is no way to make a sin undone. The only hope is that

[24] Soothill, *Three Religions*, p. 218.
[25] Melford E. Spiro, 'Social Systems, Personality and Functional Analysis' in *Studying Personality Cross-Culturally*, edited by Bert Kaplan, Evanston: Row, Peterson, 1961, pp. 93–128 (p. 120).
[26] *Ibid.* See also Hu Hsien-chin, 'The Chinese Concept of Face' in *American Anthropologist*, vol. 46, 1944, pp. 45–66.

by doing good works a certain balance between sins and meritorious acts may be established, so that sins are outweighed by merits.[27]

Just as in the west, popular metaphors were scales on which good and bad deeds were weighed, and heavenly beings charged with book-keeping.

Conceptions of salvation also reflected the diversity of traditions. In Confucianism, the good life is its own reward: virtue and sincerity lead to the perfection of oneself and others, and this is true happiness. Philosophical Buddhism and Daoism focused on enlightenment, nirvana or immortality. After a lifetime of meditation and purification the sage would transcend the world of illusion and return to the Absolute as a drop of water to the ocean. There were innumerable variations on this theme, including experiments with elixirs to transform the physical body into an immortal entity. Ideas of a paradise figured in popular Buddhism: 'There is in the west a paradise called the Pure Land, exquisitely adorned with gold and silver and precious gems. There are pure waters with golden sands, surrounded by pleasant walks and covered with large lotus flowers. Joyous music is heard, and flowers rain down three times a day.'[28]

In contrast to most forms of Christianity, however, Buddhism did not emphasize the need for repentance of acknowledgement of guilt as a precondition to receiving grace. Eberhard suggests this may arise from the experience of bureaucratic absolutism, in which good or bad deeds led to unpredictable results, entirely depending on the whims of the ruler and his administration.[29]

China also had a long tradition of millenarianism, fostered by sectarian movements that hoped to establish a paradise on earth, a project that led some of them into armed rebellion. The myth of a 'world of great harmony' has been a potent symbol in Chinese consciousness for three thousand years, the influence of which can be seen in such movements as the Yellow Turbans, the White Lotus and the Taiping, even in Mao Zedong Thought. In an environment of social deprivation and political

---

[27] Eberhard, *Guilt and Sin*, p. 19.
[28] Paul Carus, *The Gospel of Buddha*, New Delhi; National Book Trust, first Indian edition, 1961, p. 136–7.   [29] Eberhard, *Guilt and Sin*, p. 20.

oppression, religious ideals could be part of the ideology of revolt.

These few examples from the wealth of the Chinese religious traditions show that sin, suffering and salvation were an element both of philosophical élite religion and of popular culture. Here again, Christian doctrines would find resonances in the tradition, and were not totally unfamiliar. As we shall see in the next section, missionaries emphasized the doctrines of sin, damnation and redemption. Large revival meetings, where healing and charismatic phenomena could be witnessed, were equally effective in producing a highly charged atmosphere to encourage the confession of sin. One missionary reported with enthusiasm: 'It was certainly something very wonderful to see – sometimes as many as a thousand men and women broken down utterly, weeping the most absolutely sincere and bitter tears for sin . . . Hundreds would be on their faces before God at one time. Confessions, prayers for forgiveness, restitution, tears, sobs, agonizing . . . The spirit of prayer was wonderful . . . Sin, as our Chinese Christians had never known it before, was revealed in those meetings.'[30]

At their most crude, some missionaries reinforced their message with terrifying accounts of the fires of hell, which they assured audiences were in store for the damned, and with promises of the pleasures of paradise for believers. In these expositions of both heaven and hell, Christian and Buddhist imagination ran along the same lines, with descriptions of torture, legends of guardians at the gate, a book of life and other elements.[31] Here again, Christianity offered essentially only a slight innovation in a well-established tradition: public confessions also were typical of Daoist and Buddhist sects from Tang times if not earlier.[32]

---

[30] Reports of two revival meetings, in Mukden and Fuzhou *c.* 1910, cited in Lin Shao-Yang (pseudonym for Reginald Fleming Johnston) *A Chinese Appeal to Christendom Concerning Christian Missions*, London: Watts and Co., 1911, p. 98.

[31] Detailed accounts of hells are to be found in Eberhard, *Guilt and Sin*, pp. 24–60. They rival the Chinese bureaucracy in their organizational complexity. A brand new hell appeared in the nineteenth century, specifically created for Chinese who converted to Christianity.

[32] Eberhard, *Guilt and Sin*, p. 20.

It is difficult to assess what impact these particular themes make in contemporary Christianity in China. As part of the project to up-date theology in accordance with international trends, the leaders of the official church have begun to de-emphasize the Augustinian view of sin. They are also strongly discouraged from millenarian or eschatological themes, and official literature and sermons focus more on morality, social responsibility and the life of Jesus. This is another area where the house churches and itinerant evangelists are keeping alive the older tradition.

An interesting example of Christian and folk syncretism is reported in funeral practices from Fujian: all Christian families interviewed, whether Protestant or Catholic, used Christian funeral rites on the death of a relative, but they would have felt rather uneasy to leave it at that. Traditional Chinese funeral procedures have a double purpose: to provide a blessing for the one departed, but also to provide protection against evil consequences for his surviving family. The families were confident that Christian rites were sufficient to ensure entry to Heaven for the dead, but feared they would not adequately ward off possible threats from the other world against themselves. Therefore, many Christian families followed both Christian and local funeral practices.[33] The meeting of traditions throws up endless complexities and creativity. Had some interviewees focused on entry to heaven as a pragmatic benefit that might be derived from Christianity? Is this aspect of Christianity being incorporated into local folk religion, or are we at a half-way stage in the gradual abandonment of traditional beliefs?

CONVERSION

In his study of missionary work, Nishan Najarian finds that two factors were particularly important in achieving the first wave of Christian converts in China: the first he calls 'external induce-

---

[33] Chen and Li, *Popular Society*, p. 76.

ments' and the second 'internal stress'.[34] The former refers to the fact that there were certain material advantages to be gained by becoming a Christian, as indicated by the well-known phrase 'rice-bowl Christian'. (It is perhaps less well known that many Christians also faced social ostracism and occasionally persecution.) The most important material incentives were the offers of employment, as teacher, caretaker, assistant in church duties or some other capacity. Najarian summarizes the situation thus:

Underneath the missionary's sublime methods of bringing Chinese to Christ, Protestant missionaries throughout China held out certain obvious non-spiritual incentives to attract non-believers to Christianity . . . Perceiving the Chinese to be a very practical people, the missionary offered very practical inducements – food, shelter, employment, status, protection (the proverbial 'rice-bowl') – which were of direct personal benefit to the prospective convert. The non-Christian's decision to take advantage of these inducements was contingent upon the value he placed on them, rather than upon the value he placed on the missionary's doctrines.[35]

Reports from missionaries suggest that they found this a sensitive and difficult area. Some mission boards adopted strict policies against favours such as intervention in legal matters on behalf of converts. Others felt that if they declined to give help, 'we are liable to the charge of unkindness, of being indifferent to their interests, of want of sympathy'. They adopted a pragmatic, flexible approach, accepting the inescapable realities of Chinese life.[36]

This form of conversion perhaps did not give rise to serious internal conflict or crisis. The convert probably made a conscious decision to participate in certain religious practices and refrained from criticizing the church and its doctrines, and might modify his/her behaviour to conform to expectations. It is not expected in Chinese culture to affiliate to one religion exclusively. It is also widely held that Chinese culture allows a more tolerant interpretation of consistency than does western

[34] Nishan Najarian, 'Religious Conversion in Nineteenth-Century China: Face to Face Interaction Between Western Missionaries and the Chinese' in *Social Interaction in Chinese Society*, edited by Sidney L. Greenblatt, Westport: Praeger, 1982, pp. 67–111.
[35] *Ibid.*, p. 92.   [36] *Ibid.*, pp. 87–90.

society: for example, in the Chinese environment one can preserve a sense of personal worth while enacting conformity to group demands, even when one disagrees with them. In the west, one might be expected to protest or refuse to conform. Likewise there is nothing shameful in the decision to adopt the religion of one's employer or group. Many Chinese saw no inconsistency in becoming a Christian to please an actual or prospective employer. A missionary reported: 'The writer at one time had a coolie, Lao Wang, employed as gardener, who one day came to him with the announcement that he wished to join the church. "Why?" I asked. "Because I am working with you", he answered.'[37] An anecdote that illustrates this concerns a prospective Chinese student for the Wesleyan medical college. On his application form, in the space marked 'Religion?' he wrote, 'Willing to become Methodist if necessary'! Doubtless perfectly reasonable to him, if surprising to the college authorities. Having said this, long-term loyalties might well be built up through association with a church, irrespective of the original motivation, and we should not consider this kind of conversion in a pejorative sense.

More complex is the question of external inducements of a less tangible kind, in particular protection against evil, exorcism and healing. To many Chinese, Christianity appeared as a superior form of magico-religious system, and they might have no objection to testing it out, not necessarily with any intention of abandoning other beliefs. For example the famous missionary Timothy Richard recorded that in a drought: 'I prepared some yellow placards with only a few words on each, saying that if the people wanted rain, the best way was to turn from dead idols to the living God and pray unto Him . . . The result was very striking . . . deputations of elderly men would come to the inn, go down on their knees and beg me to tell them how to worship and pray to the living God.'[38]

Christianity offered unequivocal protection against evil

---

[37] Maurice T. Price, *Christian Missions and Oriental Civilizations: A Study in Cultural Contact*, Shanghai: privately published, 1924, p. 369.
[38] Timothy Richard, *Forty-Five Years in China, Reminiscences*, New York: Frederick Stokes, 1916, pp. 97–8.

spirits. Progressive westerners were scandalized that certain missionaries actually encouraged these attitudes by promoting Christianity as more effective than, but otherwise parallel to, indigenous popular religions in this respect. In the early part of the century – and perhaps still now – the Protestant tradition encompassed a variety of beliefs concerning the supernatural. A leading American Protestant, for example, expressed in 1909 his sense of shame that Protestant missionaries in Korea, China, India and Africa gave their assent to the theory of demon-possession.[39] In peasant society in late traditional China there was an almost universal animistic worldview; its exploitation by evangelists was another effective 'external inducement'. Its modern counterpart can be found in the concept of 'Power Encounter' in some Christian movements in developing countries.

In the case of 'internal conflict' the emphasis is on a psychological process: the potential convert is persuaded to feel that his present belief-system is inadequate, or inferior in various respects to a new alternative, and that he/she should adopt a new one. Of course it was not necessarily mutually exclusive with regard to 'external inducements': for example in the case of belief in spirits the distinction is hard to draw.

The key factors of successful persuasion are intensity and repetition, and evangelists made full use of both. They spent day after day, year after year, preaching, spreading literature, conversing and cajoling. Repeated use would be made of a small stock of religious words and phrases, ideally in the highly charged atmosphere of a revival meeting, and particularly a continual reiteration of the themes of sin, evil and redemption. The intensity created a kind of spiritual crisis among the audience. It was natural for most missionaries, especially before the First World War, to vaunt the superiority of western civilization, alongside which came a superior religion. Protestants almost unanimously condemned traditional Chinese beliefs and customs, such as ancestor worship. Thus the whole culture was made to appear inferior, which was easily done at a

---

[39] Professor G. A. Coe, *The American Journal of Theology*, July 1909, p. 340.

time of national humiliation. Moreover, individual listeners were constantly informed that they were sinful, wicked and doomed. It may be that the emphasis on sin and damnation was a carry-over from the nineteenth-century revival movements in Britain and the USA, the environment from which many missionaries emerged. Not all evangelists, of course, were foreign – almost all conversions since 1949, and many of those in the Republic, were a result of evangelistic activity by native Chinese – but the western legacy is important.

As well as material benefits, the new teaching also offered psychological rewards. Inquirers were continually invited to churches, which offered mysterious ceremonies in an exotic setting, strange rites reputed to be very efficacious. Missionaries were aware of deficiencies in local religious systems and were able to fill them, for example by affording contact with a great and ethically perfect God; some did not hesitate to claim detailed knowledge of life after death. Numerous converts testified to their crisis of traditional belief and the overwhelming attraction of the 'foreign religion'.

For many believers, conversion was the outcome of a quest for deeper meaning in their lives, the goal of an inner pilgrimage, resulting in a transformation of values, behaviour and world-view. At the start of the Protestant missions, some converts were men dissatisfied with Confucian self-cultivation, which they perceived to be a form of ethics, and with the rituals of folk religion. They shared a contempt for the decadence of Buddhist monks and widespread immorality in society, and considered Christianity seriously for its monotheism, doctrines of love and salvation, and revelation of God in the world. Being new, strange, and problematic in social terms, as we have seen, it naturally demanded a slow process of questioning and study to come to terms with the 'foreign religion'. By the 1920s, Christianity was a serious alternative to many thinkers in China's cities: even Chen Duxiu, later a founding member of the CCP, was attracted at one time to the 'religion of love'. Famous Christians like Wang Mingdao wrote accounts of their religious experiences that appear to confirm the 'quest for meaning' and a subsequent revelation as ultimately deciding factors.

I almost lost consciousness of being in a room, but I knew clearly that I was in the shadow of his wings. Then my whole body was liberated, my perspective on life was transformed and I discovered that tremendous power through my own personal experience. I no longer felt bitterness and sacrifice, but eternal comfort . . . Now the spirit of joy finally filled my heart I only needed to cry out 'Hallelujah' and my body immediately filled with power, my heart also, my mouth was full of praises, joy surged like the waters in oceans and lakes.[40]

After the Cultural Revolution, observers recognized a kind of 'spiritual vacuum' in China. Traditional values had long been in crisis, and most people were deeply disillusioned with Marxism. After a century of evangelization, Protestant groups were active in most provinces. Many must have heard of its power to transform lives, to give meaning, to bring comfort in a time of distress, and to offer an explanation of suffering and salvation.

CHURCH GROWTH SINCE 1979

In the 1980s a number of Chinese scholars published research on the growth of the church since 1979.[41] Generally speaking all such efforts are hampered by lack of empirical data, but the recent studies contain some valuable ideas. We have added our own findings to form table 2.

There are many interesting items here. Social and political factors (group 1) contributed to the process of unlocking the population from its traditional beliefs. Before 1949, China was humiliated by a series of unequal treaties imposed by western powers, which became in effect colonial rulers. Worse, the Japanese invasion caused millions of casualties between 1937 and 1944, and there followed a bloody civil war. For most of the period the living conditions for the majority of the population were desperate. At the same time China saw the beginnings of a

[40] David Yang, translated by Chan and Hunter, *Prayers and Thoughts*, p. 48.
[41] Papers that discuss these issues include Xiao Zhitian, 'Further Reflections on the Long-term Nature of Religion', *Religion*, Nanjing, no. 2, 1990, pp. 1–5; Luo Weihong, 'Elderly People'; Chen and Li, *Popular Culture*. Many of the explanations were also mentioned to us by scholars in China.

Table 2. *Explanations for conversion to or continued adherence to religions in modern China*

Group One: Social and Individual Stress

Connected with:	Examples:
Social conditions	Rural isolation, poverty, boredom
	Breakdown of kinship networks
	Greater social mobility
	Low level of education
Politics	Semi-colonial status pre-1949
	Disillusion with GMD/CCP
	Low opinion of government officials
	Danger of political activism
Psychological needs	Devaluation of traditional culture
	Personal search for meaning
	Need for comfort during wars/other disasters
	Ideological vacuum
Underprivileged status	Women
	Minority peoples
	Retired workers

Group Two: Continuing Influence of Religious Traditions

Traditional religions/ Buddhism Christianity	Influence of local culture, especially belief in gods and ghosts
	Congruency: ease of acceptance because of commonalities
	Generational believers
	Strong evangelism

Group Three: Perceived Advantages of Conversion

Material inducements (more in Republican era)	Money/employment/education
	Useful networks/mutual aid
Spiritual benefits	Magical powers
	All-powerful God
	Healing and exorcism
	Actualization of personal potential
	Fellowship/love/support
	Hope, faith, inner peace
Social benefits	Ecclesiastical community as surrogate family/pseudo-kinship network
	Channel to westernization or modernization

modern economy, industrialization in some areas, migrations across the continent, upheaval in national cultural life and numerous other disruptions. Communist Party rule after 1949 promoted rapid social change: agriculture was collectivized and then privatized; a huge industrial base was developed; ideology and culture were radically transformed. The countless personal tragedies, the widespread suspicion and denunciations, the deterioration of personal relationships in the Cultural Revolution – all perhaps led many people into spiritual crisis and the search for a new fellowship. The preconditions for relatively extensive conversion existed.

Other factors (groups 2 and 3) might result in religious belief rather than atheism. Even by 1979, the majority of the population, especially in rural areas, probably still retained some residual belief in elements of the Chinese popular religious tradition. The old traditions had been severely, perhaps irreparably, shaken by the events outlined above, and a severely repressive administration. Nevertheless, as soon as the reforms made an impact, the old practices revived. A theory that has been widely promoted in the Chinese press in recent years is that poverty, backwardness and rural isolation are in themselves sufficient to account for religious belief. This is simplistic and fails to answer important questions. Why do some people, at least, abandon their traditional beliefs? Why the apparent upsurge in conversions to Protestantism? If they seek something more sophisticated than popular religion, why do they not turn to Buddhism, which after all has a far deeper resonance with Chinese culture than does Christianity? Why is there a high interest in religion in some poor areas and not in others?

As regards external inducements, there have been on the contrary since 1949 strong disincentives, notably in the period of fierce repression in the Cultural Revolution. Even in the 1980s it is hard to see any significant material advantages that could be derived from conversion to Christianity, with the possible exception of some commercial networks in southeastern provinces. Likewise, it is hard in today's China to note any widespread feeling of guilt about traditional culture, and there is no opportunity for colonial evangelism. In the new context, then, we should seek other explanations, and can propose the following:

1. The Protestant religion has numerous parallels with traditional Chinese beliefs: as we have seen, it offers prayers, healing, fellowship, a system of morality, rationale for suffering and promise of salvation. Similar factors have also been discussed by two American scholars, who refer to a *congruency* with traditional beliefs; Christianity may be rather strange and new, but not totally so.[42] It requires a reorientation rather than a rejection of the past. But it is wider in scope, more universal than popular religion, which in any case was closely tied to social structures that have been shaken by socio-economic changes.

2. It has a highly flexible and successful organizational form. Two or three people can gather together and form a religiously sanctioned group; families or groups of neighbours can meet in private, or even secret; congregations can be addressed by itinerant evangelists, or self-supervising, or served by regular pastors; or people may meet in large, prestigious buildings with good facilities. This flexibility has meant that the churches or home-meetings could survive even periods of repression like the Cultural Revolution. In the 1980s the church also built up a fairly powerful and efficient national organization, under the able leadership of K. H. Ting in Nanjing. It produces literature, runs seminaries and training programmes, has secured the return of church property and has argued for increased religious freedom. Protestant organization runs from tiny cells of private home-meetings to a high profile national movement. It may reconstitute a sense of kinship in an alienated society.

3. The church benefits from the prestige of the west. In the 1980s, Chinese perception of the west made a dramatic change. Following increased contacts of all kinds, many Chinese began to value western culture, technology, ideology and fashions: in some ways a superficial appreciation, in some ways a genuine search for new ways forward. The church is well known as a symbol of and link with the west, which enhances its attractiveness.

---

[42] See Bays, 'Sectarian Tradition'; and Rubinstein, *Protestant Community*. We discuss this issue further in chapter 7.

4. Protestantism has a powerful religious, moral and philosophical message in its own right. Older people may especially value the teachings of harmony, forgiveness and restraint at this time when familiar codes of behaviour are under threat from consumerism and other developments.

5. Many Protestants today are generational believers, members of families or communities that have been Christian for some time. Concentrations of Christians are still to be found in areas where there was a strong missionary presence before 1949, the main example being the southeastern provinces, as has already been discussed. Even within these provinces it appears that church groups tend to be concentrated within particular counties, rather than evenly distributed throughout. It is also quite clear that a large proportion of city congregations are people who have been Christians since before 1949, and their children. We concur with the opinion of most researchers who regard the Christian communities in these areas as developments of earlier ones.

6. A key feature of Protestantism is its evangelistic nature. In this it is rather different from Buddhism and Catholicism, both of which tend to let non-believers find them, rather than actively seeking to convert (although Catholics in particular stress generational transmission of their faith). Protestantism in China has many skillful and persistent evangelists, who dedicate their energies to winning new adherents to the faith. It should be emphasized that this has little to do with proselytism by foreigners: for example the great 'fever' in Henan was an indigenous phenomenon. A feature of contemporary evangelism outside the official church is a strong oral culture focused on accounts of healing and miracles.

7. It is a relatively rationalistic and non-wasteful religion. As society develops and education improves, people are perhaps less willing to spend money on extravagant festivals and also less likely to believe in magic. Protestantism, which is perfectly able to survive in hi-tech and industrial societies, is not necessarily threatened by a more critical, less tradition-bound mentality.

8. The church offers attractive forms of worship, notably its congregational aspect and music. In Buddhism and popular

religion, worship tends to be an individual, separate affair. Even if many people are in one temple, they generally make individual offerings and pray by themselves. They form a group only in the sense that they happen to be there at the same time. Moreover, in Buddhism, there are few opportunities for ordinary folk to participate in proceedings: they tend to be observers, watching the clerics chanting. A church service, by contrast, is a strongly communitarian activity, both active and corporate. This is especially intense during hymn-singing. It is easy to understand why many people find emotional release or spiritual enrichment on such occasions.

9. It has a tradition of diversity. This is particularly interesting to explore in China, because the official church has adopted an ideology of 'post-denominationalism' that tends to mask this. Yet one great strength of Protestantism is its ability to offer different things to different people, to serve different nationalities, social classes or personalities. Thus in China one can find groups that value a highly charismatic style complete with glossolalia, healing and exorcism; one can find pietists and free-thinkers; one can find stern Presbyterians and liturgical Anglicans. This may be valuable in a huge continent with a variety of subcultures.

10. It can offer self-respect and enhanced personal identity to those who fail to achieve these in other spheres of life. An essential feature of Protestantism is to grant immense, one might say absolute, worth to each individual, who may conceive of him- or herself as important in the eyes of God. This affirmation of selfhood and individual value is perhaps more the case than with Buddhism with its doctrine of no-self, and Catholicism with its greater emphasis on sacraments, orthodoxy and the priesthood. In the community sense, it can be noted that Protestantism has become widespread in the minority peoples of Yunnan and Guizhou in particular, who may feel themselves devalued by the surrounding Han majority.[43]

Another factor of great significance, the prevalence of women in Protestant congregations, has been analysed by a contempor-

---

[43] See Lambert, *Resurrection*, p. 153.

ary Chinese scholar, Xu Shaoqiang.[44] He states that the sense of self-worth for women actually decreased in the 1980s, despite the increase in productivity in society as a whole. This observation concurs with others, that the revival of private farming led also to a revival of patriarchal practices that were worse for women than the ideology of the Maoist era. Lack of economic security also leads women to the church; they may pray to God for help with material needs, or else turn to the church or Christian networks for charity or jobs.

Xu also found that many people turn to Christianity in the hope that their illnesses will be cured. The author quotes a survey of believers in Henan, Anhui and Zhejiang which found that 70 per cent of believers sought spiritual healing. Women in general have a lower educational standard than men, and there is a high rate of female illiteracy. The author does not make explicit the link, if any, between poor education and predisposition to Christianity, except to note that believers on the whole are also poorly educated. Finally, an unhappy family life persuades many women, especially elderly ones, to become interested in religion. Examples given are disputes among in-laws and deterioration in marital relationships. Women, and particularly retired women, may suffer from a sense of social isolation: going to a Christian group helps them to meet others and become involved in a social network.

Xu confirms the impression that most observers have gained, namely a preponderance of women in congregations. It is relevant to note that women generally served the function of 'religious specialists' inside the Chinese family. It was the woman's responsibility to make offerings to the family's ancestors at domestic altars, and, as can be seen in Hong Kong, women attend Buddhist and popular religious temples far more frequently than men. Apparently they often do so at the request of males in their family, who consider it inappropriate to go themselves. Also, church attendance in the PRC may still lead to

[44] Xu Shaoqiang, 'Woguo jidujiaohui nuxinghua yuanyin chutan' ('Preliminary Discussion of the Feminization of the Christian Church in China'), *Lilun yu dangdai (Theory and the Present)*, no. 10, 1990, pp. 12–14. An English abstract can be consulted in CNCR 1800, 14 June 1991.

social disadvantages, such as reduced prospects of promotion at work, and Communist Party members are not allowed to join religious organizations. Thus when a family converts, the husband will not go to church until retirement, but will be happy for his wife to do so. Anecdotal evidence suggests this happens quite often. Of course, the greater religiosity of women compared to men has been noted in other cultures.

The above, and doubtless other, factors may have contributed to the relatively rapid growth of Protestant conversions since 1979. Not all the conversions are permanent. In the 1920s, many missionaries were concerned about the 'back-door' phenomenon, namely that thousands of people joined the churches, but most of them also left quite soon – in through the front door, out through the back. A Chinese churchman has noted this in the 1980s also.[45] Perhaps many were, and are, curious, attracted by novelty, trying it out, rather than definitely committed. This factor, incidentally, partly explains the enormous difficulties in collating statistics. It seems that believers who wish to see their church grow would have to focus their energies on consolidating their present attendance, as well as on attracting new interest.

This is presumably best done by careful 'nurturing in the faith', or, in sociological language, devising strategies for positive reinforcement. Both the official churches and house groups manage this to some extent. We know of TSPM pastors who take pains to converse regularly with new church members and lead them to a more serious appreciation of the faith, for example deflecting an interest in healing into quest for salvation. In home meetings there is considerable informal pressure from family or neighbourhood groups, who may consolidate their influence by helping in times of trouble, calling on recidivists and encouraging each other through exchange of stories and ideas. Having discussed these issues at a somewhat theoretical level it will perhaps be helpful to see more concrete illustrations, which are provided in the next chapter.

[45] Wang Weifan, 'Discussing the Present Situation of Christianity', *Contemporary Religious Studies Review*, no. 1, Shanghai, 1991.

CHAPTER 5

Varieties of Christian life

INTRODUCTION

In chapter 2 we described the atmosphere and organization of urban TSPM churches, based on observation in cities such as Beijing, Guangzhou and Shanghai. We may call these the show cases of the official church, and not in any pejorative sense. They are stable centres for mainstream Protestantism and offer numerous services to the members of their congregations. In their upper echelons are the personnel responsible for the political activities of the TSPM and relations with the local and national government, although little of this is apparent to ordinary believers who come to church as a place of worship. These churches are also the most accessible to foreign visitors, and many of them have personnel specially designated to help overseas guests who provide hymnals, find seats and offer to interpret. Quite often foreigners are invited to meet church workers after a service, and many have been touched by the warmth with which they were received.

Such churches, despite their influence in the large cities, are a tiny number compared to the Christian communities in China. They are to be found only in the municipalities, provincial capitals and a few other affluent cities, mostly on the coast: in the whole of China they perhaps number only around a hundred. They reflect the prosperity and high educational and cultural standards that have been achieved; but these cities are also the most closely controlled by the CCP and its agencies, and the careful political supervision is extended to religious institutions.

The modern urban experience is certainly one face of China, and an important one, but the urban population is surrounded by a vast ocean of humanity living under very different circumstances.

The material in this chapter illustrates some of the variety of Christian life to be found outside these model churches. There are unavoidable shortcomings in our presentation. First, any such reporting is unrepresentative. There are over 20,000 meeting points recognized by the official church, and countless unofficial ones. The millions of individuals involved range from highly qualified professionals to destitute migrants. It would need many volumes of case studies to do justice to the phenomenon. Second, research is extremely problematic. The groups themselves are placed at risk if they receive overseas visitors, and the government does not give permission to foreigners to conduct fieldwork. Chinese researchers are strictly limited to working under the supervision of official institutions. The only substantial bodies of research reports are believed to be those held in the Chinese Academy of Social Sciences and in the UFWD central offices. They have not been published and are not available for inspection. Third, many groups are located in remote areas with little outside contact. Usually they make no written records of their affairs, nor do the official church or government acknowledge their existence or document their activities. The following reports, then, do not claim to provide a sound basis for generalization. However, they are genuine case studies and illustrate the diversity and vitality of Christian life.

The first example is of a small church nominally registered with the TSPM. As the report shows, its condition stems from historical influences and new creativity, influenced by the current economic climate and the stimulus of contact with Hong Kong. The information was compiled at first hand by Chan Kim-Kwong.

The two sections from Xiamen provide information on two important topics: who becomes Christian and why; and the nature of house churches. The latter is particularly important because of the general dearth of informed comment. We suggested earlier that the term 'house church' should perhaps now be changed to 'autonomous Christian community', to refer to Christian groups in China other than those under the direct jurisdiction of the official church. Some may still be just family-centred, with occasional gatherings at a believer's household, but others have grown far beyond this point. They may even have an extensive national network with clandestine seminaries, publication facilities, missionary sending apparatus, and hierarchical structures with ecclesial activities in many provinces. Diversity is again an obvious feature. Some of these groups may nominally register with the TSPM, others may totally ignore, and even be antagonistic to it. Some may be a rural extension of an official church occasionally visited by officially appointed clerics, while others may be regarded as anti-revolutionary organizations hunted by police. Finally, some may be very conservative in doctrine, while others have a strong cultic nature and may even be regarded as heterodox.

In spite of the differences among them, the communities tend to share certain characteristics. They are usually vibrant in faith, evangelistic in outreach, fundamentalist in doctrine, pious in devotion, informal in liturgy, spontaneous in development and flexible in structure. Their leaders are generally lay persons with little or no formal theological training, often strong personalities with charisma. Above all, these groups seem to represent the silent majority of Chinese Christians and may be an important influence on the future of the Chinese church, a factor long deliberately ignored by the leaders of the official church, and sometimes romanticized by overseas evangelical 'China Ministry' groups. Section five reports on one of these groups, the 'Apostolic Church' located in a remote region of a province in southern China. For the safety of this group, the location is not given and some data are slightly altered.

For the situation in Xiamen and for the Apostolic Church, data collection was conducted on our behalf by various individuals to whom we are extremely grateful: we have confidence in their objectivity and commitment to accurate reporting. We were able to raise questions with them and to a limited extent check on their findings, and they also made useful suggestions for interpreting the data. For these sections we have translated and edited several reports, and added our own comments.

Finally, the testimony of Huang Detang, an itinerant evangelist who died in 1981, is a fascinating document that conveys the living spirit of grass-roots, rural Christianity. Huang's personal notebook was located in China by Mr Deng Zhaoming, who also deciphered, translated and edited it. We are indebted to Mr Deng for allowing us to quote from this unique source. The complete text, from which we have selected and further edited a few sections, is in *Bridge*, no. 51, January–February 1992, pages 11–19.

AN OFFICIAL CHURCH?

The first case we examine is a small church that is nominally supervised by the TSPM: we will call it 'Jesus Church'. It is located in a small town in southern Guangdong, in the centre of the Pearl Delta region. The local economy has benefited enormously from factories financed by Hong Kong investment. Living standards and wages are generally high: even unskilled labourers can earn several hundred yuan per month, more than professionals in most parts of China. Because of the town's proximity to the border, people can receive clear TV signals from Hong Kong and almost every family has a colour TV. The atmosphere is of a busy, rapidly expanding town, starting to enjoy a little of the prosperity that has spread to parts of East Asia in the past decade. As China is increasingly attracting foreign investment, with the commercialization and consumerism that inevitably accompany it, the relative prosperity of the southern seaboard may spread to other parts of China. Thus the experience of Jesus Church may serve as a paradigm for other churches, especially those in the new boom areas.

Presbyterians began mission work in the town in the nineteenth century, and by 1900 they had built a large church with a seating capacity of over two hundred. In the 1920s, as part of the movement for ecclesial independence, the missionary church joined the Church of Christ in China, and has since been ministered by Chinese nationals. The church later established two schools, and served as the mother church for several preaching points in the surrounding area. It had approximately 200 communicants before 1949.

In the early 1950s, as the Korean War progressed, almost all Christian workers in the region were imprisoned. The pastor-in-charge of Jesus Church was also arrested and accused of being a spy for the USA, because he had once worked with an American missionary. Several clerics were executed, and the pastor-in-charge served a term in jail, although no evidence was brought against him. After his release he was sent to teach in a high school, as was the Bible-woman of Jesus Church. Because there was no pastor, attendance dropped and very soon the church ceased to function. No Three-Self association was formed in the area. The government confiscated church properties and used them for other purposes.

In 1982, the provincial government instructed the regional office of the RAB to re-establish Jesus Church as part of the new religious policy. The RAB located twenty or thirty old believers, and asked the retired pastor (then eighty years old) and the Bible-woman (then seventy years old) to minister to the church. The government returned a small room behind the church, which had been used as a Sunday school classroom before 1949, to serve as the main church building. It could seat forty to fifty people. The main church building continued to be used as a dormitory for staff of a factory. The church was reopened in October 1982, the first to open in the region after the Cultural Revolution. No home meetings or other Christian activities are known locally.

From 1982 to 1989, the number of worshippers stayed at around thirty to forty, mostly elderly, with only a few young people. They held a weekly service and prayer meetings, and gathered for celebrations on special occasions such as Christmas, which was popular with children in the town. Many migrant workers have moved to this part of Guangdong from other parts of China, and some tried to join the church; but since they did not speak the local dialect, they usually did not stay. The church attempted to start a Bible-study group for them in Mandarin, but the Bible-woman who ran it was too ill to continue and had to abandon the project.

Jesus Church, besides taking care of its congregation, is also responsible for three surrounding rural churches. Lay preachers and the Bible-woman visit them regularly, and the minister visits once every three months to lead communion and baptism services. The three churches have no full-time cleric and operate under lay leadership. The whole region has thirteen churches served by three ordained ministers, whose average age is eighty. Up to 1989, the Church had no contact with foreign Christian groups and received extremely limited support from the TSPM.

In 1990, a group of Hong Kong Christians, along with their pastor, discovered the church by chance and paid a formal visit. The members of Jesus Church were suspicious and afraid that the Hong Kong Christians might have ulterior motives, for example wishing to interfere in the local situation. At the first meeting the church leaders did little other than to repeat official Three-Self ideological statements. The ice broke when the pastor from Hong Kong mentioned that a former minister-in-charge of Jesus Church had been a family friend. As frequently happens in China, people were gladdened by evidence of long-standing personal relationships and friendship networks. The atmosphere changed suddenly and the church members became very friendly, treating the Hong Kong Christians no longer as strangers but as part of the family.

At the time of the first visit, Jesus Church had a congregation of about thirty elderly people, with an average age of seventy-five, three or four young people, and no children. The meeting hall was a dark, gloomy room with an old foot-pedal organ: the only organist was the eighty-eight years old pastor. The church had no vestments or communion set, even though they followed Rhenish liturgy, probably because this was the only liturgical text they possessed. The atmosphere was depressed, hopeless and dying. The Hong Kong Christians proposed to donate a communion set to the church. The local believers regarded this proposal with scepticism, thinking that it would just be an empty promise. Some time later, the pastor from Hong Kong personally delivered the communion set, which was received with great emotion and gratitude.

Members of the church began to share their other problems, in particular their need for a piano, and the Hong Kong group raised funds to purchase one. There was not a single piano within a 100 kilometre radius of the town, and the closest music shop was 150 kilometres away. Eventually, the Hong Kong Christians managed to buy a piano in a town in China, and hired a truck, movers, a driver, and a piano tuner. Transporting this ensemble to the church involved negotiations of almost endless complication which will not be soon forgotten by the organizer! When the piano arrived, it was greeted with tremendous enthusiasm not only by the whole church, but also by the regional RAB director and the regional Three-Self chairman. The RAB director openly invited the Hong Kong Christians to pay more friendly visits, and particularly encouraged them to invest in the region.

In 1990, Jesus Church invited the same group of Hong Kong Christians to present a Christmas programme for local children: traditionally the church could expect to attract about a hundred children for the festivities. However in this period the government had tightened controls over religion, and many restrictions were imposed: all texts, songs and programmes had to be scrutinized by the church authorities, and no preaching or open speech was allowed. During the performances, the atmosphere was tense, and the Hong Kong Christians had to keep strictly within prescribed boundaries. It was the first time the church had invited foreigners to participate in their religious activities.

By the end of 1990, average attendance had increased to forty or fifty adults, and there were more young people and some children attending. There had been several baptisms. There seemed to be more initiative from the congregation to decorate the church, more local donations, and more optimism in general. As a result of the increasing activities, the church hall was no longer adequate in size. The government had promised to return the main church building, but had procrastinated for many years and was clearly in no hurry to do so. In the course of a lavish banquet the Hong Kong Christians expressed their concern over the return of church property to the regional director of RAB. Very soon, the local government set a deadline for the factory to vacate the building and to return it to church use. Since the building was in a poor state of repair, it really needed to be demolished and a new church constructed.

In 1991, the Hong Kong Christians paid regular visits to foster the relationship. The congregation grew to between fifty and sixty people, with many more young people asking to join the church and be baptized. The Hong Kong Christians also pledged to help with the church building project, which boosted local morale tremendously. In 1991, the Hong Kong Christians were again invited for the Christmas programme. This time they had almost complete freedom to do and say whatever they wanted, in spite of the fact that the provincial government had issued clear regulations to curb Christmas celebrations. In spring 1992, Jesus Church received the necessary authorization to construct a new church building, and the Hong Kong Christians donated money to cover the costs. They hope to finish the building by October 1992, to celebrate the tenth anniversary of their reopening.

The experience of working with this local church has led to various observations. First, personal relationships seem to be more important than formal regulations. On the local level, the policies promulgated by the government and the TSPM are implemented flexibly. If personal relationships are strong, almost anything is possible, including co-ministering in China by overseas Christians. In our experience, the policies presented in government or church documents do not necessarily reflect local reality, as can be seen, for example, in the supposed banning of Christmas celebrations, or not allowing children to attend religious activities. A related factor is that the open-door policy for economic development, in this part of south China at least, carries more weight than the policy of restricting the activities of overseas believers. The local RAB actually encourages the local church to receive overseas believers, hoping that they in turn will bring in foreign investments. Local officials are thus inclined to play down the more restrictive religious policies dictated by the central, or even provincial, governments, who do not profit so directly from investment in the coastal areas. Their strategy seems to be to encourage contact with foreigners in almost any way possible.

As for inter-ecclesial communion, this Three-Self church has a more intimate relationship with churches in Hong Kong than with other Three-Self churches in China. It seems that pragmatism, in the sense of accepting support where it is offered, supercedes regional, ideological or national affiliation. So one of the pretensions of some TSPM leaders, namely that they should monopolize inter-ecclesial communion in China, does not apply here in practice. Theologically, the church practices and doctrines are closely related to the fundamentalism of the 1930–40s. Three-Self doctrines are almost completely disregarded by Jesus Church. The members either do not understand what is written in *Tianfeng*, or simply do not care about it. They are ordered to subscribe to the journal, but according to our observation it is never read but used for a variety of purposes, such as propping up the pulpit to make it stand level on the uneven floor. Equally, Jesus Church has no history of influences from the Little Flock or similar groups, which may be the reason for the lack of autonomous church movements in the region. The fact that it joined the Church of Christ in China quite early, and thus adopted the building-centred church model, was perhaps another reason that discouraged household gatherings in the area.

Perhaps the key factor in the local situation is that Christianity is unattractive to the local youth, who have clearly opted for materialism. They can earn good money and life is comfortable. They do not seem concerned about spiritual needs, and there are many opportunities for personal gain. Most of the new converts are from Christian families, with only a few from a non-Christian background. In these boom towns, the focus of the people in general is material rather than spiritual. This may contribute to the slow growth rate of this church, and to some current problems, for example in finding a replacement for the ageing clerics. The salary for a minister, around 120 yuan, is very low compared to the income of even an unskilled worker.

Also, a pastor must have high-school education and at least two years of seminary training. Even if there were candidates willing to accept the vocation, there is only one officially approved seminary in Guangzhou, the provincial capital, with a very limited intake.

The overall impression of visitors is that there is little to distinguish Jesus Church from orthodox evangelical churches in Hong Kong. One wonders again at the TSPM claim of its distinctiveness, other than in the occasional meetings to which church workers are summoned, and the documents bearing the organization's name. Likewise one wonders at some overseas Christians who criticize churches such as this as somehow collaborating with an atheistic regime. Finally, if this is the extent of Christian influence in a typical new industrial zone, the government has little to fear from it. The church provides a focus for the religious life of a tiny proportion of the population, but it is very difficult to imagine it becoming a mobilizing force. This is not in any way to detract from its inherent worth as a centre of spiritual life and communion for a dedicated congregation.

For the Hong Kong Christians who visited Jesus Church, it was an extraordinary opportunity to listen and to learn. They could not fail to be moved by the perseverence of the community of believers in poverty and harsh conditions, in sharp contrast to the material wealth of Hong Kong churches, with their air-conditioners and electronic organs. It seemed to make the visitors more humble, more appreciative of their privileged position, more sensitive to others. It also encouraged them to study the Chinese context and to conduct further outreach work. In fact, the pastor and the other visitors feel that they have benefited more from the visits than has the congregation of Jesus Church. Such a reaction is common among overseas visitors, especially those from rich countries, who have the privilege of meeting Christians in China.

CHRISTIANS IN XIAMEN

Xiamen is a city of about one million people on the coast of Fujian. It was a treaty port, one of the earliest locations for

Protestant mission work and a key centre for western influence between 1840 and 1950. In 1980 it became one of the first 'Special Economic Zones' and has achieved rapid economic growth in the past decade. It is now one of the most prosperous cities in China, enjoying much contact with the outside world and a high standard of living. Xiamen has long been known for its rich cultural life and has a prestigious university. It also has one of the most important Buddhist monasteries in south China. The province of Fujian is noted for the vitality of folk religion, which was the traditional religious system for the great majority of the population. Our report highlights the interplay of influences, western and Chinese, Protestant and traditional among different groups of people. In theory all Christians base their religious life on the Bible. In practice, from observation in Xiamen, it appears that their views often depend on their social and educational background.

In general, the religious outlook of well-educated believers is characterized by idealism and altruism. For example, many believers who work at the university regard religious belief as a way of enriching their life and achieving moral perfection. They are not much concerned about whether God or the Kingdom of Heaven exist in a literal sense, nor do they care about 'salvation'. Rather they dedicate themselves to their profession. Some have achieved national, and even international prominence in fields as diverse as biology and history, and have received prestigious academic awards from the Chinese government. They are much respected by their colleagues. Some have even used personal income earned abroad to purchase scientific equipment and books for their departments. Certainly there may be some relationship between their attitude of active involvement in the affairs of the world, and the Christian concept of original sin. However the main motive for their activity is to testify, by their words and conduct, that a devoted believer can be law-abiding, of the highest moral standard, and a good citizen of a socialist state. Their disciplined way of life is a witness to the world. At the same time they prove that the adoption of a religious belief is not necessarily a negative, other-worldly escapism; and they practically refute the charge, held by extreme Marxist theoreticians, that religion inevitably has negative social consequences. Most such believers come from Christian families and were educated in church schools before 1949. They have a good understanding of church life, doctrines and Christian ethics. This generation has now mostly retired or passed away, and Christian influence of this sort is weaker among the younger generation of intellectuals who were educated in the atheist environment of the PRC.

By contrast, believers from a relatively low cultural and educational background have a more pragmatic attitude to faith. One can often trace a conversion in their family to some misfortune one or two generations previously, where previously the family had believed in various gods and spirits. For example, Mr Li, aged thirty-one, considers himself a Christian, but he has never been to church, has no contact with other believers and has not read the Bible. When asked why he calls himself a believer, he simply replies that his parents are certainly Christian, for which they are well known in their village close to Xiamen, and so he is too. His parents previously believed in various spirits and often went to the local monastery to offer incense. They claimed to be worshipping Buddha, but it would be more accurate to consider them as believers in local religion rather than committed Buddhists. They married young, when Li's mother was about sixteen, and their first three children all died soon after birth. This was a great blow to the family, who desperately sought assistance from the Buddha and spirits. At that time there were very few Christians in the village, where the first conversions were in the 1930s. However a zealous Christian woman showed intense concern for the material and spiritual welfare of the distressed family, and brought groups of fellow believers to their home. Li's parents were deeply impressed by the warmth of fellowship, abandoned their former beliefs and converted to Christianity. Subsequently they had several children, who all grew up strong and healthy. Li said this was surprising, but in fact the reason for their survival is that in each case the delivery was made in the maternity ward of a western hospital. The success can be credited to modern medical facilities, but this was overlooked by Li, who maintained a traditional cause-and-effect belief in spiritual intervention.

Instances of healing are, in general, meaningful to Chinese Christians as has been reported by many researchers. Traditional beliefs are deep rooted and hard to change, a fact recognized by all preachers in the course of their ministry. It is very hard to shake these beliefs by preaching, but some sort of experience, for example those allegedly caused by the Holy Spirit, makes it easy to bring about changes. It seems that many Christian activities in China are closely related to traditional cultural patterns: there is a change of conceptualization, but the latent influence of Chinese traditional values, modes of thinking and cosmological views is still at work. The particular belief may change, but the cultural legacy remains. Beneath the surface phenomena lies the pragmatic orientation of many Chinese people, for example when those who recover from illness feel that the Christian God is more efficacious and hence more practical than other gods. Pastoral workers are fully aware of this psychological characteristic and often quote a large number of such cases in their sermons to strengthen believers' faith and to attract new people to church. Likewise, testimony meetings, organized by churches or by the believers themselves, are popular.

However, such reasons are not the only explanations for conversion at present. Another common cause is that people are distressed by something, for example a crisis in personal life, a disadvantaged background, frustration at work, an injustice, disappointment in love or loss of a family member. They seek a way to free themselves from their predicament. Often they will receive guidance from zealous Christians and then accompany such Christians to church or home meetings where they receive care that they cannot find elsewhere. They are able to bare their souls to each other, and their anger or depression vanishes. They may then attend religious activities regularly and become believers.

The pastor of a local TSPM church recognized that healing was a very important factor in conversions prior to 1949. He explained that in the past people who had little medical knowledge, and who could not afford to consult a doctor or even a herbalist, had to turn to the gods and Buddha for help. Others sought the counsel of charlatans, and many quacks, sorcerers or swindlers cheated the poor of their little money: consequently the money was spent, and the sick remained sick. Some families afflicted with illness or other problems turned to the Lord because of the love and concern of the local Christians, who also helped them to have confidence in western medical science. On their recovery from illness they gave themselves to Christ, believing that Christianity was more 'efficacious' than other religions. But somehow things are different in the 1980s, especially in the cities. People may still worship various gods and the Buddha, but they also recognize the need to consult a doctor or go to hospital when they or their family members are sick. The efficiency of modern medicine is no longer a factor that can lead people to Christ, since such medicine is now commonly available and in this respect Christianity no longer holds the privileged position it did prior to 1949. Rather, people are now more influenced by the concern of the brothers and sisters, and by the warm atmosphere to be experienced in church. To be sure, the pastor also stressed that it is the Lord who moves their hearts. One such case is described here.

Mr Chan, aged sixty-one, and his wife were formerly believers in Buddhism, and they also worshipped other gods such as the Goddess of Mercy and the God of the Land. They offered incense every day and took their religious vows seriously. In the mid-1980s one of their sons obtained a position as crew member on board a Panamanian cargo vessel and subsequently, unknown to the parents, became a Christian. In 1987 the ship caught fire and sank near the Spanish coast. The son died, along with several other sailors from Xiamen. The Spanish authorities assumed responsibility for the aftermath of the disaster. Funeral services were conducted according to the various faiths of the victims, and representatives of the victims' families were invited to go to Spain. The Chan family was then informed that their son had become a Christian, and a solemn memorial service was held particularly for the Christian dead. Many local Spanish people who attended the service expressed their sorrow and concern for the victims' families. The parents were deeply moved. The fact that they as strangers, Chinese at that, were given such considerate treatment and profound sympathy, by so many foreigners, made them sigh with emotion. Also when they returned to China, the Christians in Xiamen held a memorial service for all the sailors who had died. Mr Chan and his wife wept with gratitude in the solemn atmosphere of prayer and hymn-singing in the crowded chapel. From then on they became dedicated Christians, attending Sunday service and encouraging others to join the church.

Another cause of church attendance is a kind of peer-group pressure. Some people went to church merely to accompany their friends but gradually became converts themselves. A female preacher at a local chapel said this was her background. At first she attended with friends, out of curiosity. Then she found that what was being said was reasonable; she began to attend regularly and eventually converted. A friend remarked that this had caused some conflict in her family since her parents still rigidly followed Chinese traditions, and had disowned her when she chose Christian ministry as her career. Similar cases, particularly among young women, are common in Xiamen. Local girls, before they start courting, like to go out in groups of three or four. They visit each other after school or work, and may go to cinemas, dances or restaurants together. They frequently develop common interests and hobbies such as music, singing, poetry or exchanging books. It seems quite natural for such groups of young women to attend church together on Sundays.

Other people attend Christian meetings in the hope of finding a life-partner. One man, aged thirty-four, started attending a home meeting about four years ago to seek a bride. A suitable candidate was found for him, and they started a family, becoming more committed in their faith. To arrange marriages for other people was considered a virtuous activity in traditional China. The idea still survives in rural districts of Fujian that every woman should, at least once in her life, act as go-between for a lucky couple. Perhaps still influenced by this tradition, many married women in Xiamen are glad to help others in this way, and Christian networks form a natural circle of contacts for the purpose. This was also an important social function of the religious sects that flourished in imperial China. In Christian circles it gains added importance, because many Chinese Christians emphasize that a believer should marry another Christian: persons who marry outsiders may be shunned by the Christian community.

Most of the above cases reflect traditional Chinese ideas inherent in religious attitudes, notably pragmatism. Under the influence of this powerful value system, the element of reflective thought is perhaps lacking. Questions which may preoccupy a western Christian mind, such as the final judgement or the meaning of life, seem remote to many Chinese believers. Very few become converted after thinking about such questions. A sense of passivity and lack of initiative is also observable in some Christian circles. For example, believers tend to listen passively to sermons, but seldom participate actively in discussions on doctrines.

Of course there are exceptions, people who are eager to think over and discuss doctrinal questions, some of which are in the realm of theological discourse. They have usually received some kind of higher education in philosophy or theology. Besides attending services on Sunday they will meet together on occasion to talk about their views, and they seek out specialized literature. They may also choose to attend particular small meetings for doctrinal reasons rather than for reasons of sociability or convenience. A kind of popular pragmatism may account for the underlying trend of belief in the population, but the true picture is in fact more complex and varied.

HOUSE CHURCHES IN XIAMEN

There are two main types of house churches in Xiamen. The first kind has no fixed pattern of organization and members meet informally. Frequently they are elderly believers who find it inconvenient to travel and cannot follow the usual practice of attending church. Thus they meet together in private homes with a few neighbours and family members. We could consider this a kind of intimate family prayer meeting. Participants are often members of the official church and maintain good relationships with pastoral workers who may visit them on occasion. Such meetings are unlikely to be grounds for any controversy.

The second type, which we consider here, has a stricter organizational structure with daily schedules for liturgies and other activities. Participants avoid contact with the TSPM, and they call their group 'a church'. Since 1979 these formerly covert activities, the house churches, have become more known to the public and have attracted the attention of many party officials, pastoral workers of the TSPM, and academics. One explanation for their existence is that they are the result of the Cultural Revolution. For example some TSPM spokesmen have said that the closure of churches made it impossible for believers to conduct worship and engage in open religious activities, so they turned to secret meetings. This form of organization was called the 'underground church' during the Cultural Revolution, and was persecuted by the authorities whenever discovered. But it was impossible for the government to suppress all of them, and many survive until now. A similar explanation is that so many churches were confiscated or destroyed before 1979 that there are insufficient to cope with the numbers of believers, especially those who live far from the major churches.

However, there are two other important reasons, notably the continued existence of various denominational traditions and political objections to the TSPM. As to the first, the official church in Xiamen can be considered as basically related to the Presbyterian tradition, but many of the house churches stem from other traditions, notably Baptist or 'Little Flock', suggesting that the current differences are the result of the denominational legacy. A further complication is the question of the TSPM. Among both 'Presbyterians' and 'Baptists', some individuals have joined the TSPM, others have not. In such cases, the fact that a person lives close to or far away from a particular church is quite irrelevant: house churches are sometimes found very close to TSPM churches. Choice is made on grounds of conviction, not convenience.

Let us take the area around Xiamen harbour to illustrate some of these points. There are at least five house churches, two of which have a definite organizational structure. Their members have no contact with the TSPM/CCC of Xiamen, although some of their key figures were previously pastoral workers within the TSPM. These two groups came into existence in the late 1970s or early 1980s. Both are influenced by the traditions of the 'Little Flock' founded by Ni Tuosheng. However, the 'Little Flock' has no formal organization in China, so the groups cannot be considered part of a larger institution or movement. At one meeting point the regular attendance is around thirty, and at the other membership increased to about one hundred by 1990, but the meeting was then temporarily banned by the government. Three of the key leaders had previously served sentences in a labour camp and were only released in the late 1970s. They are deeply respected by local Christians and visit several meeting points in and around Xiamen. They have the right, granted by the congregations themselves, to preach and to conduct baptisms.

Such groups adopt an unco-operative attitude towards the TSPM. One member told us that he has various points of disagreement on doctrinal issues, for example he disagrees with the role played by pastors in the official church. But most importantly he cannot accept government interference in religious matters: 'The TSPM is the brain-child of the government. I do not mean that there is anything wrong with the slogan of 'Three-Self'. The point is that the government uses it to interfere with people's religious activities. That is why I do not like the TSPM.' Many other believers expressed a similar point of view. They strongly uphold the idea that religion should be independent from politics and free from government interference. A main reason for the existence of house churches of this kind is resentment against the existing system and dissatisfaction with the CCP record on religious policy.

The official TSPM explanation for this phenomenon was given by a pastor: 'Some house church members suffered bitterly under the ultra-leftist policy of the Cultural Revolution. Some were sentenced to jail and labour camp. They have a deep discontent and can no longer have confidence in the religious policy of the government. Thus they avoid contact with the official church.' However, this is only part of the story. In fact, by the time of the Cultural Revolution, many house church leaders were already in prisons or labour camps: they were sent there after being denounced by pastors of the official church in the 1950s. After 1979, these same pastors and administrators again dominated the TSPM/CCC in Xiamen. The house-church leaders' distrust is directed specifically against TSPM leaders; as we see later, their relationship with local government officials, for example in the RAB, is quite friendly.

There are other reasons for the existence of house churches. For example, some TSPM officials allegedly have lax morals and make a poor impression on believers, who then turn to the house churches. Some complain that pastoral workers lead a comfortable life, provide privileges for their children, misuse church property and fail to provide clear financial statements. Another reason is that most of the older generation of pastors have already passed away. Some believers think that those who survived the Cultural Revolution and returned to church work in 1979 must have 'betrayed the Lord and committed apostasy'. When denounced in the Cultural Revolution, such pastors attacked Christianity, renounced their faith, and stated that their previous pastoral work was reactionary. They were speaking under duress, but nevertheless Christians are supposed to withstand hardship and should never utter a word contrary to their conscience. Some Christians thus joined the house churches being unable to forgive these pastoral workers.

In short, the principal figures of the Xiamen house church groups experienced political attacks in the past and are consequently discontented with the Party, its religious policy and organizations. They refuse contact with the TSPM and are enthusiastic in promoting house church activities. This group of committed and energetic leaders is an important factor. Their views are easily accepted by other believers who may have had similar experiences.

The house churches in Xiamen are usually called 'Little Flock' by local people. As far as we could ascertain, they are also influenced by the Baptist tradition. The number of believers in each meeting is quite stable, and few people attend several house churches: they tend to be regular attenders at a particular one. The meetings are quite small and believers become familiar with each other. Although they are close together, there is only limited communication among the various groups. Also, it was observed that in each meeting point, members tended to share similar economic and educational backgrounds. We cannot report on this in detail but can illustrate a few examples. For example in meeting point A, which has been in existence for over ten years, most members are connected to overseas Chinese families. Others who wanted to join would not be refused, but the great majority are elderly people with families abroad. Meeting point B is larger, with about thirty regular attenders of all ages, and an equal number of males and females. Many of the members are primary and middle school teachers, doctors, nurses and clerical workers. In recent years some female university students also attended. In another meeting point C the key figure is a retired doctor. Members are mainly family members of retired staff at Xiamen university, including several widows of former professors. Meeting point D is the largest group and its leaders travel to meetings elsewhere. It specializes in 'Campus Ministry' and attracted many students and faculty members. This is the meeting that was banned for a period in 1990.

In meeting point B there are two elders, and one person in charge of financial matters. In general its affairs are conducted by the two elders, who were rehabilitated in the early 1980s after release from hard labour. They preach sermons at the meetings, but all members of the group have the right to address the congregation and speak of their personal experiences. The meetings are held in a private household, and the owners of the house also play a key role in the practical arrangements. They are devoted to study of the Bible and Christian doctrines, and have achieved a good level of theological education. They are well respected and sometimes give Bible lessons to new converts.

The main worship service is conducted on Saturday evening and includes reciting of Biblical texts, hymn-singing, prayer and sermon. Similar activities take place on Wednesday evening. The Holy Communion, which they call 'the breaking of bread' is held on Sunday morning. The church also performs baptisms in a small cement pool. Candidates who ask for baptism have to thoroughly explain their motives to the congregation. Candidates must lie face up in the water, assisted by the two elders. Total immersion is required. In winter, hot water is added to raise the temperature and candidates are offered ginger tea. Candidates for baptism are also received from two other meeting points, especially meeting point D. Leaders of meeting points B and D are on close terms and share materials, including theological books from Hong Kong. They also maintain contact with house churches in other parts of China and sometimes travel to preach or pray for the sick when they are invited.

Other characteristics of these meeting points are noteworthy. One of them does not celebrate Christmas. A believer said: 'The Bible does not tell us the date on which Jesus was born. I heard that the reason December 25 was designated as Christmas Day has something to do with the sun god Apollo in the Greek legend. Christmas is not a product of Christianity, so we do not celebrate it.' In some meetings, female believers have to cover their head with a black hair-net, which indicates their obedience to men. Money for the groups comes from believers' offerings, which can be made at any time. No specific amount is fixed and all gifts are voluntary. The money is spent on church expenses, for example grape-juice (all the groups ban alcoholic drinks) and bread, transport for contact with other groups, charity work, living expenses and rent. The two elders of meeting point B dedicated their lives to God after their release from prison and have no other work. They are single and their living expenses are provided by the church.

Members are eager to lead others to Christ. They seize every opportunity to proclaim Christian doctrines and the meaning of believing in Christ. A popular theme is 'The Last Day'. For example in the prelude to the Gulf War in 1991, many Christians believed that the Last Day was approaching. But they also engage in social welfare. For example several members of meeting points A and B are medical staff, and offer preferential treatment to members of their groups, although they are also generous to other citizens. Poor believers are given free medication, and all are given very good care. The medical personnel also use the opportunity to preach and persuade people to become Christians. The low fees and good treatment make it a popular service even outside church circles.

Prayers are recited in a loud voice, with feverish excitement. The atmosphere in the meetings may strike observers as somewhat fanatical. Believers must call on the Lord loudly. Emotion runs high. Voices carry far and wide when the Wednesday and Saturday meetings take place. At one point in the mid-1980s this attracted the attention of the government, who called the principal leaders of the 'Little Flock' in Xiamen to study classes run by the UFWD. They were told to join the TSPM and warned not to worship in a fanatical way. According to one believer, a number of house church members also opposed this kind of prayer. They felt that if a person has faith, he/she has no need to express his prayer in this way: prayers should just be recited calmly. A few believers withdrew from the meetings because of this. The government intervention and disagreement among members led to some problems for the meetings, but they continue to provide numerous devotional activities for the members.

Official attitudes towards these churches are not uniform. Some officials consider them 'illegal activities' because they are held in locations that have not been officially approved. They maintain that if the house churches are not integrated into the TSPM they will become a destabilizing factor. A different view is that, according to official guidelines, activities can be defined as either 'normal religious activities' or illegal, criminal activities conducted under the cloak of religion. They point out that unregistered worship cannot be considered to fall into the second category. The fact that Christians do not join the TSPM or attend official churches does not constitute an illegal, counter-revolutionary, criminal or subversive act. Indeed if it is classified as such it will have serious negative consequences in

China, as well as leading to increased suspicion by foreign observers.

In recent years in Xiamen, the government in practice has interfered very little with the house churches except in the following circumstances. First, if they have contact with the secret service of the GMD. Second, if they have contacts with foreign Christian organizations. Third, if the group becomes too influential and controls relatively large sums of money. Fourth, if it engages in anti-communist or anti-government propaganda. The reason for the closure of the meeting point in 1990, and the detention of its leaders for a short time, was mainly because the group became quite numerous, had foreign participants, and allegedly received money from abroad.

In general, house church members say that government treatment of them has been good. For example, as mentioned, several officials were concerned about the practice of praying in an excessively noisy and emotional way, but the leaders were only called for a number of study meetings. The groups were not obliged to close and nobody received harsh treatment of any kind. Believers pointed out the contrast with previous decades. For example in the 1950s it was alleged that the GMD had infiltrated the Little Flock and that Ni Tuosheng himself was a secret agent. In general all members of the Little Flock were condemned as counter-revolutionaries and a large number were sentenced to hard labour. In the late 1970s the Party began a process of rehabilitation to exonerate those who had been treated unjustly. Many Little Flock members were rehabilitated, including some who are now active house church members in Xiamen.

Among TSPM workers, we have also generally identified two attitudes towards house churches. The more liberal believe that house church members who do not join the official church should not suffer any discrimination: they are Christians and part of Christ's body. The solution of the house church question lies in the building of more churches, to allow some of these Christians to gradually be drawn into the orbit of the official church if they so wish. The more conservative insist that all Christians must be 'patriotic', i.e. support the current government. Without any guarantee of national security, nobody can have a sense of personal security. One worker said: 'The TSPM is good, and we should not harbour misgivings just because our churches are under its direction'. She tried not to pass judgement on the house churches, but it was clear that she did not agree with their attitudes and organizational structures.

Many of the characteristics of the Protestant community in Xiamen reflect the overall atmosphere of the city. The local government is pursuing prosperity through foreign investment and commerce, and cultural life is generally open and relaxed. The general level of education is high, and there is a long-established Christian presence. Even non-Christians are familiar with the church through acquaintances or family members. This liberal atmosphere allows the house churches to operate relatively freely for the most part, provided that they do not transgress certain guidelines. House churches are well attended, although a number of official churches operate successfully in various parts of the city. However it can again be observed that there is no evidence of a tremendous explosion of interest in Christianity. The house church groups and the open churches have experienced a steady growth in membership, but Christians are still only a small minority of the population.

THE APOSTOLIC CHURCH

The Apostolic Church is located in a mountainous region, far away from any industrial and cultural centre. The church has no official documentation nor archival records, so the information is derived from interviews and personal observations. Furthermore, the leaders are far from sophisticated and not very articulate, but we attempt to present their views as accurately as possible.

Methodist missionaries undertook pioneer work here in the late nineteenth century, but by the 1920s there were only about twenty communicant Christians and before 1949 Christian life in the area was insignificant. In 1980, the official church resumed limited activities, a few persons who had become Christians during the Cultural Revolution surfaced and Christianity began to flourish. In 1984, the CCP launched the Anti-Spiritual Pollution Campaign which tightened government control over religious activities. The growth of Christian communities experienced a set back but then resumed. In this region, the clerics of the official church were not popular among the believers: they were accused of misconduct and failing to live up to Christian standards. A group of pious Christians began to pray for the future of the church. At one fasting prayer vigil, attended by many people, the believers decided to separate themselves from the leadership of the official church. They regarded this action as an act of obedience to God. They formed a new community and called themselves 'The Apostolic Church'.

The group experienced rapid growth. At the end of 1991, they had five subgroups, each comprising about 700 adult believers. Usually each subgroup is made up of villagers from a few neighbouring villages. There is still, in theory, an official church representing the Christians in the area, but it exists mainly on paper, running an empty building with very few activities. However, the government only acknowledges this official church and regards the Apostolic Church as illegal. It refused to grant members a permit to erect church buildings and so some of the villagers build large houses to serve as meeting halls.

It is difficult to obtain figures on the membership of these groups. One of their leaders said, 'Believers are like the stars in the sky. When the weather is good, you can see more; when it is cloudy, they all disappear.' He is referring to the political climate. When the government tightens control, or when there is a major political campaign, the believers do not hold meetings. So, on the surface, there seem to be no Christians around. However, when the situation is more relaxed, the believers surface to participate in various religious activities. During the past few years, these groups have experienced an increase of approximately 100 new converts per year per subgroup, a significant development.

In the smaller subgroups, the ministers are called Co-Workers; in the larger ones, Elders. Each subgroup has three Deacons to administer the offerings and financial affairs. At the regional level, there is an administrative structure to oversee all five subgroups. It is headed by two Elders who were privately ordained by a Rumanian pastor while he was visiting the group some years ago. These two Elders supervise two groups of staff who are in charge of the internal affairs and the outreach or missionary enterprise. They also maintain an extensive underground network for receiving religious materials (such as Bibles, Bible commentaries, theological textbooks, religious pamphlets, audio- and video-tapes) from overseas, as well as organizing visitors from Hong Kong and Taiwan to preach and teach.

When asked about the nature of their church, members often quoted Matthew 18:20: 'For where two or three come together in my name, there am I with them.' They favour a non-institutional model and vigorously oppose the structure of the official church that has professional clerics as leaders. They do not believe in having pastors or bishops, and stress that the only leader of the church is the Holy Spirit, not any human being. In meetings, all can pray aloud and anyone can arise to speak out if moved by the Holy Spirit, somewhat like the Quakers. There is no paid staff: all church workers are volunteers and the church is totally operated by laity. They regard this lay leadership as a democratic system under the guidance of the Holy Spirit.

One of their mottoes is 'The only guidance is the Holy Spirit', and hence they oppose any form of human intercessor, such as clergymen. They use an interesting way to test whether visitors are, in fact, true Christians who totally obey the guidance of the Holy Spirit by inviting visitors to pray aloud with them. Listening to the prayer, they feel whether or not the visitors share the same spirit as them. They have developed a certain format and vocabulary of prayer, so outsiders who are not familiar with their style of loud vocal prayer usually fail the test, and are regarded as Christians lacking Holy Spirit. When they have to make a major decision, they hold long sessions of fasting prayer vigils during which they claim to receive guidance from the Holy Spirit. Whenever they are losing arguments with other Christians, such as pastors from the official church, they warn their opponents to pay attention to the Holy Spirit.

Another *locus* of authority is scripture. Despite their lack of formal education it would be quite wrong to suppose them ignorant. Although most of them have only primary education, virtually all are passionate in their study of the Bible. Most of them know the New Testament very well, and some have extensive knowledge of the whole Bible, in many cases better than an average seminarian. When asked whether they would like to seek further education in the Bible in a theological college, they feel that there is no such need. They believe they are much better, in Biblical knowledge, than most pastors and seminarians of the official church.

They believe the authority of the Holy Spirit and that of scripture complement each other. Although they possess many useful Bible handbooks and concordances, they emphasize the role of the Holy Spirit in enlightening the believers on the meanings of the Bible. Often they study the Bible and wait for the Holy Spirit to reveal the hidden spiritual meaning. Once they receive such a revelation, they search for scriptures with similar themes and examine these verses to uncover further hidden spiritual lessons. Although they place a high view on the Holy Spirit, they are not obscurantist. On the contrary, they have many beautifully printed Bibles and Bible study textbooks: their collections are in fact superior to those held by the provincial official church and seminary. They also often listen to religious broadcasts from Hong Kong. Each year in their revival meetings, they spend much time in Bible study.

There is a group of young Co-Workers, Deacons, and Elders who are well versed in scripture and good orators. They form the teaching authority of this church. Although they are small in number, they have great influence over the believers. They seem to be the group that discerns what is the guidance of the Holy Spirit and what is not. They also decide the correct interpretation of the Scripture. In fact, this group of young people is the *de facto* authority of the Apostolic Church. The Church has no liturgy and little music, perhaps because it is a new creation of the 1980s and does not follow any previously established denominational practices. It is essentially based on prayer and Bible study.

Christians of the Apostolic Church look down upon the

official church, especially the clerics. They have four main criticisms. First, they accuse the ministers of the official church of immorality, such as promiscuity in relationships and stealing money from donations. Second, the ministers of the official church are of low spiritual quality; they do not read the Bible, and they have only a superficial knowledge of spiritual wisdom. Whenever the believers of the Apostolic Church meet official pastors in debates over doctrinal or biblical knowledge, the pastors lose the debates. Third, the ministers and seminarians of the TSPM receive pay for their poor quality ministry, whereas the Co-Workers of the Apostolic Church ask for no payment for their dedicated services. Finally, the official church only holds one service per week, a sign of spiritual weakness, whereas the Apostolic Church conducts at least four meetings per week, and several revival rallies per month. Also, each year the Apostolic Church holds several large revival meetings that attract many thousands of people. Overall, the Christians of the Apostolic Church regard themselves as spiritually superior to those of the official church.

The ministers of the official church are jealous about the popularity of the Apostolic Church and often call upon the civil authorities, notably the Public Security Bureau, to suppress it by force. Their hostility is based in part on financial considerations. Many believers have left the official church, thinking that they can only obtain salvation in the autonomous groups. This causes a loss of income to the official workers, who are angered by it. The tension is intensified by a theological dispute, which in a sense is also about social economy. Namely, the official church tends to accept 'this world' and argues for preservation of the *status quo* and obedience to the government: it can be said to represent the interests of those who have achieved a high social status. The colloquial expression for this kind of teaching is 'Shen Yifan theology' named after the Shanghai bishop who is considered an expert in church–state accommodation. By contrast, the poor peasants have a deep despair about this world, and are deeply committed to extreme forms of eschatology.

Those in the Apostolic Church, using biblical imagery, often describe the official church as 'someone who is trying to get the right of the Firstborn, yet lacks the spirit of the Firstborn'. Some even regard the official church as an apostate church with man, not God, as the head. We have also heard that many seminarians from the official church, once graduated, have joined the Apostolic Church. This reflects the popularity and the attractiveness of the Apostolic Church, but again causes resentment. All these issues naturally create animosity between the two groups of Christians.

With regard to the civil authority, members of the Apostolic Church try to obey the law, but do not want the civil authority to intervene in ecclesial affairs. They believe that so long as they pay taxes, the King of this World has no right to rule over the Kingdom of Heaven. Other than these simple guidelines, they have not yet developed a stance on the church–state issue. In general they tend to follow fundamentalist doctrines and are very pious. They believe that they receive more blessings from the Holy Spirit than other Christians in China because 'blessings comes from harshness and suffering', as one of their leaders said. Since they feel that they have been specially blessed by God, they are fervent in preaching the Gospel. They do not hesitate to break government regulations, for example the ban on propagating religion outside church buildings, by preaching in open areas, and even sending missionaries to other regions and provinces. On traditional festival days, such as the Qing Ming Festival, when the peasants come to town to join the open market, the church organizes teams of singers, story tellers, or musicians, to perform in public to attract people. As the crowd begins to assemble, a preacher will appear to replace the performers; and suddenly an evangelistic rally is in place. Such techniques have been used for centuries, for example by salesmen of patent medicines, and illustrate the church's roots in local culture.

In spite of their fervent devotion to the cause of the Gospel, these believers do not seem to become fanatics. They emphasize the concept of 'Holism' and call themselves 'Holistic Sect'. They stress the five major aspects of the Gospel: Repentance, Rebirth, Salvation, Baptism, and Filling of the Holy Spirit. This comprehensive emphasis is a reaction to Christian groups elsewhere who stress only one or two particularly themes, and become a sect such as the 'Rebirth Sect', the 'Baptism Sect', or the 'Filling of the Holy Spirit Sect'. For example, the 'Baptism Sect' charges two yuan per baptism, and teaches that the more baptisms one receives, the more holy one becomes. Also the 'Filling Sect' screams very loudly during the meetings and is disturbing to others. Therefore, the Apostolic Church opts for a more balanced view on spirituality by equally emphasizing all the major themes.

Another important element of the Apostolic Church is the emphasis on exorcism, healing, vision, and prophecy. They frequently experience the Holy Spirit through revelations or guidance received in vision. This ability does not only reside with the leaders but is shared among the peasant Christians. Exorcism and healing are major sources of attraction for converts. The peasants are pragmatic and believe only what they see in front of their eyes. When many people from a village are healed by prayer, they often convert to Christianity immediately. An old woman with the gift of exorcism reportedly exorcised more than a hundred evil spirits from one individual, a spectacle witnessed by many. Another moving experience, witnessed by the researcher, was several hundred people gathered together to conduct fasting and prayer for several days, praying for a severely ill person. The person was healed. There was another incident when a peasant did not have time to use pesticide when his wheat field was infected. He simply prayed for the field and brought in a bumper harvest, much more than if he had sprayed the pesticide. There are also reports of speaking in tongues and visions of Heaven, but these are rare.

The Apostolic Church is very concerned about the 'End of Time'. The faithful hint that the last judgement will occur in 1999: according to their calculations, this is when the second coming of Christ will take place. The official church teaches that no one, 'not even the Son', can know the date. However, the leaders of the Apostolic Church cite many examples from the Bible to show that future events can be predicted: for example, Abraham knew when God would destroy Sodom; also, among the Ten Virgins in the Gospel, one knows the time when the bridegroom would come. The peasants especially like to read the Book of Revelations and the Book of Daniel. They have a commentary on the Book of Revelations by a Dispensationalist, Ms He Muyi of Hong Kong. Moreover, they read the prophecies of Nostradamus with great interest. They often tell visitors about the signs of the 'End of Time': evil prevails on earth, the Gulf War (Babylon versus Israel), the collapse of the Northern Empire (USSR), the appearance of European Confederation (EEC) and more. They exhort visitors to prepare the lamp; otherwise, when the time comes, true believers will be in Heaven, and will be sorry to see others burning in Hell.

The predominant religion of this area is the popular form of folk religion with symbols borrowed from Daoism and Buddhism. It stresses pragmatism and polytheism. The power from the name of Jesus, in exorcism and healing, establishes Christianity not only as an alternative religion, but a more practical one than folk religion. Therefore, many peasants convert to Christianity for pragmatic reasons. Furthermore, the traditional deities are degraded into evil spirits in the new religious setting, and the peasants only need to worship one God rather than many Gods. They find this more reasonable and less troublesome. The new religious orientation allows them to carry over their traditional worldview without too much conflict, and offers a convincing explanation of various life-events, the existence of suffering, disease and so on.

Miracles and wonders are a major starting point for many peasants converting to Christianity. However, Christianity provides more than pragmatic benefits, it ultimately calls for inner freedom, to detach oneself from material gains and to sacrifice oneself in response to a higher calling. It would require a lot of nurture and teaching for the full realization of Christianity, so that eventually believers will transform from a community emphasizing magical power into a community stressing the power of love. Otherwise, Christianity may be corrupted into another form of folk religion competing with other deities in performing supernatural acts.

Life is very harsh for peasants who live in this mountain

region. There is little they can celebrate or feel happy about. However, when they become Christians, especially after they receive the Holy Spirit and the assurance of Eternal Life, they become very joyful. They feel that they are the Children of the Lord and the Firstborn in the order of salvation. Because of this conviction, their lives are transformed from inferiority, depression and hopelessness into self-confidence, pride and fulfillment. The sense of joyfulness is apparent from the bright smiles on their face. There is a transformation of their temperament after their conversion into Christianity. Many peasants display a kind of humiliation when meeting city people, especially well-educated or wealthy visitors. They seem to regard their own life as meaningless, of no significance. However when they become convinced of God's interest in their life, these poor Christians are like people setting off on a voyage on a wonderful ship. They feel at least equal to city people. The researcher observed that when talking about the Gospel they are filled with spirit, and begin to act almost like self-satisfied college boys. But when the conversation returns to daily business, they again become humble peasants.

Traditionally, conflicts between the mother-in-law and daughter-in-law are ground for major familial disputes in Chinese peasant households. Very often after they become Christians, these conflicts decrease dramatically. Also, during droughts, peasants usually conduct violent feuds for the use of water for their crops. Yet the Christians demonstrate a high degree of self-restraint and unselfishly help out each other to irrigate the fields. In many cases, the believers come from a disadvantaged or criminal social background; in other cases, they have incurable chronic illnesses. Both groups are regarded by the Church as sick, physically or socially. After their conversion, they usually demonstrate a remarkable recovery. The sick recover, and social deviants become model citizens. These transformations are common and non-believers are often impressed by these testimonies.

Life in the rural areas in China is very monotonous and severely lacking in cultural amenities. In the past, the Communist Youth League provided certain activities for the youth but it is no longer functioning, nor do the youth in general believe in communist ideology. Furthermore, because of governmental restrictions on residential registrations, many villagers may live in the same village all their life, and their talents are buried due to the lack of opportunity. However, if they join the Church, their potential can be appreciated and utilized. For example, the leaders are mostly gifted young people. Through ministry in the Church, they exercise their gifts, such as organizing, teaching, caring, propagation, mediation, which they would otherwise have no opportunity to do. Christian communities also provide the chance, particularly for talented young people, to have social activities such as fellowship, choir and other forms of music.

According to the researcher, the actual life of the peasants in such a remote, mountainous region is extremely narrow. A person is born, lives, eats, sleeps, works and dies. Is this human or animal existence? The impression is of a life without self-determination, hope, planning, expectation, 'culture' – almost a naked biological existence. This harsh and restricted life manifests itself in the social psychology: dissatisfaction, anger, jealousy, anxiety and even numbness. The Christian community's cultural and social activities are especially meaningful when one is aware of this background. The sense of fulfillment derives also from the believers' self-perception as heroes fighting a historic war against evil, their sacrifice to evangelical enterprises, their 'leadership in a huge army' as one of them said. Away from this great adventure, their horizons are limited to their house, their tedious farming and endless trivial disputes with neighbours.

Many who were illiterate have learned to read and write through study of the Bible. Some, because of their devotion to scripture, even develop into highly intellectual Bible teachers. Many, realizing the richness of Christian thought, spend most of their spare time (which is plenty) in studying the Bible and theology. It seems that Christianity gives them the incentive and means to develop their intellectual potential. However, what they lack is knowledgeable teachers to guide them into the richest sources of Christian thought.

At worst they may easily develop into a closed sect adopting some extreme doctrines or practices. We have already seen this possible tendency in their eschatology. Another example is that the Church has a strong sense of its own spiritual superiority. Their members think that that they are the best Christians, and their church, of course, the most ideal. It is partly against the official church that they make such claims. However, this sense of self-righteousness prevents them from seeing their own limitations, and from appreciating others. They often accuse the official church as the 'Brother who kills Cain', or the 'Judas who sold Jesus'. Such accusations, not without some truth, are not fair to all the personnel in the official church, nor fair to what the official church has achieved in promoting a certain degree of religious freedom in a hostile environment. Further, such rivalry generates disharmony among Christians and becomes a poor witness to non-believers in the long run.

Peasants are often very selfish, especially in poorer regions such as this. In the past, people thought that through education and communist ideology, the CCP could eradicate selfishness from the mind of the Chinese peasant. This has been proven wrong. With the collapse of the commune system, rural China disintegrated into traditional groupings that frequently clash with each other, often violently. This ecclesial community of ordinary, poorly educated peasants, shows a different spirit. The common faith can bring selfish individual households into a mutually supporting community in which the common ideology is the Gospel, and the organization is the church. It seems that Christianity can provide Chinese rural societies with an alternative means for constructing social stability. Furthermore, through the building of a religious subculture, namely the Christian community, it may raise the moral standards of peasants and, in the long run, revive the morality of the nation.

How should we evaluate this Apostolic Church? Is it a church in immature childhood, or one that has returned to authenticity, the essence of Christianity? Local believers definitely believe the latter, but there is a case for considering the former too. Two characteristics that emerge from these observations are firstly the ability of Protestantism to touch the daily life of this group of people, and secondly the extent to which it is conditioned by the extreme poverty of the villages. The key element of Protestantism here is that it *works*. The question as to whether it is a 'foreign religion' or 'indigenized' appears to have little relevance. In fact to these people, anything which comes to them from outside their county is 'from outside', even if it is a form of Buddhism or Daoism, or for that matter a new agricultural technique. Protestantism is no more nor less strange than many other things that have entered their lives. Moreover, in the case of the Apostolic Church, there are no special buildings, liturgies or even music. The key features are the Bible, prayer, the practical benefits and the teachings on eschatology. Their world is harsh and hopeless, and the church offers a fellowship that alleviates sorrow. It even promises something better, foreshadowing the 'New Heaven and New Earth'. As an extreme example of this hope for improvement, one local believer stated: 'In Heaven I will be the boss of a few counties' – an ambition that was obviously unthinkable for him on earth.

It might be easy to criticize the believers for some extreme tendencies. However the movement also represents a turn from despair to hope, humiliation to confidence, and allows an actualization of many good qualities that would otherwise be wasted. Nobody else – not the CCP nor foreign aid agencies nor any wealthy western government – seems to be interested in helping such communities improve their standard of living, their education or their cultural life. Who can blame them if they tend to exaggerate one aspect of a powerful religious message that seems to be transforming their worldview at present?

THE WITNESS OF BROTHER HUANG DETANG

Huang Detang was born in Tianyanghu township, Xiangshan county, Zhejiang Province. When he was baptized, he was given the name of Lazarus, but he confessed later that he did not understand the significance of the whole event. Years later, however, his Christian name and his baptismal commitment took on a deeper meaning when he was suddenly struck with boils on his feet, causing great pain and preventing him from walking. People began to call him 'Lame Huang'. In desperation, he thought of Jesus and asked for forgiveness. One night, he heard the Lord tell him in a dream: 'You must believe in me truly. I will heal you. You must witness for me.' Brother Huang thought of the relief of his pain and promised immediately. But the Lord said: 'A verbal promise is not enough. You must write a contract of indenture by which you offer yourself up as my servant.' Huang did not know how to write such a contract, for he had not had good schooling. He had to ask for the mercy of the Lord, and the Lord taught him in another dream, with the result that he composed the following:

An Offering Indenture

I, Huang Detang, sign this indenture by which I offer myself up forever.

Because of my own uselessness, I have boils on my feet. It is very painful and I have nowhere to turn. I can only ask my gracious savior, my Lord Jesus, to be merciful to me, a great sinner.

I now receive the precious blood of the Lord as the ransom price which has redeemed me from death to life, and I know that the Lord will heal my foot sickness, take my soul to the Heavenly Kingdom forever, and I will become a child of God with honor and glory.

Because I have nothing to repay the grace of the Lord, I will most gladly dedicate my body and soul to God. After my dedication, I am totally at the disposal of the Lord. No matter where I am sent, even without any address, I will go. Whether it is in the east, south, west or north, whether it is climbing mountains or crossing seas, whether it is cold or not, whether I am hungry or thirsty, whether I suffer want and persecution, I will follow the Lord to the end and will not be disheartened. No one in the family and among relatives and friends will be able to pose any obstacles or cause me to go back on my promise.

This indenture is the common wish of both parties and no one of them raises any objection. I sign it as evidence of my willingness.

In the original, Brother Huang did not put down the date. But below the indenture he penned the following words: 'It is I myself who want to dedicate myself most gladly to the Lord. No matter what kind of suffering comes to me, I will be glad and rejoice, I will never be disheartened. When I finish my path, I will see the Lord. Hallelujah, strengthen my faith, O Lord, let me never waver.'

Selling the 'ha-ha' song

Brother Huang was not well educated nor had he any theological training. What he did was to address people in the streets, but as the crowd gathered, he was afraid. To cover up his embarrassment, he used a mask to preach. Only after a while did he dare to face the public without the mask.

His unorthodox approach certainly aroused suspicion in the church hierarchy. At one meeting, Brother Huang was told by the pastor of his church in no uncertain terms: 'You are not trained to evangelize. You do not understand the truth of the gospel. People look down on you. It is better for you to go with Brother Wang Yongtao to the sea to catch fish. You can help him with the accounts. To generate income for the church is also rendering a service to the Lord.' Huang did not disobey. He went fishing. After a year the war with Japan reached the coast of Zhejiang, and Huang had to move inland. One evening he dreamed that he was on a high mountain, and there he saw Jesus in tears teaching a crowd. He heard the Lord commanding everyone to distribute 'ha-ha' in every place for the next five years. Awakened, he thought he had only five years to live and became very remorseful that he had forgotten his pledge to the Lord. He knelt down to ask the Lord what 'ha-ha' actually was. The Lord told him that 'ha-ha' was the whole Bible, the word of God, the bread of life.

Following that experience, he went everywhere to sell 'ha-ha'. Bewildered, people inquired about this 'ha-ha' because they thought it was funny. At this moment, he told the crowd that this precious thing was invisible, yet useful everywhere, for it was the good message of the Lord Jesus. The following is the 'ha-ha' song composed by Brother Huang:

There is a way to keep you from growing old and dying. You get it free from heaven. I assure you that everybody likes it and wants to have it, not even sin and guilt can be a hindrance to it. If you feel the need of going home, there is only Jesus who can lead you. Be truly repentant and believe, rely on Jesus as your savior; pray constantly for His mercy and His precious blood will cleanse you till you reach the door of Heaven. Then we will sit at the table with the great laughter of 'ha-ha'; we will rejoice with thousands and ten thousands of angels and saints, dancing and singing. God the Father and Jesus will sit with us. How delicious is the fruit of life! We will never grow old and die. This is the blessedness of being the elected in the Kingdom of Heaven. Everyday we laugh with a big 'ha-ha'. Brothers and sisters, do you want to share?

Giving up his gown

Once when Brother Huang was preaching, he felt moved, as if a voice were telling him: 'Love the one in the last row!' That evening he could not fall asleep. As soon as it was dawn, he inquired about the one who sat in the last row of the church. When he was led to the home of that person, he saw him bedridden. There was only a shredded quilt on his bed, and the floor was full of dirt.

Brother Huang asked him how many years he had believed in Jesus. The man shook his head, making it unclear whether he had ever believed. Then Brother Huang asked him why he turned up in the church. He said that on the eve of the Chinese New Year he was told in a dream to go to church and that Jesus would save him. Usually he was confined to bed. But on the day of the meeting, he felt much better and so asked somebody to help him to go to church.

Seeing that this man was infected with leprosy and did not believe in Jesus, Brother Huang thought that he must be a sinner and argued with the Lord: 'You tell me to love him, but I have no money. How can I love him? Should I heal him in your name?' The Lord answered: 'Take off your gown and give it to him.' Brother Huang was totally in a daze. 'Lord, I cannot do it, I am not willing. I have only this cotton-padded gown. I have great need of it. You see, it is the snowy season, the wind is cutting. I must not take it off.' The Lord said: 'If you do not give it to him, what you preach is like a noisy gong or a clanging cymbal. If you have not love, what use is it? If you have not love, you are not serving me.'

Brother Huang had to obey in tears, but as soon as he had given the gown away he felt immensely relieved. Brother Yue of Dachen was ready to give a gown to him, but he refused on the ground that he did not have the Lord's permission. Thus he was without a gown for many years and yet was not frostbitten.

A wretched prostitute

Brother Huang was evangelizing at Zhongnei. On his way home he heard a voice: 'Go and save this person!' He turned his head and saw a woman groaning on the floor of a broken down house. When asked where she was from, she said she was local: 'My father was Ya Fu, but my parents are dead now.' At a close look, she was indeed familiar. At sixteen she had gone to a brothel in Shanghai. She came home occasionally, beautifully dressed and adorned with jewels and gold. But now she was crawling on the ground, all her former glory vanished without a trace.

Brother Huang was stunned. He asked whether she wanted Jesus. 'Do you think Jesus wants such a wretch like me?' she bewailed. Brother Huang told her: 'Indeed, there is no one who wants you. But Jesus is gracious. If you only express your want for Him, He will receive you and save you.' 'I want Him! I want Him!' came her immediate answer.

Brother Huang asked her to kneel down to pray. But she could not, for she was wearing a long shirt with no underwear and she could only remain covered by staying in a seated position. Seeing that she had no other clothes to put on, Brother Huang gave her his outermost pair of work pants to cover her up.

Then she asked for *gaotuan* [stuffed dumplings of rice flour]. Brother Huang had it sent to her. He also asked two believing sisters who lived nearby to take care of her and give her porridge every day. The two sisters complained: 'Brother Huang, this woman was a prostitute. She was evil. You remember how snobbish she was! Now not even her own relatives want to bother about her, why should we take care of her and give her something to eat? Syphilis is infectious.' Brother Huang had to comfort them: 'You and I believe in Jesus. We must be different from the world. Please act as if you were helping me. I will give you the rice back later.'

The woman died less than a month later. The last bowl of porridge was laying beside her on the ground where hungry dogs were fighting for a share. Brother Huang believed she was saved because of her faith in Jesus.

Praying on a mountain

Once, three days before the Chinese New Year, Brother Huang started off for Daleishan (Great Thunder Mountain) at Xiang-shan harbour. He first overnighted at the home of Brother Chang in Yijiaqian. During conversation, Chang begged Huang to go along. He said: 'My son was seriously sick and healed by the Lord. I myself also had the blessing of the Lord. Now I keep every Saturday holy for Him. I do not work on that day. Instead, I go everywhere to tell fellow Christians to come to church the next day.'

The next morning, the two went out together, but it started raining. When they reached the foot of the mountain, Chang asked Huang: 'When are we going back?' 'The sixth day after Chinese New Year,' replied Huang. Incredulous, Chang asked, 'why didn't you tell me earlier, so that I could have brought some *gaotuan* along. Now we will have no food for days.' Brother Huang reminded him that they did not live by food alone, but by the word of God. Chang was silent for some time. Then he asked again: 'Have you ever been to Daleishan?' Hearing the answer was in the negative, he began to worry: 'You haven't been there, neither have I. Now it is raining and the mountain is high. We have neither food nor quilt. Whether there are houses there, we don't know. Where shall we go to sleep?' Brother Huang said that God would provide. Finally they reached Yangpo where they were received by believing families. After lunch, Chang decided he could not go on. 'Why?' Brother Huang asked him, 'you begged to come with me, but here you stop.' He answered: 'If I go with you, I will either starve to death or be frozen. For four days and nights without food nor quilt, it is crazy.' So he returned home.

Brother Huang went up the mountain alone. There he met a Daoist hermit who, disillusioned with life, had given up his trade as a builder and built a house in a cave on top of the mountain. When asked for shelter, he was generous, pointing to his home: 'Well, you see, I have also a quilt prepared for you.' Seeing the perplexed eyes of Brother Huang, he explained: 'Someone who used to share this room with me just left. He is a lay Daoist. As it is the Chinese New Year's eve, everybody has hurried home for family reunions. How could he have stayed here alone? He actually took the quilt with him. But not too far from here, his shoulder pole broke, so he left all his belongings here. He will come back after the New Year.'

Brother Huang was grateful for the arrangement. He went outside to pray. By then the weather had turned fine. He sang a hymn at the top of his voice. The Daoist had a disciple who was returning after he had begged for alms at the foot of the mountain. All of a sudden, he saw three people singing and dancing on the mountain top. No sooner had he laid down his load than he inquired of his master about the guests. The master told him that there was only one guest with them. Overhearing their conversation, Brother Huang was reminded of Daniel in the fiery furnace. He felt surer than ever before that the Lord was with him.

For three consecutive years he went to Daleishan to pray. In a way he admired the dedication and austere life of the Daoist hermit, yet he was thankful that Christian salvation was free of human effort.

Making his own son a death substitute

The only son of a certain church elder was going to die, and Brother Huang was called in to pray for him. He prayed from early morning to midnight, but nothing seemed to work. He became desperate and begged the Lord: 'His only son is going to die. You know how much we need his help in the church. You should not disappoint him. If you must take a son away, take one of mine instead, for I have four.' At dawn, the son lived again.

Again, some one from Sanmuyang was dying, his coffin already prepared in his house. Brother Huang was called in to pray. He forced the Lord to heal again, pleading that this man was helpful in the development of the church at Tuci. And again, he asked the Lord to choose from his sons. A third time, when the wife of Zheng Xianming was seriously ill, he made the same plea.

Later, when Brother Huang brought his fourth son Fonghan to visit his eldest son Fongcao in Nanjing, Fonghan died. He was not only the youngest, but also the brightest. Therefore, Brother Huang had to argue with the Lord: 'If you had planned on taking him away, you should have done it when he was young! Now he is twenty-three years old and full of hope. Don't you see how difficult it has been to bring him up so far?' The Lord answered: 'You yourself asked me to choose from them. You pleaded with me three times. I look around and found him the most suitable. He hasn't married yet. If I had chosen another one, would you not find it more difficult to accept?' Brother Huang was silenced, for he fully understood what he had promised the Lord.

Comments by Deng Zhaoming

Brother Huang personally jotted down many stories, mainly in his own dialect and quite often unintelligible because of his educational level. The above testimonies have been chosen from his personal notebooks and rearranged. They are not exhaustive. Yet, from these stories, one already has an understanding of a rural evangelist in China, his grasp of the Bible and his relationship with God. Like other rural preachers, his approach to theology was earth-bound, indissoluble with the context in which he lived. For example, dreams were an important channel through which to receive God's revelation. At the same time, he believed he could communicate with Jesus at whatever time and in whatever place. Quite often he would not decide to do anything before he prayed to the Lord. Sometimes he left home without eating even though the table had been set. He claimed that it was the will of the Lord, but he could never explain why. The strong points of an evangelist like Brother Huang are not his knowledge of the Bible nor the content of his sermons, i.e., not his outward appearance, but his devotional piety and his burning loyalty to the Lord. He, like so many other rural evangelists in China, spared no efforts to travel the length and breadth of his country for the sake of the gospel and following the example of his Lord, he stayed with fellow Christians and tried to solve some concrete problems as best as he could.

To appreciate the widespread influence of Brother Huang, one need only hear of the tribute paid to him upon his death on 15 April 1981 at the age of ninety-six. On the day of the funeral, though it had not been advertised, more than 400 people gathered to take part in the procession. He was a devoted Christian who had suffered greatly in his life and was honoured for his sacrifices.

CHAPTER 6

Buddhism and Catholicism

BUDDHISM IN THE 1980S[1]

The fate of Buddhism between 1949 and the start of the Cultural Revolution has been documented by Holmes Welch, to whose work the reader should refer.[2] To summarize, in the early 1950s the CCP organized a new Buddhist organization known as the China Buddhist Association (CBA). As with the TSPM, its leaders were specifically chosen for their willingness to co-operate with the CCP; it was rumoured that some of them were underground Party agents. Understandably this caused resentment among other Buddhist leaders, who felt the new organization was unrepresentative and too politicized. Government agencies implemented a programme of control and consolidation of Party leadership in religious circles. Many monasteries had been important landholders, and subsidized their activities by income from rent and *corvées*. The loss of property in the land reforms of the early 1950s led to the collapse of their economic structure. Many monks returned to lay life, under pressure from cadres, through poverty, because their monasteries were closed, or through choice. Some were sent to labour camps, many were maltreated, others executed. Buddhist publications were obliged to change their contents to support the Party line rather than preach orthodox Buddhism. Lay believers were too frightened to visit temples. With increasing speed the whole Buddhist establishment crumbled.

---

[1] The next three sections are based on Alan Hunter, *Buddhism Under Deng*, Leeds East Asian Papers, 1992. We are grateful to Thomas Hahn and Julian Pas for helpful comments on an earlier draft.
[2] Welch, *Buddhism Under Mao*.

By 1966 only a few monasteries survived: they had been kept alive that long only because the government used its 'tolerance' of Buddhism as a diplomatic tool when dealing with Asian neighbours such as Burma, and to keep Taiwan out of international organizations. Even these remnants soon ceased to function. A handful of city temples were placed under military protection and escaped some of the turmoil; others in remote locations suffered less systematic vandalization. But by 1978 temples and monasteries existed only as empty shells, or had been converted into factories and warehouses. Doubtless many believers kept some kind of personal faith in private, and there was a limited amount of academic activity concerning Buddhist history, but to outside observation, at least, Buddhism was dead.[3]

In 1978 Buddhist activities resumed after almost thirty years of repression, and their status was formalized in the Fourth National Congress of the CBA, held in Beijing in December 1980. A programme for the restoration of Buddhism was announced by the CBA's chairman Zhao Puchu, endorsed by senior Party officials, and reported in the media. The main elements were revival of the CBA itself; repair of monasteries; establishment of training schools; new ordinations; publication of Buddhist literature and development of contacts with overseas Buddhist organizations. The CBA of the 1980s was essentially a reincarnation of the organization that had ceased to operate in 1966. Zhao Puchu and other senior figures retained their posts. It again published a journal[4] and acted as liaison between government and believers. The CBA kept a low political profile and had no major conflicts, either with the government, internally or with foreign critics, at least as far as one can tell from documents available to date.

However the picture is far from idyllic. Observers estimated that only around 25,000 monks survived by the early 1980s, compared to about half a million in the 1930s. Most of them had been in labour camps, or worked as peasants, for many years

---

[3] *Ibid.*, pp. 379–80.
[4] Although its name changed, from *Xiandai foxue*, '*Modern Buddhism*', to *Fayin*, '*Voice of Dharma*'.

previously. The great majority were over sixty, and many much older, since there had been almost no ordinations since 1949. Many were in a decrepit state through poverty, age and maltreatment, and the monastic tradition could only survive if it received an influx of young monks; had repressive policies continued, monastic Buddhism could have died out. As it was, the CBA urgently established a number of Buddhist academies as one measure to educate a new generation of monks. According to one estimate, the grand total of graduates for all academies for ten years to 1990 is still only about 1,100, hardly enough to replace the elderly monks who are obliged to leave.[5] Moreover, some of these young graduates are keen to pursue further studies abroad and may succeed in emigrating through Buddhist networks.

The number of new ordinations is certainly higher, although precise figures are not known. A recent estimate by Thomas Hahn suggests around 4,000 from 1982 to 1986, and speculated that the total number of new ordinations, including that of graduates from the Buddhist academies, might be in the region of 10,000 between 1980 and 1990.[6] Those who do not attend one of the Buddhist academies receive training of variable quality inside the monasteries from the older monks/nuns. Thus, although the number of monks is certainly a problem, Buddhism seems to be assured of survival for another generation at least.

As regards doctrine, the CBA on the one hand promotes a rather syncretic form of rationalistic, this-worldly Buddhism, with constant exhortations to serve the people and contribute to the development of socialism. An illustration of this is the slogan calling for joint practice of meditation and productive agricultural work. In most of our conversations with Chinese Buddhists they regarded these doctrines as something of a formality to appease government bureaucrats, and told us that more

[5] Fang Litian, 'Fojiao yu dangdai Zhongguo shehui' ('Buddhism and Contemporary Chinese Society') in *Taixu tingsheng yibai zhouian guojihui yilunwenji* (*Collected Papers from International Conference on the Centenary of the Birth of Taixu*), edited by Fok Tou-hui, Hong Kong: Fazhu chubanshe, 1990, pp. 350–62 (p. 352).

[6] Thomas H. Hahn, 'New Developments Concerning Buddhist and Taoist Monasteries', in *The Turning of the Tide: Religion in China Today*, edited by Julian F. Pas, Hong Kong: Oxford University Press, 1989, pp. 79–101 (p. 93).

traditional doctrines were taught in most monasteries. In practice, three main schools are dominant: Pure Land, Chan and Esoteric Buddhism. They are not mutually exclusive, and quite often one monastery teaches two or even three schools' scriptures. Alternatively, a monk may spend some years in a primarily Chan monastery and then perhaps move on to a Pure Land one. Scriptures and commentaries from most major teachers appear to be quite readily available. However, the traditional lineages of practice and scholarship have been broken up, perhaps irretrievably. There is a risk that the teaching of Chinese Buddhism may become a superficial generalization, rather than an authentic transmission.

Foreign contacts were beneficial to Chinese Buddhism through the decade, and did not prove controversial. We met several monks, nuns and lay Buddhists from Taiwan and Hong Kong who visited China regularly, and they all carefully avoided disputes with the authorities. They were generous in donating money and educational materials, but never attempted, as far as we know, to support any 'anti-CBA' Buddhists. Nor did they publish criticism of Chinese religious policy. The general attitude seemed to be that the situation was difficult enough already, so they would be careful not to make it worse. As Buddhism entered the 1990s, it seemed to be relatively stable, certainly as far as relations with the state went.

THE REVIVAL OF MONASTIC LIFE

Starting in 1979, the various provincial governments, under instructions from the Party centre, ordered that monasteries be repaired. The number and location was decided after consultation with officials in the UFWD and the RAB, and with senior monks, many of whom were released from labour camps or other forms of detention. The rationale is easily understood in the context of post-Mao reforms and religious policy: it was meant to promote tourism and to increase popular support for the programme of economic modernization, reflecting the shift from the politics of class struggle to those of national unity.

The first to be repaired and reopened were a number of key

monasteries in each province, most of which had a long history and often a heritage of art and architecture. After the restoration of these well-known monasteries, work began on smaller local ones. As to quantity, the numbers are still kept secret by the Chinese government, perhaps embarrassed to admit both the huge decline between 1949 and 1979, and the great popular enthusiasm since then. Figures which can be collated are far from definitive but give an indication of scale: we would estimate somewhere in the region of 2,000 monasteries for Han areas of China, of which about 200 might be quite important. They would be served by some 20,000 monks, most of whom are ageing, but with some replacements in the pipeline.

The large monasteries inherit Buddhist traditions which have doubtless been modified, but still continue in forms easily recognizable from the older literature. Among their functions are the training of young monks, reception of pilgrims, tourists and other visitors, performance of ceremonies, scripture reading, meditation and publication. On the whole their material condition is excellent. There is plenty of vegetarian food, the buildings are in good condition, sometimes bordering on the opulent, they are much visited, publications are readily available. One can enter into conversation with monks and most of the monasteries appear genuine hives of religious activity.

Reservations about these places have been expressed, both by visitors and monks, which generally refer to over-exposure as tourist locations, corruption due to money, and government interference. Monks are obliged to keep the temples open for long hours every day, to sell tickets for entry, to show visitors around, provide toilets and food. Thousands of the tourists have no interest whatsoever in Buddhism, and a few are openly disrespectful. Thus for most of the day the monasteries' forecourts are inundated with workers, schoolchildren and soldiers, smoking, spitting and posing for photographs. Some locations are far worse than others: a few monasteries are tourist destinations pure and simple, and some are even administered by local government offices as such, without any pretence at fostering a religious life.

The problem of corruption through money is perhaps more

insidious. We spoke at length to a person who for ten years had been quietly supporting monasteries by taking in donations from Hong Kong. He said that he had stopped doing so because by 1990 it was only contributing to a sad development. Many monks had become more interested in money than religion. Unscrupulous people had realized that they could become rich by soliciting donations from overseas individuals and institutions. Funds were either donated for building projects or paid in exchange for ceremonies such as masses for the dead. Much of it was not declared and went into private pockets. Another source informed us that this was not only the case for overseas visitors, but also some monasteries had begun to rake in large sums of money from the local population in exchange for performing rites. According to him, some young men became monks for a few years solely in order to save money to get married. The problem has become sufficiently serious to attract criticism from the CBA.

Finally, surveillance of monks is quite intrusive. Government agencies are concerned to keep tabs on the situation, so most monasteries house one or several Party members who lead a monk's life without being believers themselves. They often work on the admission door, registration section or have similar duties, and report to the local authorities anything unusual or suspicious. As far as one could tell this network is rather efficient, and many people have the impression that monks are unable to talk freely about their situation. The whole period between 1949 and 1979 is a taboo subject that people are frightened to discuss. There is a surface appearance of goodwill and harmony, but in some places there may well be an underlying atmosphere of suspicion and fear. Naturally, contact with foreign visitors is handled with especial care.

However, it would be mistaken to suggest that these problems, serious as they are, invalidate the whole enterprise of the larger monasteries. They have their problems, but they seemed to us, with some reservations, religious centres rather than tourist resorts or state agencies pure and simple. And if one wants to find a more reflective and austere form of traditional Buddhism, one is more likely to do so in quieter spots. The majority of small monasteries that reopened were to serve local communities, and to be places of retreat and meditation. Sometimes they are situated quite close to the larger monasteries and are supported by them, although often not mentioned in the tourist literature. In such small, quiet monasteries one can see the more transcendent, other-worldly religion. Monastic rules are kept strictly and visitors are not particularly welcome. Some of these places are simply huts in the countryside inhabited by one or two lone individuals: the eremitic tradition is by no means lost, even in modern China.

Thus monasteries have many facets: they are centres of learning and of a religious tradition, yet at the same time museums; show-pieces for traditional arts and crafts; moneymaking enterprises and sacred space. Buddhism cannot live without them, and it manages to live with them, making the best of hard times. Conversations with monks suggest that there is a genuine religious vocation operating, various problems notwithstanding. One monk we met lived in a small monastery. He was in his early thirties, a high-school graduate, extremely well read in Chinese literature, who had worked on a provincial newspaper for fifteen years. There was no history of Buddhism in his family, he had come across it by chance through reading. Over the years he had become disillusioned with his job, and he said he had seen through the pleasures and pains of family life: 'It takes tremendous effort here to raise a family. Not only money, but child-care, shopping, house-work. Also we constantly have to entertain relatives and pay respect to our elders. Between work and home I found there was no room for meditation. I felt that kind of life was useless, a waste of time.' He was not at all anti-communist, unlike most people one meets in China, in fact he rather approved of socialist ethics and preferred austerity to consumerism. But he felt he needed to absorb the scriptures and spend many years in meditation practice, and monastic life allowed him to do so. His family had been rather upset, but had eventually agreed, and he had simply visited a dozen monasteries until he found one where he felt happy. He thought it had been the best decision of his life.

Another monk was the son of a devout Buddhist who had

become a nun when her husband died. He had become a monk at age twelve and practised in secret locations in the countryside during the Cultural Revolution. He had trained with some of the most famous teachers in China in the 1980s, and then decided to retire from the monastic circuit. 'They are too big and busy for serious practice', he said. He had collected some donations from devotees and was building a small hut on a mountain. He spoke about the future of Buddhism in China: 'I don't care. True Buddhism can never be destroyed. A few people with certain karma are attracted to it, this number may rise or fall. It often has done in Chinese history. Now it is not developing and not falling either as far as I know. It doesn't matter. The essence can never disappear while there is still a need among human beings, but it might change its name.' He said that certain spirits on the mountain protected the monks in meditation there. Visitors could only meet certain monks, depending on the state of their karma. 'I seldom talk to people', he said.

LAY BUDDHISM

Outside the monastic system, we may first consider the intellectual and academic interest in Buddhism, which was quite high through the 1980s. In a few cities there are lay Buddhist groups for intellectuals, which meet once or twice a month to exchange views and circulate publications, organize talks by famous monks or conduct other activities. Numbers are small and activities restricted; the groups have to be cautious and are not influential. More generally, educated people are well aware of the place of Buddhism in Chinese culture, and there have been numerous recent editions of Buddhist classics, discussions of its philosophy, influence on literature and art. Some of these works are published by Buddhist associations and others by academic publishers. It seems that the government takes a liberal attitude to this activity, perceiving it, one supposes correctly, as no particular threat: it is a good example of religion as a private affair, and therefore to be tolerated. The one great lacuna is that the public is still not allowed to study or speak openly about the history of Buddhism in this century, where the CCP would be shown in a very dim light.

There are also Buddhist families in the general population. These devotees may not be well read but they may have quite a serious and regular commitment to Buddhist practices. One of the most common would be to visit a temple a few times a month, taking offerings, burning incense and asking for blessings. Such people might become familiar with a few monks, and occasionally ask them for advice on personal matters or instruction on religious questions. Some people practise vegetarianism, if not full-time then on certain days of the month as a sign of respect. (The full practice of vegetarianism is seen as a requirement for monks and nuns, not for lay believers.)

An attractive aspect of Chinese Buddhism is its tradition of pilgrimage. In particular, Buddhist groups love to visit the Holy Mountains, which hold the largest concentrations of monasteries and have been pilgrimage destinations for hundreds of years. Each centre receives hundreds of thousands of visitors yearly. Many visitors have a genuine religious purpose in mind, and diligently burn incense and offer prayers at the main monasteries. Others are simply tourists, usually organized coach-parties from work-units. From the believers' point of view they are probably a nuisance, although they do bring cash into the local economy.

Believers come either individually, in small groups of family and friends, or in large groups organized by lay Buddhist societies. The majority appear to be female, and middle-aged or elderly. Some come to 'redeem a vow', where a devotee had promised at a temple to make the pilgrimage if certain wishes were granted. Another reason is to obtain blessings which would be beneficial either for religious life or material welfare. Pilgrimage sites are thought to have specific virtues, being the earthly home of various Boddhisattvas. Among the devotional practices we have seen are lighting of incense and candles, divination, prostrations, attendance of services, purchase and study of scriptures and interviews with monks. A common practice is the 'offering of virtue', which means a financial contribution to a good cause. For example in many temples one can contribute money towards building or maintenance costs and have one's name inscribed in a ledger. Another practice is the writing of a petitionary prayer on a piece of cloth which is tied to a tree in a temple compound. We noticed dozens of these in a temple in Wutai, and were told the majority were requesting the birth of a male child.

A similar expression of the more popular kind of religiosity is attending ceremonies and festivals, such as the eighth day of the fourth lunar month, which is celebrated as the Buddha's birthday. Thousands of people pour into major temples, from the city centre, the suburbs and surrounding rural areas. Their main concern seems to be to light incense and candles and perform prostrations before images of the Buddha. They will also listen to the monks chanting, eat vegetarian food, hear discourses and generally spend time in the temple compounds. It has been estimated that around 30,000 people visited the Jade Buddha temple in Shanghai over a two-day period in 1990; the atmosphere was almost carnival-like, with everybody in excellent humour. The following description is from Xiamen in 1988:

Thousands of people were working their way through the temple complex day and night, whole families, old people, young people, an almost equal number of men and women. Most of them were offering incense before the various sacred images and burning spirit money in the big bronze kettles; others were simply curious visitors. It was an astonishing sight, as if thirty-nine years of Socialism and Marxist propaganda against religion had never happened. I stood transfixed for nearly an hour, watching faces, intent, focused on the tasks of lighting incense and moving from image to image.[7]

Buddhism has made a profound, perhaps ineradicable, contribution to the formation of the Chinese psyche and national culture, which is an entire field of study in itself. Expressions such as 'karmic connections between people' are part of everyday conversation, and countless Chinese have been brought up in households where members of the older generation are to some extent Buddhist. A friend of ours is an administrator in a major university, and a few years ago he came

---

[7] MacInnis, *Religion in China Today*, p. 135.

across a particularly nasty piece of corruption among some university administrators. By chance he also acquired irrefutable documentary evidence of the situation and the damage that had been caused. Moreover he would probably have gained promotion by reporting it to higher authorities. Before doing so he mentioned the affair to his mother, who is a Buddhist devotee. She insisted that he take no action. In her opinion, bad actions would reap their own bad consequences, and it was better simply not to develop any karmic links with such people, even if one thought one was helping. Being a good Confucian, he followed her advice and, as the Chinese say, let events take their natural course. We never did discover the outcome. But it strikes us as one small example of the impact of this philosophy, or at least one interpretation of it, operating at the heart of a modern Chinese institution.

BUDDHISM AND THE PROTESTANT CHURCH
— SOME COMPARISONS

Let us first consider the quantitative side of the question, as always bearing in mind reservations about the accuracy of data. By the late 1980s the number of registered Protestant believers in open churches was around five million. To this must be added an unknown number of the curious, the uncertain, and those outside the TSPM. The official church establishment counted around 7,000 churches, 15,000 meeting points and 15,000 clergy. Again one should bear in mind their unofficial counterparts. In terms of gross numbers, then, one can suggest that the size of the two religious establishments, and the numbers of committed believers, are of approximately the same order, based on our estimates of 2,000 monasteries, 20,000 or more monks and a maximum of five million lay believers (assuming no increase since 1949). We cannot pursue this too far, because a church and a monastery have different functions, the statistics are so vague and definitions so problematical: but it is remarkable, given their entirely different histories, that organized Chinese Buddhism and Protestantism are now somewhat similar in dimensions.

However, two outstanding differences are the place of the

religions in popular culture, and the growth rates. For the first, it is clear that perhaps tens or even hundreds of millions of Chinese citizens retain some kind of residual influence from Buddhism. At its most basic this may be to have pictures of a Buddhist deity together with Daoist or other icons in one's home. Other expressions may be a brief visit to a temple on a public holiday, going on a visit to a pilgrimage destination or eating in vegetarian restaurants. Also one should note the impact of Buddhism on Chinese attitudes to life, on language, literature and art. The depth and breadth of Buddhism's influence in contemporary Chinese culture is a topic which demands further exploration. Christianity has few of these resonances. However, one could draw a clear line between this kind of cultural influence and specific commitment to the Buddhist religion.

On the question of change, one would have to conclude that Buddhism has, if anything, declined. Certainly the monastic population has decreased dramatically since the 1930s; no figures are available for lay believers, but all the indications are that they have declined also. Protestant believers on the contrary have increased by at least tenfold in the same period. Incidentally it is interesting that at least three provinces, Jiangsu, Zheijiang and Fujian, figure high on the list for proportion of believers to the general population, for both Protestantism and Buddhism. It would be interesting to explore the reasons for this. Another geographical consideration to be explored elsewhere is the concentration of Buddhists in Tibet, Qinghai, Gansu, and Yunnan, among non-Han peoples. If the 'Chinese Empire' begins to crumble as the Russian one has done, would there be a strong revival of Buddhism tied to ethnicity and demands for national independence in these regions, as with Islam in Xinjiang?

Has there been any antagonism between Protestants and Buddhists? Again this is an area on which no serious study has been made. We have heard anecdotal evidence that Christian and Buddhist families are reluctant to inter-marry and will occasionally cast aspersions on each other in provinces like Fujian, where both are quite influential. But we would guess in most parts of China both sets of believers are relatively isolated compared to the rest of the population and could hardly expend much energy on sectarian rivalry. On the other hand some Buddhists, aware that their religion has been losing ground in recent years, have called for a programme of evangelization to compete with that of the Christians.

With regard to state relations, both religions were governed by the same regulations. The top leaders, K. H. Ting and Zhao Puchu appear to have an excellent working relationship and have frequently attended meetings together, both inside and outside China. They also use their positions in state bodies to similar effect. Zhao has the reputation for being compromising in his public statements, but outspoken and tough in his private negotiations with senior officials. Like Ting, his position over the years has won him admirers and critics, for similar reasons.

The regulations mean that 'normal' Buddhism is quite legal and can be practised without punishment. At times one reads allegations that corrupt practices are creeping in, for example the practice of monks leaving monasteries to perform ceremonies for cash in neighbouring villages. Such matters are occasionally aired in Buddhist publications and presumably dealt with by local government agencies. Unfortunately we have not seen any information concerning possible relations between Buddhism and secret societies, which might also give rise to state intervention. But in any case, what is missing is the atmosphere of suspicion and hostility that one senses in government attitudes to Christianity. An excellent illustration of this is provided by a report in an overseas edition of a mainland newspaper, intended to impress Hong Kong readers in particular. In spring 1991 Jiang Zemin, Secretary General of the CCP Central Committee, visited the famous Baima Temple in Luoyang. 'During the tour, Jiang Zemin had a chat with the accompanying monks, discussing Buddhist history and creed with them. The General Secretary stopped for a while in front of the two couplets put up in a hall of the temple . . . Jiang Zemin told his companions to jot down the couplets.'[8] Such a relaxed,

---

[8] Zhao Derun, 'Jiang Zeming Discusses Corruption with Luoyang Monk' in *Liaowang*, overseas edition, 17 June 1991, translated in *China Study Journal*, vol. 6 no. 3, December 1991, p. 70.

or even positive, presentation of a top leader's interaction with Christians is at this moment unlikely. Interviews in China with various officials and scholars led us to believe that although the formal legislation and regulations concerning the two religions are virtually identical, the atmosphere and overall feeling of officials are somewhat different. Buddhism is seen as less of a threat, somehow more Chinese, more reasonable, less subversive, less likely to cause trouble.

A major reason for this is the international dimension. The TSPM has been subject to constant monitoring by overseas Protestants, some of whom have taken the trouble to set up substantial programmes of research and publication. Roman Catholic researchers likewise have kept world opinion informed about developments in the Chinese Catholic church. Much of this comment has been neutral, academic and objective in tone, and some of it quite positive. Nevertheless there have also been sharp criticisms of the top leadership and its policies, leaked internal documents have been published, and allegations made about the integrity of some church officials. In short, foreign Christians have assumed the right to comment on the situation in China. But no organization in the Buddhist world plays a similar role. Paradoxically, this may possibly serve believers in China better than a high-profile critique abroad: the political temperature is lower.

This difference may also be understood in the general context of fear of western ideology. To the CCP, it appears unlikely that ideological or political threat will come from the Confucian countries of Japan and Korea, while Taiwan and Hong Kong are special cases. None of them have been noted for vigorous export of notions such as human rights and democracy, which inspired the last anti-government protesters. According to the CCP analysis, the threat comes from the west in general and the USA in particular, and thus is tied to Christianity far more than Buddhism: this opinion was strengthened by events in East Europe and the Soviet Union. Finally, the government will not have failed to notice the growth trends mentioned above, namely that while Buddhism is still quite influential, it is relatively static. If there is to be dynamic growth of a religious alternative it appears to be Protestantism.

We will not attempt a comparative study of Christianity and Buddhism *per se*, but venture a few remarks. On the social level, the distinctive forms of organization are different. For Christians it is normatively the individual as part of a congregation, which should be supervised by a pastor and linked to the universal church. The flexibility of this form of organization is a great advantage, since it can encompass the formal congregations of the official church, which have a clear line of hierarchy up to the World Council of Churches; and can also include home meetings served by travelling evangelists. The sense of belonging and community is very strong.

The Buddhist equivalent is different. A central feature is the monastic life, which so far has no counterpart in Chinese Christianity. It doubtless has advantages and disadvantages. In terms of numbers, the monastic community forms a substantial, committed body of religious professionals. Just as the Christians did, they were able to withstand the battering of thirty years' severely anti-religious policy and survived to train a new generation. But the individual believers, it seemed to us, although they were committed personally, did not have such a strong sense of affiliation. They would be quite happy to worship in any temple, and would usually do so alone, or simultaneously with people they did not know.

In this area we can suggest a significant difference between the two religions, which is seen even more clearly in relations with believers from other countries. In Protestantism, the concept of the universal church, and hence universal communion and fellowship, is a strong motivating force. The concepts may be theological or metaphysical in origin, but they lead to corporate solidarity and even to political action. This can easily have an international impact, as the ecclesial dimension overrides national identities. These concepts are not strongly developed in Buddhism, which tends to be decentralized; the concept of the *sangha*, community of faithful, has rarely had practical implications. Further, the Christian understanding of the Kingdom produces a spirituality that is more likely to result in political activity than the Buddhist notion of the illusory nature of the world.

As regards lay people, Buddhism can offer a reflective and individual approach to spirituality, particularly with people like university intellectuals, who have more interest in the philosophical than the religious aspects. In the case of less educated people, it is probably the sense of well-being through belief in deities like Guanyin that leads them to the temple. These approaches to spirituality have a different feel to the collective atmosphere of congregational singing and prayer. Buddhism can still provide a collective and emotional inspiration, as noted in section three, particularly in pilgrimages and festivals. The occasions which appear to be congruent with this in the Christian traditions are various periods of pilgrimage and celebration in the Catholic year, for example the ascent of Sheshan by the fishing people around Shanghai. Another event is the celebration of Christmas, which is becoming ever more heated despite government attempts to cool down popular enthusiasm. Reports from Christmas 1991 mentioned 20,000 people attempting to attend mass at a Beijing church on Christmas Eve.[9] Perhaps, given time, Christmas will 'indigenize', and that should provoke a lot of noise, fun and human fellow-feeling, as Chinese religious celebrations tend to do. What would be made of it by the rather earnest and puritanical British missionaries of the Victorian era, it is hard to say. Both Buddhism and Christianity, then, seem able to provide the setting for a mass emotional release. Their ability to continue doing so may prove an important factor in their future.

What can one conclude from the whole picture? Buddhism is more deeply rooted in traditional Chinese culture and enjoys a more relaxed relationship with the State. The famous monasteries are in working order, increasing numbers of monks and nuns are being ordained, and will be able to take Chinese Buddhism forward into the next century. Intellectuals can find a wide range of materials to study on the philosophy and religious

[9] CNCR 1898, 3 January 1992.

practices, and less educated people can enjoy the facilities for displays of popular religiosity. Buddhism enjoys continuity – with the faith and the institutions that existed before 1949, and stretching back to classical China. In this sense one can talk about a revival of Buddhism since 1979, a revival which has been modest rather than spectacular, but firmly rooted. However, one should also be aware of something that may be harder to notice: namely the tremendous disruption of the tradition that has occurred. Continuity may be superficial, and mask deep changes, for example in the loss of transmission.

The Protestant churches' growth has been far more spectacular, and one should not really call it revival, since it is for the most part a new phenomenon. It is too early to say that the religion is as deeply rooted as Buddhism. Undoubtedly it is in some areas, where there have been communities of faithful believers for many years, who stood firm throughout the worst periods. Similarly there are certain individuals, some of them well known, who one can guess will remain pillars of faith as long as they live. On the other hand one suspects that some of the groups that came into being during the 'Christianity Fever' of the mid-1980s may have less staying power. They may either disband, or perhaps stray further into the fields of 'Christo-paganism'.

At present both religions are contributing to the psychological well-being of Chinese society. In fact if one talks with believers in Christian or Buddhist circles it is quite inspiring. They seem to be more positive and confident than many non-believers, neither carried away by consumerism, despondent about corruption nor cynical about life in general. It is a sign of a degree of maturity in the Chinese communist system, that some officials recognize that these people are as good citizens as anyone else, that they deserve respect and the right to practise their religions without interference. Since Chinese people have long been known for their accommodating attitude to differing beliefs, perhaps in the future they will have a role to play in the interaction between the two religions. That, incidentally, will raise the topical question of the universality of the church and its understanding of other religious traditions: it will be interesting to see what becomes of that.

THE ROMAN CATHOLIC CHURCH IN CHINA

Catholic missionary strategy was different from that of the Protestants: the key policy was to create a secure environment for believers through the ownership of land in Catholic villages. Converts were encouraged to migrate to these villages, and this laid the basis for the rural communities of Catholics that are still central to the Church today.[10] Inside the villages the communities became deeply committed to the faith, closely knit and, as it turned out, able to resist repression. On the other hand, the system caused resentment and led to an isolationist mentality, drawing a line between Catholic communities and the surrounding culture. It also meant that many Catholics were, and still are, from poor rural families with low levels of education. In addition, certain occupational groups became Catholic, important examples being fishing peoples in the lower Yangtze basin and in villages on the southeastern coast, and there were substantial Catholic populations in the treaty ports and Beijing.

The Catholic hierarchy in China before 1949 promoted an ultra-conservative theology isolated from European modernism. Likewise, it had little contact with national intellectual life, and there was considerable hostility between foreign and Chinese priests. In the Civil War of 1945–9, the Church openly supported the GMD against the CCP, consonant with the Vatican's anti-communist stance. Senior Catholics made belligerent speeches and hurriedly prepared for an underground existence. Two initiatives were the creation of a large organization for lay Catholics, the Legion of Mary, and the rapid ordination of a large number of Chinese priests in early 1949. No accommodation was sought with the communists, and the Vatican refused to recognize the new government in 1949.

Following directives from Rome, the Inter-Nuncio Archbishop Riberi issued instructions to Chinese Catholics prohibit-

---

[10] In this chapter 'the Church' is used for convenience to refer to the Roman Catholic church in China.

ing them from associating with the communists, joining the army, participating in social programmes, attending schools or reading government newspapers and literature. Catholic leaders rejected CCP demands for control over the Church in the early 1950s. In March 1951 Riberi attacked the principle of the 'Three Self' and condemned a statement calling for the autonomy of the Chinese church: he declared that anyone following a 'patriotic' movement would be excommunicated. He was deported in September 1951, and in the following four years all missionary personnel were expelled from China or imprisoned. Attempts by Rome to control the Church were interpreted by the CCP as imperialist interference in Chinese affairs, and as reactionary sabotage. Chinese Catholics were caught in a dilemma: either to obey the Church and risk punishment by the government, or participate in socialist construction and risk excommunication.

The CCP had difficulty in persuading either clergy or lay persons to co-operate, and no rapid solution comparable to that for Buddhists and Protestants was found. The Catholic community was subjected to persecution, particularly in the 1955 Anti-Counter-Revolutionary Campaign that also targeted Protestants who refused to join the TSPM. Intransigent leaders were incarcerated and replaced by more malleable ones, effective resistance was crushed, and by 1957 the CCP was finally able to announce the formation of a 'patriotic organization', in many respects similar to the TSPM, namely the Chinese Catholic Patriotic Association (CCPA).[11] The CCPA recognized the Pope's spiritual authority, but denied him any right to interfere in Chinese affairs. Crucially, the CCPA asserted its right to conduct episcopal consecrations without approval from Rome. In response, Pope Pius XII issued an encyclical letter that condemned the CCPA as a schismatic and rebellious church, and urged loyal Catholics to act against the CCPA.

The period from 1951 to 1979 was one of martyrdom for many Catholics. The Church was a prime target of the repressive religious policies. Historically it was aligned with the

[11] Referred to by some authors as the CPA or CPCA.

GMD and the imperialist powers; it asserted that the head of the Church was a foreigner, namely the Pope; it rejected the right of the CCP to influence matters such as selection of church officials; the communities were tightly knit and hard to manipulate. Inevitably, most churches were closed, Catholic publishing stopped, clergy laicized or imprisoned and public practice of the religion ended. The Cultural Revolution completed the business, as with the Protestant community. Churches were confiscated, and some priests and believers treated with great brutality. All services stopped with the exception of a few in Nantang cathedral, Beijing, for the diplomatic community.

Little is known about the survival of Catholicism during these years, but the traditions were kept alive in Catholic families. When open religious activities recommenced in 1979, it was found that the Catholic community was still ardently devoted to its religious life, and moreover many children had been initiated into the faith in the intervening years. There was also a deep suspicion of the CCP and of the official organizations that were reimposed to control the Church.[12]

THE CHURCH IN THE POST-MAO PERIOD

After 1979 public services were again permitted. The initial response was not enthusiastic, and low attendances were reported at the major Catholic churches in 1980, probably because believers were sceptical of the government's sincerity. In the next few years there was a major recovery of religious life seen in the revival of churches, publications, seminaries, foreign contacts and pilgrimages; however the divisions in the Church, Sino-Vatican relations, and state–church relations remained problematic. This led to a new outbreak of confrontation in 1989, which we consider below.

Church authorities responded in various ways to the new policy. The key question was that of personnel. The Church suffered an acute shortage of priests after 1955: all foreign priests had been expelled, many Chinese ones had died, no new ones

[12] Chan, *Contextual Ecclesiology*, especially pp. 450–8, provides bibliographic references for the above account. Hanson, *Catholic Politics*, covers the 1950s in some detail.

were trained. In 1982 there were about 1,300 priests in China, all of them elderly. Despite the opening of new seminaries, it was estimated that by 1997 the number of clergy from the elder generation would be less than 300, while the total number of new priests would be only around 400.[13] The sacramental needs of the Catholic community will thus remain a major concern for many years. As with Protestants, Catholic communities in many locations are inevitably self-supervising and have only limited contact with religious professionals. There was progress also in printing and recovery of church property.[14]

A striking aspect of the Church until the late 1980s was the preservation of pre-Vatican II traditions, such as the Tridentine Mass and the tonsure. Almost all masses were conducted in Latin with priests facing the altar. The Latin Missal was reprinted and widely used. The daily routine of seminarians basically followed the pattern established in the late 1940s, as did their curriculum. Most grass-roots believers apparently felt that refusal to change their traditions was a symbol of faithfulness and perseverance. Typical attitudes were that 'the same masses are celebrated, the same prayers are said'; or 'we have not forgotten any of the teachings we learned before'; or 'we believe in the Church: One, Holy, Catholic and Apostolic'. They thereby emphasized loyal adherence to orthodox Catholic faith; probably unbeknown to most of the congregations, orthodoxy itself had meanwhile changed.[15] Nevertheless by 1990 changes were starting to occur, and apparently spreading rapidly. Foreign visitors began to introduce new ideas and practices, especially through the major seminaries. In 1990, the largest church in Shanghai offered one mass every Sunday in the vernacular, although it also offered one in Latin. Recent reports suggest that the changeover to the Chinese mass has become widely accepted both in official and unofficial circles.

A related issue is the celibacy of clergy. There are many married Chinese clergymen, including bishops as well as priests,

---

[13] See *China Study Journal*, vol. 6 no. 2, August 1991, p. 51; and *Zhongguo Tianzhujiao*, (*Catholic Church in China*), no. 4, 1991, pp. 23–9.
[14] Lambert, *Resurrection*, p. 179; *China Study Journal*, vol. 6 no. 2, p. 51.
[15] *China Communication* (Singapore), no. 7, July 1984, p. 7.

although it is not clear how many of the marriages are valid in a sacramental as well as civil manner. A group of priests in a northern diocese explained their predicament in a letter addressed to the Pope: 'Many of us are married, but in all cases these marriages are invalid, and in many cases the marriages are not consummated. It is under considerable duress that we went through the ceremony, and we intend to have these marriages civilly dissolved at the first opportunity.'[16] The 'considerable duress' doubtless refers to the insistence of CCP officials that the persons concerned marry, a tactic which was also used with Buddhist monks, presumably to reduce the number of religious professionals and to damage their credibility. Chinese Catholics place a strong emphasis on the vow of celibacy, and they refuse to accept these married clergy. For the faithful, the celibacy of the priesthood is treasured as a symbol for the continuity of tradition and loyalty to Rome.[17]

Thus far, the picture is relatively positive and comparable to the revival of the Protestant church. For much of the decade there was a genuine relaxation of control and a spontaneous resurgence of Catholic practice. Despite certain reservations, the official organizations presided over a successful recovery. However, the rift in the Church that dated back to 1949 was not healed. In 1979 pro-government Catholics, working under the RAB and UFWD, revived the CCPA, the functions of which were to supervise religious activities, rally Catholic support for the government, appoint personnel, promote the autonomy of the Chinese church and cultivate foreign contacts. In 1980 two other bodies were formed, the National Administrative Commission of the Catholic Church in China and the Chinese Bishops College. The three organizations are technically separate, although in practice they work together closely, and top leaders hold posts concurrently in the three hierarchies. The Chinese Catholic church is in theory an autocephalic church independent of foreign authority. Chinese leaders maintain that the early church, according to the Bible, was governed by the collective leadership of the apostles and not by an individual, and

[16] Joseph Spae, 'Catholic Life in a Chinese Village', *China Update*, September 1982, supplement no. 1 (for private distribution), p. 9.
[17] For further details see Chan, *Contextual Ecclesiology*, pp. 145–55.

that their organizational structure has biblical justification.[18]

Such structures are familiar from our earlier discussion of the Protestant situation. The new bodies were similar to the Protestant CCC, and were supposed to be a more acceptable form of supervision over the church than the overtly political CCPA. Like the TSPM/CCC, the organizations represented the interests of Catholics when dealing with various government agencies, for example helping to restore churches and to rehabilitate Catholic prisoners. They appear to have been modestly successful in persuading ordinary believers of their good faith. The pro-government Catholic structures began to expand, attract support from believers and form a self-sustained ecclesiastical community. However, resentment of the CCPA carried over from the 1950s to the late 1970s, and many, perhaps most, Chinese Catholics declined to co-operate with the organization. It is impossible to assess the relative strength of the two groups. Some observers estimate that 20 per cent of Catholics co-operated with the CCPA, while others put the figure at only 2 per cent.[19] The CCPA frequently issues statements expressing its whole-hearted support for socialism and for the CCP, and was not slow to praise the suppression of the democracy movement in 1989.

In the same period, pro-Roman Catholics were creating what amounts to a parallel church. They re-established contacts with the Vatican and organized independent activities such as pilgrimages, regional councils, training programmes and the production of devotional materials. In order to build a hierarchy loyal to Rome, some pro-Roman bishops, who did not participate in the CCPA or affiliated groups, secretly consecrated new bishops and ordained priests, and even organized a national episcopal conference, placing a strong emphasis on loyalty to the Pope. This challenged the ecclesiastical authority claimed by the patriotic associations, and also ignored official regulations. Further, some pro-Roman priests instructed believers not to attend masses in the open churches because priests there belonged to the CCPA.[20]

---

[18] *Catholic Church in China*, no. 1, November 1980, p. 21.

[19] *Correspondence* (Hong Kong), no. 12, May/June 1983, p. 8.

[20] Various reports of these activities were published outside China in the early 1980s, for example G. Dunne, 'The Prisoners of Shanghai', *China Update*, no. 6, Winter 1983, pp. 46–56.

From 1979 the government knew of the existence of pro-Roman Catholics, but at first did not take any serious action against them. For a period there was a certain amount of mutual toleration, partly because both tendencies – pro-Roman and pro-government – were preoccupied by pressing issues such as the reopening of churches and training of new priests. But as the unofficial activities escalated, the government decided it could no longer tolerate them and started to tighten controls. A series of arrests of pro-Roman bishops, priests and laymen took place in 1981 and 1982, after which the pro-Romans acted more discreetly. Some went underground, some joined the open church. The charges against those arrested varied, but were all related to civil and political crimes, for example 'hampering production and modernization', 'collecting intelligence reports', 'carrying out incitements' and 'colluding with foreign countries'.[21] On occasion, Chinese officials admitted that the refusal to break with Rome was the underlying reason for the crackdown. As could be expected from discussions earlier in this book, most western observers interpreted these arrests as violations of religious liberty and human rights. They praised the arrested Catholics as martyrs for their faith and prisoners of conscience. The Chinese government regarded it as legitimate action to preserve social order against 'a small minority who persist in their reactionary position and publicly say that they prefer to be controlled by foreign authority'.[22]

The contradictions between pro-government and independent groups are parallel to those in the Protestant community, but the Catholic situation is complicated by a further issue, namely the international dimension. The understanding of ecclesiastical authority by the Chinese government and the Vatican are diametrically opposed.[23] Needless to say, the CCP rejects any claims of the Vatican to authority over believers. Rome appears to uphold the tradition of imperialism against which the Chinese people had struggled: the Vatican was believed to have supported Spanish, German, Italian and Japanese Fascism before and during the Second World War,

---

[21] For details see Chan, *Contextual Ecclesiology*, p. 178.
[22] *Ibid.*, p. 180.   [23] *Ibid.*, pp. 104–8.

and the GMD in the Chinese Civil War. It was the second nation, after Japan, to recognize the puppet government of Manchuko in the 1930s, and did not support the Chinese in their anti-Japanese war of 1937–45. After 1949, the Vatican refused to recognize the government in Beijing as legitimate ruler of China, but rather that in Taibei; in 1992 it was the only European state to do so. Not surprisingly, the Vatican is regarded as a hostile political entity.

Through the 1980s there were attempts to resolve the interlocking problems of the divisions between Chinese Catholics and the rift between the Vatican and Beijing. At times both sides made conciliatory gestures and initiated talks through intermediaries. Beijing's primary demand was that the Vatican should break off relations with Taiwan and recognize the People's Republic as the only legitimate government of China; in return for this they would recognize the spiritual authority of the Pope in the Church, while retaining some practical powers in Chinese hands. This would have opened the way to a reconciliation between the factions inside China. However, every time a *rapprochement* appeared close, it foundered. This was to some extent due to intransigence on both sides, but also to a mutual lack of understanding that resulted in insensitive actions. In the event no serious progress was made and the Church remained divided.

Nevertheless, Chinese Catholicism was flourishing at the end of the 1980s. Officials admit to around three and a half million believers, with some 50,000 new converts every year. A significant difference with the Protestant community is that the Catholic church is numerically strongest in provinces of north China, particularly Hebei which has perhaps a quarter of the national Catholic population, a legacy of missionary history. Unofficial observers have put numbers at around five million who sometimes attend open churches, and another five million who are resolutely 'pro-Roman'. Presumably the discrepancies are similar to those discussed with reference to Protestants. We cannot judge the accuracy of the various estimates. No one, as far as we are aware, has put forward claims of massive growth comparable to those made concerning Protestantism.

CATHOLIC RELIGIOUS LIFE

After 1979, Catholics demonstrated a deep desire for public expression of faith and for sacramental worship. In the early 1980s, priests in rural areas devoted their time to performing sacraments, especially mass, confirmation, baptism and communion. These had been forbidden for at least twenty years in most places, and ordinary believers were desperately keen to revive them. At every major feast day, churches were packed with worshippers waiting to receive the Eucharist. Believers sometimes travelled hundreds of miles to attend church. Formal services are still central to the whole life of the Church, and an aspect that foreign visitors can share relatively easily. Observers in the early 1980s had the interesting opportunity to see liturgy that had hardly been practised elsewhere for a decade. In recent years they could witness the result of reform, with services conducted in modern Chinese and congregational participation. The services in open churches are evidence of the vitality of orthodox Catholicism. As with Protestantism, foreign visitors are frequently struck by the depth of emotion and spiritual feeling they witness.

Pilgrimage also revived. In 1980 a few priests from Shanghai, newly released from prison, announced that the Virgin Mary would appear at Sheshan in March. In spite of pressure from the CCP and the CCPA, over ten thousand pilgrims went to this important religious centre. Most of them were fishing people and peasants, some from far away. They made their way on their knees up the hill and performed devotional acts of prayer as they passed by the shrines, chanting, singing hymns and lighting candles. Similar pilgrimages were reported from elsewhere.

Catholic villages, many where churches had been closed for thirty years, began to organize devotional gatherings. These were grass-roots efforts, that only later were facilitated, or regulated, by officials from the CCPA. Devotional objects such as holy pictures, medallions, rosaries and crucifixes were much venerated. Some were privately produced, others came from dioceses and were made available to local Catholics on feast days. Holy water was also much in demand. The following is a vignette of Catholic devotion from 1980:

At the back of the church there were two peasant families. One put up a small picture of Our Lady, and lit candles before it. The other family put up a mirror with a small holy picture attached, and lit two rows of candles in front of it. These two families were kneeling in front of the pictures. I saw some people from the city kneeling in silence with tears on their cheeks.[24]

In pre-Vatican II Catholic life, sacraments were at the centre of practice, devotional objects were treasured and regarded as essential for spirituality, pilgrimage and Marian devotion were extremely popular. Since the Chinese church had not been exposed to reform and was isolated from the Catholic world, it is understandable that these should be prominent features of the revival. Further, the CCP policy of restricting religious life to the personal sphere precluded the social dimension of Catholic teaching, such as social ethics. Chinese Catholic spirituality is characterized by eschatological orientation, with a strong emphasis on death, judgement, heaven and hell, which again reflects older traditions. As Lambert notes, these are parallel to the Protestant house church concerns.[25] Another aspect of Catholic spirituality that cannot be ignored is the witness of those who spent many years in prison: a classic example is the autobiography of Archbishop Dominic Tang (Deng Yiming), imprisoned from 1958 to 1980.[26] Harrowing descriptions of the Chinese *gulag* were written by Catholic prisoners.

There has been renewed interest in Catholic social service of various kinds, and official journals publish reports of medical and psychiatric surgeries, cultural tuition, painting, dental health training, repair of electrical equipment, teaching of pre-school age children and many other initiatives.[27] Church

---

[24] Wang Shaojin, 'A Catholic Pilgrimage in China', *Religion in Communist Lands*, no. 10, Spring 1982, pp. 91–6 (p. 96). For the preceding paragraphs see Chan, *Contextual Ecclesiology*, chapter 3, 'The Life of the Chinese Church'.

[25] Lambert, *Resurrection*, p. 183.

[26] Dominic Tang, *How Inscrutable His Ways: Memoirs 1951–1981*, Hong Kong, privately printed, no date.

[27] *China Study Journal*, vol. 6 no. 1, April 1991, pp. 45–6 translates one such item.

organizations have also helped Catholic aid agencies, such as CAFOD, to initiate programmes in China. These efforts would probably increase if government constraints were lifted. The official Catholic journal, like its Protestant counterpart, also makes much of Catholic contributions to productivity, public morality and economic progress.

As public activities resumed many young believers sought participation in a formal catechumenate before official initiation into the Church by confirmation or validation of baptism. In some areas there were new converts from non-Catholic families, who also required catechetical classes. These were rapidly established in the major centres such as Beijing, Tianjin and Guangzhou. It was apparent that children had been baptized and received Catholic faith from their parents when regular ecclesiastical activities had been suspended: children of Catholic families usually knew the basic beliefs and practices of the faith, such as the sign of the cross and recitation of the Rosary.

The future of Chinese Catholic spiritual life will depend to a great extent on the orientation of seminary graduates. Training is mostly provided by elderly Chinese teachers, complemented in some major seminaries by highly qualified overseas personnel. Although many classes are taped, and the transcripts scrutinized by government agencies, such teaching is securely in the mainstream of orthodox Catholicism.[28] However the government is determined to include political study in the curriculum. A lengthy article in the official Catholic journal in 1991 bears the title: 'Ideological political work must be put in first place among all our work in the seminary.'According to the author, political indoctrination should focus on patriotism, socialism and opposition to bourgeois liberalization. In particular, seminarians could be used by hostile foreign subversive forces: 'financial subsidies, ideological corrosion and overseas studies try to fight with us for the younger generation'.[29]

Overall the political indoctrination has only limited impact.

[28] *China Study Journal*, vol. 5 no. 2, August 1990, p. 16.
[29] *Catholic Church in China*, no. 4, 1991, pp. 23–9. English summary in CNCR 1863, 4 October 1991.

At the heart of the Church the dedication of priests and lay persons, doubtless both inside and outside particular hierarchies, is extremely moving. The following was written recently by a priest who returned to his vocation after thirty years in the wilderness of labour-camps:

Late at night I was half-asleep in bed. The Cathedral clock had chimed ten. I heard somebody knocking at the door of the priests' quarters. Who could it be at such a late hour? Perhaps it was a Catholic asking a priest to go to his family to administer Extreme Unction. I put on an overcoat and went downstairs. I opened the door and saw an unfamiliar middle-aged lady looking very frightened. Before I could say anything, she rushed inside and closed the door. I had to step backward in a hurry.

'Are you a priest?' she asked nervously.

'Yes, I am. Who are you looking for?'

'I am not a Catholic, Father, but I wish to talk to you,' she said hesitatingly.

'It's all right. Do come in.'

She sat down and told me her story. She was a pianist, married with three children. Recently her husband suffered a nervous breakdown. He turned the house into chaos and caused trouble day and night. Instead of helping, her relatives and neighbours laughed at her and gossiped about her. Fortunately her children had gone away for their studies. She tried to endure the situation and hoped to convince her husband to receive medical treatment. He refused to go and his mental disorder seemed to intensify. Just an hour before, he had taken a knife from the kitchen threatening to kill her. She had to run out of the house. She was all in tears as she said, 'I ran aimlessly in the street, wondering where I could turn to. There is really nowhere I can go. I suddenly stopped and saw a Catholic church in front of me . . .'

What could I do for this poor lady? I took her to the Church Guest-house for the night. We would see what could be done the next day.

Lord, I am your unworthy servant. I have only done what I should do.[30]

As with Buddhism, it is often difficult to distinguish between genuine continuity and a kind of new development, modelled on a fragment of the past that has somehow survived. An example is

---

[30] Tan Tiende, 'My Life' in *Family News of the Catholic Church in China*, edited by Yeung Cho Woon, Hong Kong: Holy Spirit Study Centre, 1990, pp. 8–51 (p. 49).

the revival in the 1980s of convent life. The Catholic religious orders appear to have been abolished in China in the 1950s, and as far as we know have not been reinstated. Yet convents exist, often led by elderly nuns who received their spiritual formation before 1949. One wonders what their status is now with regard to the religious orders, and what kind of spirituality operates in these convents? Will the orders be revived in China? What are the implications of their abolition?

DEVELOPMENTS AFTER 1989

Until early 1989 many Catholics still hoped for an early settlement between Beijing and the Vatican, and between 'official' and 'pro-Roman' churches. But between 1989 and 1992 several developments in the Chinese Catholic world made this impossible: the emergence of a militant 'underground'; increasing weakness of the pro-government Catholic organizations; greater tension between Beijing and the Vatican; tighter controls on believers. The problems are linked both with international developments and events earlier in the decade.

In late 1979 the Vatican granted exemptions to underground pastors, mostly concerning canonical regulations for the celebration of sacraments, in recognition of the difficult conditions under which they worked. Following urgent requests from China, it also gave permission to certain bishops – those who were steadfastly loyal to Rome – to nominate and consecrate their successors, and even to select bishops for neighbouring dioceses. As Tang puts it, this was seen as 'the green light to build a church in opposition'.[31] There were at least fifty consecrations by 1989, and a large number of ordinations. Sources close to the Vatican have informally indicated that this may have been a mistake: many of the newly consecrated bishops were unsuitable for their posts, or lacked experience. Of the secretly ordained priests, many were very young and poorly educated. Some were apparently mostly zealous in promoting sectarian rivalry with their official counterparts rather than in

---

[31] Edmond Tang, '1989, A Year of Confrontation', in Hunter and Rimmington (eds.), *All Under Heaven*, pp. 69–79.

serious pastoral care: 'as regards their theology and understanding of canon law, it is to be observed that they have become more and more militant and intolerant, to the point where their teaching has to be called outright heretical'.[32]

According even to relatively pro-Roman observers, such as a Taiwanese bishop quoted by Edmond Tang, the underground priests, commonly known as 'little black priests', created considerable trouble: 'these young priests were more specialized in acts of denunciation and "knowledge" about excommunications than in the doctrines of the Church or pastoral work among the faithful. They publicly denounced other pastors and preached that the sacraments administered by the "patriots" were invalid.' The bishop concluded that:

The Holy See must come out with sanctions and regulations to ensure that underground bishops do not unnecessarily ordain new bishops and priests . . . These 'little black priests', so-called by the Christians, do not spread the Gospel; instead they foster hatred amongst the faithful. They do not preach God's word; instead they engage in name-calling and labeling other people. Obviously the church is divided; hence, the Christians are scandalized and have no wish to go to church.[33]

Tensions had been brewing beneath the surface since 1979 at least. In 1989 they came into the open in a series of incidents between Catholics and government forces. Security forces attacked Catholic villagers and underground seminaries in Hebei, causing several deaths, and arrested scores of bishops and priests throughout China between 1989 and 1992.[34] The arrests emphasized the widening breach between underground forces and the official hierarchy. In November 1989, for example, a conference of underground bishops and priests was held in secret in Shaanxi province, with the aim of establishing a clandestine Chinese Bishops Conference which would be in full unity with

[32] George Evers, 'The Catholic Church in China', *China Study Journal*, vol. 5 no. 3, December 1990, pp. 12–14.
[33] Cited in Tang, 'Year of Confrontation', pp. 75–6.
[34] For example, nine bishops and twenty-three priests and lay persons arrested in December 1989 and January 1990; novices and seminarians physically assaulted by police in December 1990. Reports in *China Study Journal*, vol. 5 no. 1, April 1990, p. 54; vol. 6 no. 2, August 1991, p. 57.

Rome, and would form an effective, explicit opposition to the CCPA. Several 'loyal' bishops circulated statements openly critical of the CCP, its religious policy, and the 'patriotic organizations'.

Control over the Catholic church became an important item on the religious policy agenda. The guidelines of current policy were stated in a circular known as 'Document 3', published on 9 March 1989, that originated in the CCP Central Committee. Its main thrust is that Chinese Catholics must be autonomous and not accept directives from the Vatican. The Vatican must break diplomatic ties with Taiwan and not interfere in religious affairs in China. All bishops must be appointed unilaterally by the (official) Chinese church, which must be financially independent and self-supporting. The document admits the existence of bishops and priests appointed in secret by pro-Roman clergy, and insists that they must recognize the leadership of the Party.[35]

A new round of controls over pro-Roman groups had thus already been initiated before the democracy movement of spring 1989. The Church was not involved in the movement, but the swing to hard-line policies inevitably led to increasing implementation of repressive policies. The Hong Kong news agency UCAN reported on a crackdown that started in December 1990 in Hebei in particular, when clerics were detained, and various reports emerged of arrests, harassments, closure of seminaries. Sometimes the pressure extended not only to 'pro-Roman' activities but even to institutions operating under CCPA auspices.

Meanwhile the Vatican appeared to be in an increasingly confident mood. In June 1991 it revealed that the Pope had appointed a Chinese Catholic Bishop, Ignatius Kung Pin-mei, as cardinal *in pectore*, or in secret, in June 1979. (Kung was at the time a prisoner in Shanghai, and steadfastly loyal to Rome. He served a thirty-three year sentence before his release at the age of eighty-seven.) The CCPA immediately denounced the an-

---

[35] A synopsis of the document is in Edmond Tang, *The Catholic Church in the People's Republic of China*, Leuven, Belgium: Pro Mundi Vita Studies, no. 15, June 1990, pp. 24–6.

nouncement as a violation of the principle of independence and self-administration.[36] In September 1991 a senior Jesuit announced that a large number of Chinese bishops, including many in the CCPA, were in secret communion with the Pope, and simply bowing to force of circumstances for the time being. This was a direct challenge to the credibility of the CCPA. On the diplomatic level, Sino-Vatican negotiations reached an impasse following 4 June 1989. One interpretation is that the Vatican foresaw the end of communism in China, following its demise in East Europe, and thus had no need to make any concessions, rather preferring to wait, or perhaps even to encourage opposition. For the moment, the situation is confused and tense. Probably it is the local communities of Catholics themselves, who have already borne the burden of oppression for four decades, who will continue to be confused and demoralized by political arguments.

By 1992, the CCPA and the government had reportedly lost a great deal of credibility, not only among the 'Catholic masses' but even among members of the CCPA itself, as evidenced by the large number of bishops allegedly loyal to Rome. It relies entirely on the power of the secular authority, backed by force where necessary; instead of a 'united front' organ, however flawed, it has become purely an administrative agency. This has isolated the pro-government hard-liners at the top of the organization, and is leading to increasing reconciliation among other Catholics, the vast majority of whom are loyal to the Vatican. However, because of the distortions caused by repression and political manoeuvering, there is still a great deal of tension in Catholic circles that will require years of patient effort to dispel.

CATHOLICS AND PROTESTANTS

To return to the main theme of our study, what can be learned about the Protestant church and its place in Chinese society from the Catholic experience? And, incidentally, what are the

---

[36] *New China News Agency*, Beijing, 18 June 1991.

implications for the CCP and the Vatican, and what lessons emerge for viewing the Protestant and Roman Catholic traditions generally?

The Catholic church in China has been deeply influenced by its history prior to 1949. Its traditional anti-communism has been maintained by the Vatican, by officials of the underground church and presumably members of the congregations. It is in fact almost unique in China as a social group that has never accepted communist rule. The majority of believers did not bow to the 'patriotic' association, and there have been numerous instances of passive or active rejection. Even the CCPA itself has many members who secretly support the underground church; their reason for participation in the CCPA is only that open seminaries and churches would otherwise be impossible.

Most Catholics still recognize a non-Chinese institution, namely the papacy, as head of their church. The *locus* of authority is thus outside China. This attitude gives them additional strength and motivation to resist communist claims to control the national religious life. Linked with this is an extreme traditionalism, symbolized by insistence on celibacy for the priesthood. Even if the Vatican reverses its policy on celibacy, which seems unlikely at present, it would surely take many years for this to be acceptable in China. On the other hand, curiously, congregations are not strongly opposed to abortion or contraception, which is another dividing line between reformists and conservatives in western Catholicism. These issues are rarely raised by Chinese Catholics of any persuasion, and it is thought that most believers simply follow national guidelines on birth-control.

The Protestant community was historically less overtly anti-communist: conservative missionaries tended to be apolitical and some liberals even co-operated with the CCP. There is in Protestantism a different conception of the universal church, and no *locus* of authority in any one personage or institution. Thus the question of authority over the Chinese Protestant churches was handled simply by ending the missionary presence and carefully controlling interaction with foreign church organizations. The majority of overseas Protestants have refrained from attacking the Chinese government, and only a few evangelical organizations have made sorties into China; even then, perhaps with very occasional exceptions, they have not claimed authority over indigenous groups. Also, the question of international diplomacy is for the most part absent, with the exception of human rights issues. Their impact cannot be compared to that of the overseas Catholic interest in China, although both 'undergrounds' – Protestant and Catholic – receive substantial aid and resources from abroad.

The Catholic church in China is characterized by its strong communities and generational transmission, again a legacy of missionary history. Often whole villages or sections of towns are largely Catholic, and children are inducted into the faith even at times of repression. Some reports suggest that families are finding it hard to maintain this faith now that more distractions abound near the affluent cities. Growth appears to have been slower than for Protestants in the 1980s. Increase in Catholic numbers perhaps results more from population growth within established communities, rather than from evangelism outside them. There has been no talk of a 'Catholic fever', and the expression 'Christianity fever' refers to the Protestant situation.

Socially, Protestants are more dispersed. More of them are converts, and fewer have grown up in tightly-knit faith communities. Geographically the two religions are stronger in different areas of the country: Catholicism in the north, although with a strong presence in Fujian; Protestantism in the southeastern provinces and Henan. However in some cities and provinces, for example Shanghai and Fujian, there are relatively large concentrations of both. Shanghai has around 120,000 of each. Fujian perhaps 250,000 Catholics and 650,000 Protestants. In such places, both of which were important areas of foreign influence, Christianity as a whole provides a real religious alternative for a substantial part of the population.

In religious practice, we have reported greater diversity among Protestants. This may be because of lack of data, but it may reflect important differences between the two traditions. In Protestant traditions greater emphasis is placed on personal religious experience rather than formalized liturgical structures, and, as we have seen, personal study and interpretation of the Bible are strongly encouraged. Healing or prayer for it may be attempted by anyone, and the sense of the priesthood of all believers is strongly held. In contrast, Catholic spirituality is linked above all to the major sacraments and Mass, and to a hierarchy of authority culminating in Rome: the Church still tends to be relatively institutional and monolithic. The Bible is used for recitation rather than personal study, and priesthood is reserved for those men appointed to it. Healing and exorcism have hardly been reported, perhaps because they should only be conducted by clergy, who are in short supply. Yet by necessity the Catholic community is if anything even more self-supervising and lay led than the Protestant: there are only about a thousand priests for the whole community, and hundreds of thousands of Catholics may see a priest only rarely.

It is easier for Protestants to accommodate to the surrounding environment. They have no need to seek authorization for their personal interpretations of scripture or doctrine, and may form independent sects. No ecclesiastical authority can legitimately criticize or control them, even if they engage in practices considered by some to be heterodox. (An irony of the situation is that the TSPM, a communist united front organization, is responsible for maintaining Protestant doctrinal orthodoxy in China.) It appears that the Catholic church retains its identity more strongly, but consequently is less adaptable. Similarly, its greater emphasis on sacraments results in greater orthodoxy, but at the expense of wider propagation. On the whole the Protestants, with their greater flexibility, may find it easier to spread their influence, but harder to retain orthodoxy.

As for the CCP, it probably sees its task as damage limitation. One supposes that few CCP leaders have much sympathy for the Catholic faith or for the Vatican as a political entity. But pragmatically they have to deal with a community of believers and with international politics. As we have seen, their tactics throughout the 1980s have been quite predictable and consistent. They try to promote the CCPA and to 'win over' as many of the masses as possible. Supervision in the official churches and seminaries is maintained as strongly as possibly, probably more than in the Protestant equivalents. Since total control is impossible, the Party turns a blind eye to 'pro-Roman' activities as long as these are relatively low key. When the latter start to be provocative or to influence large numbers of people, it uses force to repress them. Police action is probably a reluctant choice, since it immediately produces international criticism, which the Beijing government avoids where possible, although not at the expense of losing control of any situation in China itself. In the longer term the CCP would like to resolve the diplomatic impasse with the Vatican, but not at the price of humiliating concessions. The diplomatic dimension may become more important depending on developments in Hong Kong and Taiwan.

The Catholic church in China raises many questions. The standpoint of the official Chinese Catholic church is that it can remain a legitimate part of the universal church, while still rejecting papal authority over a whole range of issues. Thus it maintains that the papacy has no right to assert authority over appointment of bishops. In light of the disagreements in world Catholicism over matters such as celibacy, birth control and liberation theology, this raises a crucial point: what right does a pope have to impose his wishes on a local church? This perhaps explains the enormous pains which the Vatican has taken to ensure its influence in China. Were the official church in fact to become united, popularly supported and independent, it would indeed be a significant challenge to Rome, perhaps a model for others to follow.[37]

Curiously it is the CCP which has been the Vatican's saviour in this situation. The mass of believers is so alienated by the treatment they have received from the government that they do not consider the official church as a legitimate representative. On the contrary, loyalty to the Pope is a symbol of opposition to the current regime. If the Catholic masses did genuinely support

[37] A relatively sophisticated presentation of the 'official' case is made by Bishop Tu Shihua in *Catholic Church in China*, no. 3, 1990, part of which is translated in *China Study Journal*, vol. 5 no. 3, December 1990, pp. 52–4.

the official church, and the latter developed further friendly relations with churches in the USA or Germany, one wonders what would be the consequences for the Church of Rome.

CHAPTER 7

Into the 1990s

THE CHURCH IN 1992

We have seen that the state of religion in China is much influenced by political considerations among the top leadership of the CCP. The liberal regime of the 1980s allowed a period of rapid growth for the Protestant church, and revival of other religious activities. Then in 1989 a hard-line tendency gained control of the Party apparatus after the suppression of the democracy movement. The new leadership maintained that stability was the most urgent national priority, and imposed more repressive policies in the cultural field, coupled with a slowdown of economic reform, sharp criticism of western interference, and attempts to promote communist ideology. In the first few months of 1992 it was reported that reformists were staging a comeback, apparently under the leadership of Deng Xiaoping himself. Signals appeared in the 'People's Daily', where a lead article argued for increased import of western capital, technology and management expertise; it even endorsed the development of a capitalist sector in the economy. The struggle between the two lines was set to intensify in preparation for the Fourteenth Party Congress, scheduled for later in 1992. Deng was allegedly planning to discipline leftists for sabotaging his reform programme, and would then introduce a second wave of market reforms. Senior officials concerned with cultural and educational policy were rumoured to be facing dismissal.[1]

[1] See many reports in the Hong Kong press of the period, for example *Far Eastern Economic Review*, 5 March 1992, p. 20.

The 1992 disagreement reflected previous ones: reform or conservatism, encouraging foreign investment or closing the door, imposing Party control or relaxing it. Alongside the central issues of economic development and political control, cultural policies, including those on religion, were inevitably affected. The period from 1989 to 1992 was one of increasingly strict regulation over religious activities. Many priests, bishops and lay persons in the Catholic Church were arrested, while Protestants were more closely supervised and government agencies tried to hinder the spread of religious influences. Internal documents from the Party Centre, the State Education Commission, the RAB, the UFWD, provincial governments, the TSPM/CCC and other agencies laid down strict limits to religious activities. Typical regulations were those adopted on 21 August 1991 in the province of Henan, where Christianity had spread fast: all religious institutions had to operate from a fixed place with a responsible management; they should be approved by the government and have a legitimate source of income; there must be no proselytism outside the designated buildings, and it was forbidden to hear broadcasts or watch videos from outside China.[2] House churches reported increased surveillance, pressure to cease meetings and arrests of travelling evangelists.

On the other hand, more liberal views were still made known. In January 1992, Bishop Ting expressed concern about recent indiscriminate closures of home worship gatherings in several areas. He revealed that the RAB was currently drafting further regulations, and hoped that they would be fair and reasonable, and that 'the excessive methods which have been carried out in some areas will be corrected'.[3] Moderate policy recommendations also emerged from research units such as the Chinese Academy of Social Sciences, which rejected the simplistic picture of home meetings as being subversive or infiltrated by foreigners. Such voices strongly argued against the use of force and urged dialogue between officials and believers in case of disputes. There were also reports that senior church officials and

---

[2] CNCR 1934, 13 March 1992.
[3] Amity News Service (Hong Kong), ANS 92.1.5.

academics were using their personal contacts behind the scenes to restrain hard-line proposals. In short, the arena of religious policy, like that of other national policies, was characterized by tensions between 'reformist' and 'hard-line' tendencies. The hard-liners had gained a temporary advantage, but were by no means in complete control. This doubtless created a confusing situation for officials in agencies such as the RAB, not to mention for the believers themselves.

Since about 1987 there has been speculation that the government will promulgate a law on religion to formalize the policies articulated in Document 19. By 1992 there was still no sign of its appearance, although research was invested in studying religious legislation in other countries and soliciting views within China. Such a law would perhaps be a step forward, but one suspects that there would still be much room for interpretation depending on political priorities. As far as we can foresee, the Chinese government will continue to supervise all religions, in particular to vet personnel appointments and to ensure political loyalty. This will be done with more or less flexibility depending on the national political situation, and it does seem unlikely that the government will resort to wholesale persecution. Based on recent experience, Catholics may be the most antagonistic to this kind of supervision, and Buddhists the most accommodating.[4] In all cases, the extreme minority status of religious believers makes it impossible for them to overtly challenge such controls with any prospect of success. Of course a major change in religious policies might occur if communist power were to collapse as it did in Russia and East Europe, but the consequences of this for China would be totally unpredictable.

The national Christian conference held in January 1992 forms a convenient point to end our account of the official church. The following are extracts from its press release:

The Fifth National Chinese Christian Conference (NCC) closed in Beijing on January 6th, calling for renewed emphasis on younger

---

[4] Some groups of Muslims may also come into increasing conflict with the central government. We do not have space to take up this question here.

leadership, church order and commitment to the Three-Self principle of self-government, self-support and self-propagation. In the largest and most broadly based Protestant gathering since the beginning of the reform period in 1979, 273 delegates from 29 provinces . . . gathered in Beijing for the week-long meeting . . .

Bishop K. H. Ting [Ding Guangxun] was re-elected head of the two national Christian organizations, the National Committee of the Three-Self Patriotic Movement of the Protestant Churches in China (TSPM) and the China Christian Council (CCC) . . .

Government officials including Ren Wuzhi, director of the RAB, and Qiao Shi, member of the Standing Committee of the Political Bureau of the CCP, also presented their greetings at the meeting.[5]

The conference also approved a 'Church Order For Trial Use in Chinese Churches' which had been in preparation for more than four years. The order incorporates ecclesiastical perspectives from a variety of traditions according to the principle of 'mutual respect'.[6]

The atmosphere of the conference was restrained, although there was much enthusiasm for the ordination of forty-five new pastors which took place in a nearby church. Commenting on the conference, Deng Zhaoming noted that progress on rejuvenating church leadership was still slow, although elected members over the age of eighty were now very few. The decision-making bodies of the church remained basically the same as after the 1986 conference both structurally and in terms of personnel. 'Many of the elections represent a shuffling of the same core group of people, rather than a rotation in which new people are brought in and older ones retire . . . The average age of the vice-chairpersons and the vice-presidents of the two standing committees must be well over seventy. The average age of the standing committees is a little younger but not much.'[7]

The publication in December 1991 of the 'Church Order for Trial Use in Chinese Churches' affords opportunity to analyse the current ecclesial status of the CCC.[8] It provides useful definitions of the church, believers, sacraments, ministry and organizational questions, and as an outline document seems

[5] Qiao Shi is also director of China's security services and police force.
[6] Amity News Service (Hong Kong), ANS 92.1.1 and ANS 92.1.2.
[7] *Bridge*, no. 51, January–February 1992, p. 4.
[8] *China Study Journal*, vol. 7 no. 1, April 1992, pp. 71–6. The same issue, pp. 68–71, translates the constitutions of the CCC and the TSPM as of March 1992.

fully in accord with Protestant tradition. However, several issues are still in need of clarification. It may be that the CCC has not yet taken a decision on them, since they go to the very heart of the problem of enabling the church to operate in the particular political environment of Chinese 'communism'.

First, there is no church creed, so the parameters of affiliation are not clear. Are the True Jesus Church or Seventh-Day Adventists, for example, considered members of the 'Chinese church'? This is related to a second question, the lack of clarity concerning the CCC's status as a national church. Again, what is the relationship between the CCC and other Christian communities in China? Does the CCC claim to be an established church, to speak on behalf of all Chinese Christians, or to be one amongst several organizations of equal status? A third point concerns church–state relations. According to the document, churches should 'observe the Chinese constitution, laws, regula-tions and government policies'; 'clergy should be patriotic and law-abiding'. Should this be taken to mean unconditional obedience and support for all laws and policies? Or is there still scope for following the voice of conscience in the event of a conflict? Finally, the ecclesial status of episcopal consecration within the CCC is not defined. The 'Church Order' states that three bishops, who take part in the laying on of hands, are required for the consecration of a new bishop. Some Chinese bishops such as K. H. Ting were consecrated in the Anglican tradition and presumably claim Apostolic succession. Is this true for those bishops consecrated by them? What is their status with regard to the Lambeth Conference? Does each have a diocese?

Issues such as these are still unresolved. Nevertheless it seems that the TSPM/CCC, at least for the present, is set on a steady course. One may regret that more reforms did not take place, but neither were severe restrictions imposed, nor any liberal figures ousted. Under the circumstances this maintenance of the *status quo* may be considered a reasonable achievement: there is less talk now of reform of the TSPM itself, but pressures for radical change will certainly re-emerge when a more liberal climate returns. In many respects the Chinese church can now be considered a 'respectable' mainstream conciliar Protestant church, with orthodox doctrines and ecclesiology. Its acceptance into the WCC in 1991 symbolizes international recognition of this status, although there was considerable opposition inside the WCC to the admission of the CCC, and of course the WCC itself is by no means representative of the whole of world Protestantism. More conservative evangelical organizations tend to have more sympathy for the house churches and still have reservations about the official church: that it is infiltrated and controlled by an atheist regime, that it collaborates in suppression of 'true Christians', that it would collapse without CCP backing and that it continues to publish pro-government rhetoric. As an example of the latter, the final resolution of the 5th NCC called for 'all colleagues and fellow-Christians throughout China, to rally closely around the Chinese Communist Party and the People's Government'. This was presumably unavoidable to placate government observers. However, as Deng Zhaoming asks, one wonders how much room is left for the church to rationalize its relationship with the state without sacrificing its Christian identity.[9] At least with the increased flow of information from China in recent years, outside parties have a better basis on which to form their own judgement about these issues.

As always it is more difficult to be confident about the situation of the house churches. Numerous reports reached Hong Kong after 1989 that repressive measures were being implemented and that many meetings were fragmenting into smaller and more private groups. However the number of known arrests by 1992 was still relatively small – perhaps less than fifty all told – and all the indications are that the house churches and autonomous communities continue to flourish. It is hard to predict even in the short term what will happen. The extent of the movement is a new phenomenon, and at present it seems to be quite well organized, benefiting still from the prestige of the west and Hong Kong, as well as from practical links and broadcasts. It may well be that the 'fever' has abated

[9] *Bridge*, no. 51, January–February 1992, pp. 5–6.

or will do so shortly, but this would still leave many millions of people touched by Christianity in the 1980s for the first time.

One supposes that such evangelists and pastors as there are will be busy ministering for this community, let alone expanding. Consolidation may in the long term be more productive for Protestant churches than another period of rapidly growing interest. It would allow time for the promulgation of orthodox doctrines in congregations that to date have had limited exposure to them. Qualified personnel would have the opportunity to preach and establish a familiarity with standard forms of worship. Bibles, other written materials and broadcasts would continue to make an impact on the local communities. It is difficult to imagine that a new faith could strike deep roots in millions of people in too short a time. One suspects that a very rapid growth would lead to superficial affiliation that might not be meaningful in the longer term.

It is important not to exaggerate the differences between the official and unofficial groups. In theology and doctrinal orientation there is little substantial difference. Some materials imported from outside China are possibly more conservative than those produced by the TSPM/CCC, and the latter continue to publish mandatory pro-CCP statements, but the distinction is fine. In the longer term one should perhaps emphasize the middle ground between the 'official' and the 'house' churches, rather than their differences. It may be possible to bridge the gap by building churches under local control, sensitivity to particular communities, and confidence building measures on both sides. The new church order presented at the NCC, reported above, is a far more conciliatory document than the demands for monolithic unity issued in the 1950s, and points the way to increasing negotiation about local freedoms. However such reconciliation is more difficult at a period of repression when the question of collaboration with a hostile state administration arises.

Another open question is the extent to which syncretism between Christianity and local religious traditions will occur. A letter from a group of Christians in Henan to the editor of *Tianfeng* voiced typical concerns about an unorthodox sect that was spreading its influence in their district: 'These people get going in the evening, finding a suitable place in which they cry and shout, saying that they are confessing their sins . . . They urge people to attend their assemblies, to join their organiz-ation, and not to go on worshipping in a church. Some people who have been along to take part in their activities have come back with reports that they have seen a big tiger, a great snake, and the Lord wearing white garments.'[10]

Some sects are allegedly creating disturbances to social order. An internal report on the development of Christian sects in China noted that reactionary organizations within Protestant-ism have revived secret meetings and conspiratorial activities: 'The 'wilderness sect' and the 'disciple society' . . . have recruited more than 30,000 followers in the Ankang district and more than 10,000 in the Yunyang district. Many times they create disturbances during their meetings, attack the local government, and beat up security officials and members of the working group. They seize firearms and cause serious casualties . . . Moreover there are criminal groups which make use of religion to rape women and defraud people of money and property.'[11]

China is in religious as well as social ferment: the events of the last ten years have produced profound changes to the picture of religion in China. A crucial development has been the ending of systematic persecution. Had this continued for another decade, the future for all religions in China would have been bleak indeed. But Christianity, popular religion and Buddhism have managed to stage a recovery, including in the key area of educating another generation of pastors, monks and priests. Religious personnel may be far from sufficient, but they will keep the religions alive.

The state of folk religion is an extremely important topic that has so far received little scholarly attention. Popular religion in

---

[10] *Tianfeng*, January 1990, translated in *China Study Journal*, vol. 5 no. 2, August 1990, p. 67.

[11] Quoted in *Freedom of Religion in China*, Asia Watch, January 1992, p. 79. As many as nine provinces are mentioned as affected by such sectarianism: Henan, Fujian, Zhejiang, Anhui, Hebei, Shanxi, Shaanxi, Inner Mongolia and Heilongjiang.

all its many forms was, if anything, persecuted even more severely than institutional ones; yet the examples of Hong Kong and Taiwan show how tenacious it is even in modern urban environments. Its potential for revival is enormous, as can be seen in the liberal provinces such as Fujian. However we cannot speak with confidence even of the present, let alone the future.

Among the organized religions, Protestantism has developed a much firmer base in the population. If it is still considered a 'foreign religion' this is no longer a stigma. On the contrary it is rather dynamic and successful, both in an orthodox form and, as far as one can tell from fragmentary evidence, as an element in the revival of Chinese sectarianism. So far, it must be said, it is not an important factor in intellectual life. But the way in which Christmas, for example, has become a national festival, shows how the Chinese are still willing to allow new input into their religious culture. Protestantism is still very much, it should once again be emphasized, the religion of a small minority of the population. Nevertheless it has grown into a convincing religious alternative for millions of Chinese believers, a part of the religious scene in China that is recognized as legitimate even by its critics in the state apparatus, and a movement that seems to be regarded with respect among the broader population.

CONGRUENCY, INDIGENIZATION, TRANSFORMATION

Let us now take note of some questions posed by a scholar from CASS, Professor Tang Yi. At the end of a paper on the contemporary church, Professor Tang speculates on three possible models of development for Christianity in China:

First, the Christian faith may eventually conquer China and Christianize Chinese culture. The secular, human-centred mentality may eventually be supplanted by the transcendent, Christ-centred spirit through a radical change in the Chinese outlook on history and human nature . . . After a lapse of two thousand years, China may turn out to be a converted Roman Empire II . . .

Second, Christianity may eventually be absorbed by Chinese culture, following the example of Buddhism. It may eventually be adapted to the human-centred mentality and become a sinless religion of the Chinese genre . . . In effect, a different religion may result . . .

The third way is for Christianity to retain its basic Western characteristics and settle down to be a sub-cultural minority religion in China. In the end the public will get more used to it and accept all its religious ideals, including its prophetic message, as a complement to . . . Chinese civilization without any fear of jeopardizing the mainstream culture. This is, for all practical purposes, the most likely solution.[12]

Tang thus opts for the 'subculture' model as the most likely outcome. With regard to Catholicism this does seem a reasonable assessment. The Roman Catholic church in China has had deep roots in particular faith communities, some for several hundred years, that were not destroyed even by the many years of severe repression. On the other hand it has shown little sign of breaking out of this network of communities and winning new converts, as Protestants have done relatively successfully.

It is too early to suggest that Protestantism is moving away from its role as subculture and beginning to influence mainstream Chinese culture as a whole. As Tang points out elsewhere in his paper, this is possibly nothing to do with political pressures: despite more freedom in Taiwan, and enormous investment of missionary resources, Christian belief there is marginal to mainstream Chinese society. But one may raise further questions. For example what is meant by 'mainstream Chinese culture'? There is a vast gulf between the culture of city intellectuals and that of the peasants. There is also a great difference in the latter's culture, depending on the current political and economic policies and local traditions. It is probably true that Christianity has no great role to play in the industrial cities, especially when religious activities are carefully supervised by an antagonistic bureaucracy. It may have a more significant presence in parts of the countryside, where much of the population has a long tradition of religious belief. In rural

---

[12] Tang Yi, 'Chinese Christianity in Development', *China Study Journal*, vol. 6 no. 2, August 1991, pp. 4–8. It is worth recalling the point made by Rubinstein that Christianity in Taiwan has remained very much a minority religion. Where it is partially successful is precisely when it integrates with the indigenous religious tradition and accommodates to the cultural environment, as Buddhism did many centuries previously.

areas, it is more accurate to describe 'mainstream Chinese culture' as centred around belief in spirits rather than being purely 'human-centred'. The distinctions between 'conquering', 'indigenizing' and 'becoming a subculture' may need further clarification.

The concept of indigenization has been important since the 1920s in China, and it also rose to prominence in Asian and African Christian thinking in the 1970s. Central to the question is whether Christianity retains the essence of its faith while becoming fully integrated into a 'new' (non-western) culture. Students of Chinese culture have long been interested in a related question, sinification, especially with regard to Buddhism in the Tang dynasty and Marxism since the 1920s. In both these cases a foreign philosophy was adopted by significant numbers of Chinese, and transformed in the process.

In his paper 'Christianity and the Chinese Sectarian Tradition', Daniel Bays discusses the commonalities in belief between Christianity and aspects of the Chinese religious tradition, for example salvation, paradise, moral behaviour and other issues we have considered in some detail already. He notes that in organization structure, forms of worship and social functions the Christian groups followed a model that was familiar to the local population. In some Chinese sects, for example, the distinctive form of organization was the congregation, centred around a charismatic local leader who was responsible for healing and preaching. This congregation was often an independent entity, linked to a larger, decentralized organization such as the White Lotus Sect. Forms of worship included liturgies, singing, reading of scriptures, preaching, offering of money and celebratory rituals.

In terms of social function, such groups provided a community with a sense of belonging, a subculture within a larger culture, to satisfy 'the sense of longing for smaller, more immediate social groupings that many members of a large society may feel, especially in turbulent and insecure times'.[13] Bays notes the importance of locality and lineage ties, ethnicity

---

[13] Bays, 'Sectarian Tradition', p. 42.

and occupational groupings within congregations, both Christian and sectarian, and also their importance as a sphere of women's activity. Part of this was a stress on healing, mutual aid and group solidarity. Such parallels may be termed 'congruence', which is defined by Rubinstein:

> The task of the cultural transmitter, whether government assistance agent or missionary, is to adapt the cultural patterns of one society to the needs of another. He can do this only if he can first find congruence, that is, find the existence of key parallel cultural patterns and structures. Once this has been done, he can show his clients, his target audience, that though the cultural/religious system he represents seems quite alien to their cultural or religious systems, there are still numerous points of congruence. If he is successful, then much of the battle is won. His host audience may now be ready to acknowledge that the new belief system or theology is at least acceptable. Congruence is the key to understanding the Chinese acceptance of the True Jesus Church.[14]

Rubinstein focuses on somewhat different issues from Bays, providing yet more commonalities: use of canonical scripture, whereby scripture is quoted first, followed by comments showing relevance to daily life, or else the issue discussed, then discussion confirmed by quotation; belief in demons and angels; celebration of Eucharist (ritual use of food); gift of Holy Spirit (glossolalia, healing); assertion of uniqueness and orthodoxy. Incidentally a Chinese audience would not be surprised to hear Christians proclaim that theirs is the true doctrine while others are heterodox, or that they are possessed by a Holy Spirit while others are possessed by inferior ones: such claims are made by most sects.

From what we have seen, it seems fair to suggest that Christianity can be accepted by many Chinese as something not totally strange, but rather as a continuation or enhancement of familiar traditions. It may also be a more universal, prestigious, credible and better organized alternative. An important factor in its spread is the intense, evangelizing oral culture supported by written materials and, more recently, radio broadcasts. At the heart of the matter is that Christianity can provide the

---

[14] Rubinstein, *Protestant Community*, p. 129.

answer to life's quest, a spiritual experience which leads to utter certainty and conviction. Belief in Christ and the Christian God is susceptible to analysis in sociological terms, but also demands understanding as a religious phenomenon.

Returning to the questions raised at the start of this section, what is a likely fate for Protestantism in the context of Chinese culture? One important issue is its possible transformative impact for those communities where it becomes accepted. The process of adaptation can surely not be considered a one-way avenue. In fact, one may not feel too comfortable with the concept of sinification itself, the notion that, for example, Buddhism was slowly but surely 'made Chinese'. In the process, Buddhism also made China what it is. The same point can be argued with Marxism. The philosophy and political practice mutated into Chinese forms, but Chinese society itself underwent a tremendous transformation under the impact of Marxism. Protestantism has certainly adopted characteristics determined by the indigenous religious traditions, but equally in the long term it is likely to make an impression upon them. Some key areas may be the prophetic impulse, and impetus towards social and political involvement; individual rather than community responsibility; increased emphasis on literacy; the turning away from a basically animistic worldview to a religion of salvation.

There are relatively few examples in the Chinese religious traditions of social or political thought. One exception is the occasional outbreak of Messianism, where rebellions have adopted quasi-religious ideologies to underpin their revolt against the empire; some Buddhist monasteries were also active in welfare efforts. However the Christian tradition has long upheld the right, or the duty, of the individual to act in the socio-political arena, even against the state when his/her conscience demands. The examples – from the prophets of Israel to contemporary theologies of liberation – do not need rehearsing here.

At one level this is connected with political tradition. On another, it relates to an essential feature of the Christian religion, namely the concept of the relationship between the individual and God, which has its roots in both Judaic and Greek philosophy.[15] Christian ontology also encourages a more positive involvement in social issues than that of Daoism and Buddhism, which insists on the illusory nature of the world. The Protestant tradition, with its stress on the right to personal interpretation of scripture and individual responsibility in religious matters, emphasizes these differences even more than the Roman Catholic.

Another key area that should be investigated further is the attitude towards Holy Scripture among Chinese Protestants compared to followers of traditional religions. Especially in the periods of repression, the house churches placed tremendous emphasis on the Bible, around which were organized many church activities: preserving copies from destruction, copying enormous quantities of scripture by hand, clandestine printing and distribution. Great importance is attached to Bible study, which motivates numerous uneducated believers to become literate. In a sense the Bible is a symbol of faith, but it is much more than that. First, it is a unifying factor, which cuts through the divisions in the Christian community: all sects we have encountered, although they may differ in interpretation, accept the Bible as the source of their faith. Second, it promotes literacy, and even a form of personal research and reflection, as readers are allowed to develop their own views of the texts. This may be a significant contrast to other religions. Some indigenous Chinese traditions were not text-based at all; others held certain scriptures in reverence, but reserved recitation and study to professional clergy. A comparison of the lay study of religious texts in China could well be rewarding.

Finally, some Protestant churches in the west have gone far down the road of secularization of belief, for example virtually abandoning the idea of a transcendent deity and his/her incarnation in the figure of Christ. In less modernist theologies, there has been at least a denial of most forms of animism, and disbelief in devils and ghosts. Likewise many Protestants are extremely sceptical of miracles, in the sense of unexplained

---

[15] See Carver Yu, 'The Relevance of Christian Humanism to the Quest for Democracy in China' in Hunter and Rimmington (eds.), *All Under Heaven*, pp. 108–14.

contravention of the 'laws of nature'; of scriptural inerrancy; the value of church rituals; in short of many vestiges of medieval thought that have survived into the twentieth century. It has been argued by some scholars that the Protestant enterprise as a whole is part of the enormous project of modernization, the transformation from a magical to a rationalistic culture, from an agrarian pre-scientific society to an urban technological one. Perhaps some similar development will be observed in China if the church continues to penetrate into the fabric of traditional religious culture.

FINAL THOUGHTS

There is a vigorous debate on the social functions of Protestantism: the role of the Protestant in the growth of capitalism; whether movements such as Methodism promoted democracy, individualism and peaceful social change, ultimately contributing to modernity and secularization; if Pentecostalism is an escapist path that inhibits social responsibility, or a means of empowerment.[16] The twentieth century has shown that the connection between Protestantism and capitalism is contingent rather than causal. Many areas of the world – spectacularly Japan – have seen economic advance with almost no evangelical Christianity. Another case in point is South Korea, a formerly Confucian country that in the twentieth century saw a massive increase in Protestant church growth, and also rapid economic development. It might at first sight provide an example of Protestantism stimulating economic growth, but, after a survey of local studies from Korea, David Martin concludes that there is little evidence of economic changes in Korea specifically connected to, still less caused by, the spread of Protestantism. It

---

[16] Apart from Weber, important participants in these debates have been Elie Halévy, Edward P. Thompson and Peter Berger. An extended recent commentary and bibliographic references can be found in David Martin, *Tongues of Fire: The Explosion of Protestantism in Latin America*, Oxford: Blackwell, 1990. With reference to Asia, see *Max Weber in Asian Studies*, edited by Andreas E. Buss, Leiden: E. J. Brill, 1985; and Christian Jochim, 'Some Observations on the Current Debate about Confucianism, Protestantism, and Economic Modernization', paper presented at the IAHR conference, Beijing, April 1992.

is true that Christian converts had a reputation for being industrious, but so did many other groups in the community.[17]

Qualities such as moral responsibility, trustworthiness and willingness to reinvest profits are to be found in many non-Protestant cultures, for example in the Confucian and Buddhist countries of the Far East. Here the requisite ideological transformation was that the traditional Confucian, with his distaste for practical activities and obsession with tradition, should become an efficient administrator or technocrat. It was also necessary that the transcendent, world-denying orientation of Buddhism did not inhibit a sense of enterprise. Scholars have argued that where institutions and government policies were favourable to the growth of capitalism, for example in Meiji Japan, there was no need for a specifically Protestant ethic to motivate entrepreneurs.[18] The most one can conclude about the correlation is that Protestantism certainly does not hinder economic progress, as some religions might do. The linkage can best be stated in terms of frequent concurrence: 'evangelical religion and economic advancement do *often* go together, and when they do so appear mutually to support and *reinforce* each other'.[19]

With regard to politics, the situation is even more ambiguous: some Protestants have supported Fascist governments, others communist ones; some are totally apolitical, others committed to political action; in many countries different Protestant groups have held diametrically opposed views. In the traditional Protestant spheres of influence – North Europe and the USA – one can distinguish three main strands of political orientation, albeit with numerous subdivisions. First is the Anglican or Lutheran kind that is close to state-churchhood and has links with a ruling élite. Such established churches have naturally tended to be traditionalist and conservative in orientation, adopting the theological stance that government is God-ordained, for which scriptural justification is adduced in

---

[17] Martin, *Tongues of Fire*, pp. 135–56.
[18] See the discussion by Robert N. Bellah, 'Reflections on the Protestant Ethic Analogy in Asia' in *The Protestant Ethic and Modernization: A Comparative View*, edited by Samuel N. Eisenstadt, New York and London: Basic Books, 1968, pp. 243–51.
[19] Martin, *Tongues of Fire*, p. 206.

passages such as Romans 13:1: 'the powers that be are ordained of God'. Second, at the opposite extreme, is the dissenting sect which may be apocalyptic, pacifist, egalitarian, liberal or socialist, while a third stance is for strict separation of spiritual and social life, an apolitical quietism. These traditions also find statements in scripture to support their views: for example Revelations 13 has often been adduced as justification for anti-governmental political action. The twentieth century has likewise seen a variety of political orientation in Protestant movements outside the traditional homelands. In Latin America, Protestants have supported both National Security governments and opposition movements, while others have opted to stay out of the political arena. In South Africa Protestants were much involved in the struggle against apartheid and also active in support of it. Each community can only be considered in light of its own particular history, social constituency and political situation.

In the field of culture we find somewhat more consistency within Protestantism. First, Protestantism coincides historically with the breakdown of a monopolistic culture, classically, in the case of Europe, with reaction against Roman Catholicism. As European society saw the beginnings of pluralism, Protestant groups were an expression of increased autonomy for particular nations, for the individual and for voluntary associations. The formation of fraternities beyond local or blood ties was an enormously important step. The dissenting churches created a free space in society where sections of the working population developed special skills, such as public speaking and music, and greatly increased their social interaction. Historians have attributed to Methodism in England, for example, many contributions to modernity in the shape of education, health, work discipline and women's status. This has led some writers to suggest that Protestant tradition is in essence part of the long-term secularization of western society, contributing to the 'decline of magic', diminished belief in the supernatural and ultimately decline of belief in God.[20] Protestantism is obviously

[20] See Paul Badham, 'Some Secular Trends in the Church of England Today' in *Religion State and Society in Modern Britain*, edited by Paul Badham, Lewiston, NY: Edwin Mellen Press, 1989, pp. 23–33.

not the only way a society can make the transition from a traditional agrarian culture to an urban industrial one, but it certainly was an integral part of the process in the Anglo–Saxon world.

Scholars are justifiably reluctant to apply theories from western precedents to China, but with due caution we will see whether such cultural developments may be relevant. Contemporary China is an example of the fragmentation of a monopolistic culture, or rather of a hybrid of monopolies: the underlying pattern of traditional culture, the former imperial system and Marxism–Leninism. Both the culture and the political scene are now in the process of differentiation, and we are witnessing the rapid formation of civil society, the growth of individualism and collapse of collective controls. The democracy movement in 1989 had serious limitations, but signalled a new relationship between society and the individual. The difference between 1989 and the Red Guard rallies of only twenty years previously was astounding, and this after just one decade of western influence, consumerism, TV and the nuclear family. The old monolithic authority survives for the time being but must inevitably change sooner or later: the effort to prolong it, the promulgation of Maoist thought in newspapers and the upgrading of revolutionary heroes, has become a nationwide farce. The context for a growth in Protestantism seems to exist.

As one might expect, there is no evidence that the new churches are significant in promoting capitalist development. It is true that there are contingent connections. A few of the businessmen in south China, especially those from Hong Kong, are Christians, and Christian networks are engaged in commerce and investment, for example in Wenzhou. One hears occasional reports that to succeed in business in the latter city you must be a Christian. But this is an exceptional case, and not an integral part of China's emerging industrial growth. The most industrialized area of southern Guangdong does have a small Christian presence, but it makes no particular impact on local industries. The next major investment venture – the opening of Pudong Special Economic Zone in Shanghai – will have even less. The Chinese are quite capable of becoming entrepreneurs and fully fledged capitalists without the need for the 'foreign religion'. In fact, our observations suggest that overseas Chinese Christians become businessmen rather rarely: they prefer to be educationalists or work in professions such as medicine. This is probably a result of fundamentalist ethics that regard commerce and accumulation of wealth as worldly, in opposition to the spiritual life. Committed believers tend to despise business activities. In more extreme cases, they may even prefer a life of poverty as expression of their faith.

Because of its current importance, we have dealt thoroughly with the political dimension of the churches. We found a range of positions comparable to those elsewhere in the world: support for the *status quo*, resistance and apolitical quietism. As far as we know there were few cases of Protestants being involved in the 1989 anti-government protests. Some seminarians were involved in the democracy movement, but the student body at Beijing's Yanjing seminary voted not to participate in the demonstrations: the seminary was one of very few educational institutions in Beijing that was not represented in Tiananmen, for which it was praised by the government. This, like the official pronouncements of the TSPM, is a typical state–church position. On the other hand, many people find their religious activities designated illegal, both in the relatively orthodox house churches and in the sectarian groups. If they continue to meet, they constitute an implicit challenge to the state, which demands obedience throughout the cultural realm.

In the cultural dimension we can note some parallels with other countries. Martin observes that in the spectrum of Korean Christianity, two main trends are quite distinctive from a sociological perspective. One might be called a 'modernity package'. Earlier in the century, for some members of the educated classes Christianity was a more attractive alternative than traditional Korean Confucianism or Japanese militarism. Protestantism, introduced for the most part by American missionaries, was closely associated with learning English, with business or commerce, with emigration and educational opportunities and a network of social welfare organizations such as hospitals. After the Second World War this spirit was maintained in the traditional denominations, often through family networks.

At a more popular level the great outburst of church growth came after 1945, and was an interaction between Protestantism and the underlying culture of shamanism in the religious field, and an expression of collective solidarity in the social field. As well as offering spiritual comfort at a time of disorientation, the religion afforded solidarity and social support. A breakthrough was achieved when church groups formed a social base in their own right, for example by being able to find work and housing for new migrants to cities. These groups are a mixture of the old and the new. On the one hand they exhibit classic signs of pre-industrial religion, such as belief in an all-pervasive spirit world. On the other, Protestantism may introduce new elements, for example less emphasis on minor miracles. Very similar dynamics can, incidentally, also be seen in developing countries such as Brazil, where Pentecostalist Christianity merges with the underlying religious culture of the poor – in Brazil's case spiritism – and a rapidly expanding social network.[21]

These trends correspond to the profound changes that have taken place in world Protestantism. Anglo–American churches experienced massive expansion outside Europe in the nineteenth century, through mission work undertaken at the height of imperialist expansion. In the past fifty years they have experienced a continuous decline in numbers and influence in the home countries, with the exception of right-wing fundamentalism in the southern USA. The churches they founded are still active in many developing countries, but on the other hand there has also been a great upsurge of inventive, autocephalous and indigenized Protestant movements in Africa, Latin America and the Pacific area.

Both these forms are found in China. Many of the older generation of converts were attracted by the 'modernity pack-

---

[21] The class base of these movements – i.e. the assertion that lower classes are more attracted to spiritist or shamanic syncretism – is far from established, and must be viewed with caution. For example in contemporary Hong Kong it is frequently members of the middle class who are attracted to Pentecostal meetings.

age'; one need only think of the thousands of doctors, nurses and other professionals who emerged from the great liberal institutions of the 1920s and 1930s. They learned English, related well to westerners, and often visited or studied abroad. This generation still forms the backbone of many urban congregations in particular, and continues to influence younger members of their families. Still today, many of those intellectuals who study the Bible or attend church seem to be attracted by western aspects of the religion of America and Europe. On the other hand, the interaction of Christianity and local beliefs is an important factor in the spread of Christianity among the rural poor in the past decade.

One irony is that precisely now, when Protestantism is growing in China, the economic power of Europe and the USA is declining dramatically in East Asia. Japan is the major economic force in the area, and the events of 1989 increased its dominant position with regard to China. Western investment fell sharply after 4 June, and is still affected by problems regarding the use of prison labour, human rights questions, and other issues. Japan participated in the international response to China for a while, but was quicker to re-establish both governmental and commercial ties. It is investing heavily in China and successfully promoting its strategy of building factories and extractive industries in countries with low labour costs, at the same time providing them with income to buy Japanese manufactured goods. It seems inevitable that Japanese capital, technology and organization will be crucial to China's economy. Much of the future of East Asia depends on the outcome of this partnership; it is unlikely that anything the USA and Europe can do, short of military action, would do much to change the process.

However the vast majority of young Chinese, particularly the educated in the cities, are far more interested in western culture than in Japan, as can be observed in literature, philosophy, politics – or religion. Chinese intellectuals admit that Japan has an advanced technology and industrial base, but they have little respect for its culture; on the other hand they are still strongly attracted to the ideas of democracy, consumerism and individual freedom which they perceive as western. Claudio Veliz has proposed the idea that much of the world in the future will be 'made in England, in the sense that the English language, pastimes, and attitudes created during the industrial revolution, and transmitted through America, have an enormous influence all over the world'.[22] This certainly seems to be the case in Chinese intellectual life, and in many aspects of urban society. (Whether Japanese economic power will change this cultural pattern remains to be seen. Perhaps Veliz' thesis will need to be revised: the world of culture may perhaps be 'made in England', but the material world will issue from Japanese-owned factories.) In this sense, the adoption of Protestantism is in line with a broader trend of cultural diffusion.

Whatever happens, it seems that Chinese Protestantism is now a sustainable force. Protestants may constitute only 1 per cent of the population, but the population is so huge that even 1 per cent is more than ten million people. They are represented by a national organization and have created a certain social space for their activities. Moreover they can count on support from outside, particularly from the USA, and will shortly receive a boost of vitality from the incorporation of Hong Kong – with a large, active and committed Christian community – into the mainland. Apart from the CCP itself, what other social groups in China can form such a collective body, with a tendency to shared ideology, bonding, international connections and ability to sacrifice?

We are frequently tempted to ask, in a secular Europe where churches are seen as increasingly irrelevant, whether religion still has any meaning other than as an individual pastime. Is it just a leisure activity, like a tennis club or poetry circle? Professor Martin suggests two areas in which Protestantism, even at its most quietist, is at least potentially important for the future of a society. First, becoming a religious believer may be a symbolic rejection of official ideology, and can be felt as a form of spiritual empowerment. As a strategy, however unconscious of it the participants may be, this may be the most appropriate course of

---

[22] Claudio Veliz, 'A World Made in England', *Quadrant*, vol. 27, no. 3, March 1983, pp. 8–19.

action in conditions where a confrontation with the *status quo* could only be doomed, where political passivity is a precondition for survival. 'The evangelical believer is one who has symbolically repudiated what previously held him in place, vertically and horizontally. He cannot overturn the actual structures, but he can emigrate.'[23] Many Chinese believers have made this kind of spiritual emigration from a structure they cannot openly challenge.

Second, religious associations can generate a latent power that may only become activated after many years, or decades. Examples are the power of speech, increased social activity for women, a spread of supportive small group activity, a more methodical approach to life, even better standards of diet, hygiene and childcare, or less alcoholism. This leads to the formation of cells of a new society, still invisible in the framework of the old, that are slow to reach fruition but nevertheless active.[24] Even critics do not deny the impact of movements such as Methodism, although they warn against the assumption that the spread of Protestant values is necessarily a force for social progress. Edward Thompson, for example, castigates the Methodists' 'pitiless ideology of work', the inculcation of submission to authority, the teaching of blessedness through poverty, the lurid obsession with sin, the indoctrination of children in the 'box-like, blackening chapels [that] stood in the industrial districts like great traps for the human psyche'.[25] But even Thompson acknowledges the sustained organizational dedication and the high degree of personal responsibility that the movement engendered.

Some Christian teachings are certainly frustrating to those interested in radical social reform. It is too early to assess the long-term effects of the twentieth-century explosion of Protestantism in developing countries. In China the story has only just begun. At the moment the activity is largely confined to the

[23] Martin, *Tongues of Fire*, p. 285.
[24] Compare the parable of the yeast, Matthew 13:33.
[25] See Edward P. Thompson, *The Making of the English Working Class*, London: Gollancz, 1963, p. 368, and in general chapter XI, 'The Transforming Power of the Cross' for his assessment of Methodism.

private sphere, at least in part because the government does not permit religious organizations to build up social networks. The process may also be slower because, unlike countries of Latin America and Africa, China has successfully defended itself against massive proselytism by US evangelical agencies. But China may become an increasingly important part of the world Protestant community, and moreover one which strongly upholds beliefs about eschatology and other matters that are not now fashionable in western Europe. In this it would be aligned with the majority of the world Protestant body, two-thirds of whose membership is in developing countries. In this constituency, the position of the majority is a conservative, neo-evangelical theological orientation, an indigenous ecclesiology, a deep concern for eschatology and an emphasis on signs and wonders. We suggest that these were also major characteristics of the Chinese Protestant revival of the 1980s.

Bibliography

Abbott, Paul R. 'Revival Movements', *China Christian Yearbook*, 1934, 175–92.

Amnesty International. *Violations of Human Rights in China: A Summary of Amnesty International's Concerns in 1991*, London 1991.

Anderson, Robert M. *The Vision of the Disinherited: The Making of American Pentecostalism*, New York: Oxford University Press, 1979.

Asiawatch. *Freedom of Religion in China*, New York, 1992.

Badham, Paul. 'Some Secular Trends in the Church of England Today' in Paul Badham (ed.) *Religion, State and Society in Modern Britain*, Lewiston, NY: Edwin Mellen Press, 1989, 23–33.

Bates, Miner Searle. 'The Chinese State and Religion, with Particular Reference to Christianity', Columbia University Seminar on East Asia, 29 November 1967.

    'The Church in China in the Twentieth Century' in William J. Richardson (ed.) *China and Christian Responsibility*, New York: Maryknoll Publications, 1968, 46–72.

    Gleanings from the Manuscripts of M. S. Bates: The Protestant Endeavour in Chinese Society, New York: The China Programme, NCCCUSA, 1984.

Bays, Daniel H. 'Christianity and the Chinese Sectarian Tradition', *Ch'ing Shih Went'i*, vol. 4 no. 7, June 1982, 33–55.

    'Christian Revivalism in China', paper presented at the Institute for the Study of American Evangelicals, Wheaton College, March 30–April 1, 1989.

Bellah, Robert N. 'Reflections on the Protestant Ethic Analogy in Asia' in Samuel N. Eisenstadt (ed.) *The Protestant Ethic and Modernization: A Comparative View*, New York: Basic Books, 1968, 243–51.

Burns, John P. 'China's Fight Against "Bureaucracy": Reform of the State Council, 1981–82' in Chi-Keung Leung and Steve S. K. Chin (eds.) *China in Readjustment*, Hong Kong University Press,

    1983, 283–305.
Burns, John P. (ed.) *The CCP's Nomenklatura System: A Documentary Study of Party Control of Leadership Selection, 1979–1984,* Armonk and London: M. E. Sharpe, 1989.
Burns, John P. and Rosen, S. (eds.) *Policy Conflicts in Post-Mao China,* Armonk: M. E. Sharpe, 1986.
Bush, Richard C. *Religion in Communist China,* Nashville: Abingdon, 1970.
Buss, Andreas E. (ed.) *Max Weber in Asian Studies,* Leiden: E. J. Brill, 1985.
Butterfield, Fox. 'A Missionary View of the Chinese Communists (1936–1939)' in Liu Kwang-Ching (ed.) *American Missionaries in China: Papers from the Harvard Seminars,* Harvard East Asian Monographs, 1966, 249–301.
Cambridge Encyclopedia of China, edited by Brian Hook and Denis Twitchett, Cambridge University Press, second edition 1991.
Cambridge Handbook of Contemporary China, edited by Colin Mackerras and Amanda Yorke, Cambridge University Press, 1991.
Cambridge History of China, edited by John K. Fairbank and Denis Twitchett, Cambridge University Press, 1978–.
Carus, Paul. *The Gospel of Buddha,* New Delhi: National Book Trust, first Indian edition, 1961.
Chan Kim-Kwong. *Towards A Contextual Ecclesiology: The Catholic Church in the People's Republic of China, 1979–1983,* Hong Kong: Phototech Systems, 1987. (Distributed by the Chinese Church Research Centre, PO Box 312, Shatin Central, NT, Hong Kong.)
    'A Chinese Perspective on the Interpretation of the Chinese Government's Religions Policy' in Hunter and Rimmington (eds.) *All Under Heaven,* 38–44.
Chan Kim-Kwong and Hunter, A. (eds.) *Prayers and Thoughts of Chinese Christians,* London: Mowbray, 1991.
Chao Ti'en-en, Jonathan. 'The Chinese Indigenous Church Movement, 1919–1927: A Protestant Response to the Anti-Christian Movements in Modern China', Ph.D. thesis, University of Pennsylvania, 1986.
Chao Ti'en-en, Jonathan and van Houten, R. *Wise as Serpents, Harmless as Doves: Christians in China Tell Their Story,* Pasadena: William Carey Library, 1988.
Ch'en Jerome. *China and the West: A Study of Social and Cultural Change,* London: Hutchinson, 1979.
Chen Zemin. 'These Ten Years', *China Study Journal,* vol. 7 no. 1, April 1992, 8–13.
Chen Zhiping and Li Shaoming. *Jidujiao yu Fujian minjian shehui*

(*Christianity and Popular Society in Fujian*), Xiamen: Xiamen daxue chubanshe, 1992.

China Ministry Department *Gurou zhi qin* (*My Kinsmen According to the Flesh*), Hong Kong: China Christian Communications, 1989.

Cohen, Paul A. 'The Anti-Christian Tradition in China', *Journal of Asian Studies*, vol. 20 no. 2, February 1961, 169–80.

Covell, Ralph. *Confucius, the Buddha and Christ: A History of the Gospel in Chinese*, Maryknoll: Orbis Books, 1986.

Davis, Deborah and Vogel, E. (eds.) *Chinese Society on the Eve of Tiananmen*, Cambridge, MA: Harvard University Press, 1990.

Deng Guo. 'Socialist Revolution on the Journalistic Front', *Xuexi* no. 8, 18 April 1958.

Deng Zhaoming. 'Church Unity in Shanghai', *Bridge*, no. 48, July–August 1991, 3–7.

(ed.) 'The Witness of Brother Huang Detang', *Bridge*, no. 51, January–February 1992, 11–19.

Dunne, G. 'The Prisoners of Shanghai' *China Update* no. 6, Winter 1983, 46–56.

Eberhard, Wolfram. *Guilt and Sin in Traditional China*, Berkeley: University of California Press, 1967.

Evers, George. 'The Catholic Church in China', *China Study Journal*, vol. 5 no. 3, December 1990, 12–14.

Fang Litian. 'Buddhism and Contemporary Chinese Society', in Fok Tou-hui (ed.) *Taixu tingsheng yibai zhounian guojihui yilunwenji* (*Collected Papers from International Conference on the Centenary of the Birth of Taixu*), Hong Kong: Fazhu chubanshe, 1990, 350–62.

Feuchtwang, Stephan A., Hussain, A. and Pairault, T. (eds.) *Transforming China's Economy in the 1980s*, Boulder: Westview, 1988.

Forsythe, Sidney A. *An American Missionary Community in China, 1895–1905*, Cambridge, MA: Harvard University Press, 1971.

Fulton, Austin. *Through Earthquake, Wind and Fire: Church and Mission in Manchuria, 1867–1950*, Edinburgh: St Andrews Press, 1967.

Fung, Raymond. *Households of God on China's Soil*, Geneva: World Council of Churches, 1982.

Garrett, Shirley. *Social Reformers in Urban China: The Chinese YMCA 1895–1926*, Cambridge MA: Harvard University Press, 1970.

Goullart, Peter. *The Monastery of Jade Mountain*, London: John Murray, 1961.

Gu Zhibin. *China Beyond Deng: Reform in the PRC*, Jefferson, NC: McFarland, 1991.

Hahn, Thomas H. 'New Developments Concerning Buddhist and Taoist Monasteries' in Julian F. Pas (ed.) *The Turning of the Tide: Religion in China Today*, Hong Kong: Oxford University Press,

1989, 79–101.

Hanson, Eric O. *Catholic Politics in China and Korea*, Maryknoll: Orbis Books, 1980.

Hinton, William. *Shenfan: The Continuing Revolution in a Chinese Village*, New York: Secker and Warburg, 1983.

The Great Reversal: The Privatization of China 1978–1989, New York: Monthly Review Press, 1990.

Hood, George. *Neither Bang Nor Whimper: The End of a Missionary Era in China*, Singapore: Presbyterian Church in Singapore, 1991.

Hsu, Francis L. K. *Religion, Science and Human Crises*, London: Routledge and Kegan Paul, 1952.

Hu Hsien-chin. 'The Chinese Concept of Face', *American Anthropologist*, vol. 46, 1944, 45–66.

Hunter, Alan. 'Continuities in Chinese Protestantism, 1920–1990', *China Study Journal*, vol. 6 no. 3, December 1991, 5–12.

Buddhism Under Deng, Leeds: Leeds East Asian Papers, 1992.

Hunter, Alan and Rimmington, D. 'Religion and Social Change in Contemporary China' in Hunter and Rimmington (eds.) *All Under Heaven*, 11–37.

(eds.) *All Under Heaven: Chinese Tradition and Christian Life in the People's Republic of China*, Kampen, Holland: J. H. Kok, 1992.

Jia Lusheng. 'The Second Channel', translated extracts and introduction by Guo Xiaolin, *Index on Censorship*, vol. 18 no. 2, February 1989, 20–2.

Jochim, Christian. *Chinese Religions: A Cultural Perspective*, Englewood Cliffs, NJ: Prentice Hall, 1986.

Jones, Francis P. *The Church in Communist China: A Protestant Appraisal*, New York: Friendship Press, 1962.

(ed.) *Documents of the Three Self Movement*, New York: National Council of Churches, 1963.

Kinnear, Angus. *Against the Tide*, Wheaton: Tyndale, 1978.

Lam Wing-hung. *Wang Mingdao yu Zhongguo Jiaohui (Wang Mingdao and the Chinese Church)*, Hong Kong: China Graduate School of Theology, 1982.

Lambert, Anthony P. M. 'Counting Christians in China: Who's Right?', *News Network International*, 14 April 1989, 28–36.

The Resurrection of the Chinese Church, London: Hodder and Stoughton, 1991.

Lampton, David M. (ed.) *Policy Implementation in Post-Mao China*, Berkeley: University of California Press, 1987.

Lee Chun-kwan. 'The Theology of Revival in the Chinese Christian Church, 1990–1949: Its Emergence and Impact', Ph.D. thesis, Westminster Theological Seminary, 1988.

Lin Shao-Yang. (pseudonym for Reginald Fleming Johnston). *A Chinese Appeal to Christendom Concerning Christian Missions*, London: Watts and Co., 1911.

Lu Dingyi. 'Speech on the Twentieth Anniversary of the New China News Agency', *Renmin shouce*, Beijing: Dagongbao, 1958.

Lu Guangwen. 'We Must Guard Against Heterodox Sects', *China Study Journal*, vol. 6 no. 2, August 1991, 72–3.

Luo Zhufeng (ed.) *Zhongguo shehuizhuyi shiqide zongjiao wenti*, Shanghai: Shanghai shehuikexueyuan chubanshe, 1987. Translated into English by Donald E. MacInnis and Zheng Xi'an, *Religion Under Socialism in China*, New York and London: M. E. Sharpe, 1991.

Lutz, Jessie G. *Chinese Politics and Christian Mission: The Anti-Christian Movements of 1920–1928*, Notre Dame, IN: Cross Cultural Publications Inc., 1988.

MacInnis, Donald E. *Religious Policy and Practice in Communist China: A Documentary History*, London: Hodder and Stoughton, 1972.
  Religion in China Today: Policy and Practice, Maryknoll: Orbis Books, 1989.

MacRobert, Iain. *The Black Roots and White Racism of Early Pentecostalism*, London: Macmillan, 1987.

Mao Zedong. 'Questions of Tactics in the Present Anti-Japanese United Front', *Selected Works of Mao Tse-tung*, volume 3, London: Lawrence and Wishart, 1954.
  'Letter to Journalists' *Xinhua banyuekan*, 25 January 1959, 160.

Martin, David. *Tongues of Fire: The Explosion of Protestantism in Latin America*, Oxford: Blackwell, 1990.

Myers, James T. 'Review of Wickeri *Seeking the Common Ground*', *China Quarterly*, no. 127, September 1991, 636–8.

Najarian, Nishan. 'Religious Conversion in Nineteenth Century China: Face to Face Interaction Between Western Missionaries and the Chinese' in Sidney L. Greenblatt (ed.) *Social Interaction in Chinese Society*, Westport: Praeger, 1982, 67–111.

Ogden, Suzanne. *China's Unresolved Issues: Politics, Development and Culture*, Englewood Cliffs, NJ: Prentice Hall, 1989.

Patterson, George N. *Christianity in Communist China*, Waco, TX: Word Books, 1969.
  The China Paradox: Christ Versus Marx, Milton Keynes: Word Books, 1990.

Peck, Graham. *Through China's Wall*, London: Collins, 1941.

Petty, Orville A. *China. Laymen's Foreign Missions Inquiry, Volume Two, Supplementary Series, Part One*, New York: Harper and Brothers, 1933.

Price, Frank. *The Rural Church in China: A Survey*, New York:

Agricultural Missions Inc., 1948.

Price, Maurice T. *Christian Missions and Oriental Civilizations: A Study in Culture Contact*, Shanghai: privately published, 1924.

Rees, D. Vaughan. *The Jesus Family in Communist China*, Exeter: Paternoster Press, 1959.

Richard, Timothy. *Forty-Five Years in China, Reminiscences*, New York: Frederick Stokes, 1916.

Robinson, Lewis S. *Double-edged Sword: Christianity and 20th Century Chinese Fiction*, Hong Kong: Tao Fong Shan, 1986.

Rubinstein, Murray A. 'Taiwan's Churches of the Holy Spirit', *The American Asian Review*, vol. 6 no. 3, Fall 1988, 23–58.

The Protestant Community on Modern Taiwan: Mission, Seminary and Church, Armonk, New York and London: M. E. Sharpe, 1991.

Schoenhals, Michael. 'Unofficial and Official Histories of the Cultural Revolution', *Journal of Asian Studies*, vol. 48 no. 3, August 1989, 563–72.

Sha Guangyi. 'A Survey of the Situation of Seminary Graduates in Jiangsu Province', *China Study Journal*, vol. 6 no. 2, August 1991, 75–80.

Smith, C. Stanley. 'Modern Religious Movements', *China Christian Yearbook*, 1935, 97–110.

Soothill, William E. *The Three Religions of China*, London: Oxford University Press, second edition 1923.

Sovik, Arne. 'Church and State in Republican China: A Survey History of the Relations Between the Christian Churches and the Chinese Government, 1911–1945', Ph.D. thesis, Yale University, 1952.

Spae, Joseph. 'Catholic Life in a Chinese Village', *China Update*, supplement no. 1, September 1982.

Spiro, Melford E. 'Social Systems, Personality and Functional Analysis' in Bert Kaplan (ed.) *Studying Personality Cross-Culturally*, Evanston: Row, Peterson, 1961, 93–128.

State Council of PRC, (Press Bureau). *Human Rights Conditions in China*, Beijing, 1991.

Tan Tiende. 'My Life' in Yeung Cho Woon (ed.) *Family News of the Catholic Church in China*, Hong Kong: Holy Spirit Study Centre, 1990, 8–51.

Tang, Dominic. *How Inscrutable His Ways: Memoirs 1951–1981*, Hong Kong: privately published, no date.

Tang, Edmond. *The Catholic Church in the People's Republic of China*, Leuven, Belgium: Pro Mundi Vita Studies no. 15, June 1990.

'1989, A Year of Confrontation' in Hunter and Rimmington (eds.) *All Under Heaven*, 66–79.

Tang Tsou. *The Cultural Revolution and Post-Mao Reforms*, University of Chicago Press, 1986.

Tang Yi. 'Chinese Christianity in Development', *China Study Journal*, vol. 6 no. 2, August 1991, 4–8.

Thompson, Edward P. *The Making of the English Working Class*, London: Gollancz, 1963.

Thompson, Laurence G. *Chinese Religion: An Introduction*, Belmont: Wadsworth, 1979.

Ting, K. H. *No Longer Strangers: Selected Writings of K. H. Ting*, edited by Raymond Whitehead, Maryknoll: Orbis Books, 1989.

Van Slyke, Lyman P. *Enemies and Friends: The United Front in Chinese Communist History*, Stanford University Press, 1967.

Varg, Paul A. *Missionaries, Chinese and Diplomats: The American Protestant Missionary Movement in China, 1890–1952*, Princeton University Press, 1958.

Veliz, Claudio. 'A World Made in England', *Quadrant*, vol. 27 no. 3, March 1983, 8–19.

Wang Shaojin. 'A Catholic Pilgrimage in China', *Religion in Communist Lands*, no. 10, Spring 1982, 91–6.

Wang Weifan. 'Wu Yaozong and Wang Mingdao', *Tianfeng*, September 1989, 12–13.
'Discussing the Present Situation of Christianity', *Dangdai zongjiao yanjiu*, no. 1, Shanghai, 1991.

Welch, Holmes. *Buddhism Under Mao*, Cambridge, MA: Harvard University Press, 1972.

Whyte, Robert. *Unfinished Encounter: China and Christianity*, London: Collins, 1988.

Wickeri, Philip L. *Seeking the Common Ground: Protestant Christianity, The Three Self and China's United Front*, Maryknoll: Orbis Books, 1988.

Xiao Zhitian. 'Further Reflections on the Long-term Nature of Religion', *Zongjiao*, no. 2, Nanjing, 1990, 1–5.

Xu Shaoqiang. 'Preliminary Discussion of the Feminization of the Christian Church in China', *Lilun yu dangdai*, no. 10, 1990, 12–14.

Yu, Carver. 'The Relevance of Christian Humanism to the Quest for Democracy in China' in Hunter and Rimmington (eds.) *All Under Heaven*, 108–14.

Yu, David. 'Religious Studies in China at Crossroads', *Journal of Chinese Religions*, no. 18, Fall, 1990, 167–72.

Index

agriculture, 22, 29–30
Amity, Foundation, 80, 151
    News Service, 14
anti-Christian movements, 109–10,
    136–7
Apostolic Church, 81, 178, 199–210
autonomous communities, 81–8, 178

baptism, 196
Baptist, 79, 192, 195
Bates, Miner Searle, 107, 126
Beijing, xvi, 12, 25, 45, 238
Bethel Mission, 128
Bibles/Bible study, 2, 6, 73, 78, 201–2,
    208, 254, 270
broadcasts, 11, 41, 86, 101, 258
Buddhism, 23, 25, 142–3, 148, 159–61,
    210, 219–35, 270, 272
    academies, 221
    doctrines, 221–2
    monasteries, 222–6
    ordinations, 221
    overseas contacts, 79, 222, 232
    and Protestantism, 172–3, 229–35
    relations with state, 93, 106, 220
bureaucracy, 33–4

campaigns, 1, 21–2, 39, 44, 200
Catholic Church in China, 16n., 23,
    236–56
    celibacy, 239–40
    mission strategy, 236
    priests, 238–9
    and Protestantism, 251–6
    sacraments, 244–5
    seminaries, 246
    spirituality, 245, 247
    relations with state, 26, 237–56

censorship, 10, 11, 41
Chao Ti'en-en, Jonathan, xv, 15, 25n.
charismatic phenomena, 128–35, 152–5,
    205
China Buddhist Association, 219–22
China Christian Council see also Three
    Self, 6, 16, 58–65, 72–80, 260–2
China Inland Mission, 119, 136
Chinese Catholic Patriotic Association,
    237, 240–54
Chinese Church Research Centre, 15
Chinese Communist Party, 23–43,
    108–13
    and democracy movement, 31–2
    factions in, 32, 34
    four principles, 31, 33
    ideology, 35
    morality, 156–8
    policies, 32–6
    post-1989, 96–7, 254–8
    rise to power, 10, 109–13
    secret section, 23, 89, 112
Christian Study Centre on Chinese
    Religion and Culture, 15
Christmas, 182–3, 196, 234
church buildings, 3, 55, 72–3, 81, 182–3
Church Order (1991), 260–1
church–state relations, 47–65, 93–104,
    106–8, 135, 204
clergy, 60, 84, 201, 233, 238, 254
Confucius/Confucianism, 155–7, 159,
    167, 272
congregations, 73–4, 116, 145, 233
congruency, 171, 265–71
consecrations and ordinations
    Buddhist, 221
    Catholic, 248–9
    Protestant, 81, 260

consumerism, 157, 274
continuities, 135–40, 172
conversions, 163–8
Council of Churches for Britain and
    Ireland, China Department of, 15
Cultural Revolution, 1, 11, 14, 22, 27,
    39, 83, 192, 194, 220, 238

Daoism, 23, 148, 159, 206, 210, 270
democracy movement, 1989, 32, 45, 95,
    102, 275
Deng Xiaoping, 2, 22, 31–2, 257
Deng Zhaoming, xv, 16, 217, 260
denominations, 25, 74, 113–26, 192
devolution, 116–18
diplomatic issues, 45
    Sino–Vatican, 242–3, 254–5
    Sino–US, 10, 79
Dispensationalism, 76, 84, 139, 206
Document 3 (1989), 250
Document 6 (1991), 100
Document 19 (1982), 49–51, 88, 259

Eastern Europe, 4, 96–7, 232
ecclesiology, 139–40, 255
education, 73, 125
eschatology, 76, 131, 205, 210, 245
espionage, 50, 57, 102
ethics/morality, 8, 155–8
evangelical groups, 4, 178
evangelism, 20, 114, 126–35, 166, 172,
    204
exorcism, 76, 146–9, 205

Fujian, 67, 71, 121–2, 137, 144, 230
funerals, 163

guilt, 160–2
Guomindang, 5, 25, 198
    relations with Protestants, 105–13

healing, 7, 76, 145–52, 174, 188–9, 254
heaven/hell, 161–2
Hebei, 34, 58, 119, 137, 243
Henan, 56, 68, 70–3, 82, 113, 121, 130,
    155
heterodoxy, 7, 254
Holy Spirit, 128, 155, 201–2
Hong Kong, 4, 15, 16, 81, 278
house churches, 3, 64–5, 81–8, 138–9,
    191–9, 262–3
Huang Detang, 210–17
human rights, 19, 36–47, 242

hymns, 75

independent churches, 119–23
indigenization, 265–71
industry, 30
information, 10–13, 39–42
intellectuals, 34
Islam, 20, 23, 97, 230

Japan, 232, 271–2, 277
Jesus Church, Guangdong, 179–85
Jesus Family, 121, 130
Jiang Zemin, 96, 99, 100, 231
Jiangsu, 69, 122, 137, 230

Korea, 5, 21, 25, 81, 232, 271–5
Kung Pin-mei, Bishop, 250

labour camps, 39, 43, 103, 245
Lambert, Anthony, xv, 17, 52, 69–71,
    95
lay church workers, 116–18, 137–9, 254
Li Chuwen, 60, 112
Lin Xian'gao (Samuel Lam), 56, 91–3
Little Flock (Local Assemblies), 67, 82,
    117, 120–3, 131, 193
liturgy, 6, 196, 239
local (especially provincial) regulations,
    51–3, 258

Mao Zedong, 11, 22, 31, 111
Martin, David, 271, 275, 278
Methodism, 273, 279
methodology, 8–13, 70
millenarianism, 161–2
missionaries, 74
    attacks on, 24, 107, 110
    and Chinese church, 81, 113–26
    conversion tactics, 163–8
    and politics, 107

Nanjing, 13, 76
Nanking Incident (1927), 110
Nanking Road Incident (1925), 108
National Christian Conference (1992),
    20, 259–62
National Christian Council, 24, 128
nationalism, 108, 118
Nee, Watchman (Ni Tuosheng), 82,
    121–2, 129, 136, 198

Pentecostalism, 82, 120–1, 146–8, 153–5
persecution, 1, 83, 103

pilgrimage, 227–8, 234, 244
police, 47, 56–8, 103
power evangelism, 152, 166
prayer, 75, 141–5, 197
Protestantism
  and culture, 164–5, 188, 265–70, 273
  definition of, 66
  growth of, 68–71, 168–75
  and politics, 4, 93–104, 272–3
  and popular religion, 8, 68, 132–3,
    143–4, 263–5
  social functions, 168–75, 267–8, 271
Protestants in China
  pre-1949, 105–40
  1949–1979, 1–2, 22–7
  geographical distribution, 67–71
  in Cultural Revolution, 1, 192, 194
  leaders, 88–93
  numbers, 3, 4, 66–71, 118
  organizations, 58–65
  relations with non-Chinese, 5, 78–81,
    87, 261

qigong, 147, 150

rationalism, 172
reform programme of 1980s, 28–36
Religious Affairs Bureau, 24, 54–5,
  93–103, 182, 222, 240, 259–60
religious policy, 12, 34–5, 47–53,
  105–13
religious studies, 13–18, 177
repentance, 128–9
revivals, 126–35
  Manchurian, 126–7
  meetings, 129, 204
  theology of *see also* Sung, John, 128
Riberi, Archbishop, 236–7
'rice-bowl Christians', 25, 117, 164
Richard, Timothy, 165
rural churches, 26, 114–16
rural reconstruction, 125, 128

salvation, 158–63
sects, 56, 267
self-actualization, 173, 208
seminaries, 76, 95, 246, 275
sermons, 75–6, 124
Shanghai, xvi, 3, 25, 26, 73, 84, 94, 244
Shen Yifan, Bishop, 90, 98, 203
sin, 158–63
social control, 36–47
social gospel, 123–6

socialism, 38–9
social sciences, 10
social welfare, 80, 126, 197, 245
Soviet Union, 24, 109, 232
Spiritual Gifts Society, 129–30
statistics, 66–71, 137–8, 175
Sung, John (Song Shangjie), 82, 127–9,
  131–2, 147
syncretism, 8, 68, 82, 163, 263–5

Taiwan, 8, 15, 81, 102, 266
Tang Yi, 265–6
Thompson, Edward P., 279
Three Self Patriotic Movement, 24–5,
  55–65, 72–82, 93–103, 176–8, 184,
  193, 254
Tianfeng, 14, 24, 72, 78, 93, 184
Ting, K. H., Bishop, 2, 24, 55–63,
  85–90, 93–8, 125, 231, 258–61
tourism, 41, 43, 101
True Jesus Church, 67, 120–3, 130,
  153–5

underground churches, 70, 241–2, 253
United Front, 18, 48–50, 111–2
United Front Work Department, 49–55,
  59, 177, 197, 240
United States of America, 10, 79, 139,
  232
Universal church, 233, 252

Vatican, 248–51, 255

Wang Mingdao, 82, 91–2, 129, 136
Wenzhou, 2, 8, 67, 274
Wickeri, Philip L., 17
women/gender issues, 6, 61, 173–5
World Council of Churches, 79, 233,
  262
Wu Yaozong, 92, 112

Xiamen, 73, 130, 185–99
Xiao Qian, 117
Xinjiang, 20, 83, 137, 230
Xu Yongzhe, 56, 65n.

YMCA/YWCA, 58, 108, 112, 125
Yenan, 89, 111
Yunnan, 137, 173, 230

Zhao Puchu, 93, 95, 231
Zhejiang, 1, 67, 71, 121–2, 137, 210, 230
Zhou Enlai, 23, 99, 111